Sir Alec Douglas-Home

John Dryden: a critical biography

Arthur James Balfour: the happy life of the politician, Prime Minister, statesman & philosopher, 1848–1930

Churchill and Beaverbrook: a study in friendship and politics

Rhodesia and Independence: a study in British colonial policy

Music's Great Days in the Spas and Watering-places

The Greek Passion: a study in people and politics

Sir Alec Douglas-Home

by KENNETH YOUNG

Statesman, yet friend to truth! Of soul sincere,
In action faithful, and in honour clear;
Who broke no promise, served no private end,
Who gained no title, and who lost no friend.

Alexander Pope, on James Craggs, Secretary of State

Fairleigh Dickinson University Press
Teaneck   Rutherford   Madison

© Kenneth Young 1970

First American Edition 1971

Library of Congress Catalog Card Number: 76-167748

Associated University Presses, Cranbury, N.J. 08512

ISBN 0-8386-1041-2

Printed in Great Britain

To PHYLLIDA YOUNG, darling daughter

Contents

Illustrations
Between pages 116 *and* 117

Preface

In addition to the usual sources of information, printed and verbal, I have had the advantage and pleasure over the years of seeing Sir Alec Douglas-Home off as well as on duty, picnicking by the Tweed, at family lunches at the Hirsel, relaxing at private parties. During the preparation of this book, I have also benefited from long, tape-recorded conversations with him, and have been able to ask him the baffling questions that sometimes frustrate the biographers of subjects no longer alive.

Many of Sir Alec's replies were so flavoured with his personality, so characteristically candid, that I have dovetailed them into the narrative as direct quotations. These passages present a speaking likeness of the man himself, his spirit, gaiety and high intelligence; to turn them into *oratio obliqua* would be to lose their freshness and sparkle.

Used as I have used them, they add, I believe, an extra dimension to the biography. Not only does the living subject keep breaking in to explain and elaborate events in his past, but also to comment on them from his present, sometimes different, standpoint. Through these time-shifts the 'then' and the 'now' coalesce as indeed they do in the consciousness of every individual.

Sir Alec has also allowed me to use a number of documents, notes, photographs and letters. But I must make it clear that the background of national and international events against which I have told the story of his life, the inferences drawn, criticisms made and conclusions reached are mine, alone. He is in no way responsible for his biographer's emphases, lapses or *lacunae*.

It is impossible to portray Sir Alec without his wife at his side for this was a marriage made in heaven. Lady Elizabeth deserves a biography to herself. If she were not so utterly feminine and altogether human, she might be described as the dynamo of the Douglas-Homes, powering their pursuits, at once electric and magnetic. For the present,

I can only thank her for her illuminating comments and for the warmth of her friendship to my wife and myself.

To my friends in the Borders, Major Cox and Mr and Mrs S. J. L. Luczyc-Wyhowski, my thanks for being the most intelligent and stimulating of hosts, and for suggesting approaches to this book I should never have seen for myself.

From Sir Michael Fraser, C.B.E., Deputy Chairman of the Conservative Party Organization, I have had, through our friendship, the benefit of his shrewd political insight and his encyclopaedic knowledge of the history of Conservatism.

Many of Sir Alec's colleagues and friends have delighted to talk to me about him, but to the following I owe particular debts of gratitude for help of various kinds:

The Earl of Antrim; the Earl of Avon, K.G.; Viscount Blakenham; Miss Angela Bowlby; Lord and Lady Clitheroe; Henry and William Douglas-Home; Lady Caroline Douglas-Home; Edward du Cann, M.P.; Prof. Sir Keith Feiling; Selwyn Lloyd, M.P.; Sir John Masterman; Dominik Luczyc-Wyhowski; Lord Ogmore; Lord and Lady St Oswald; Lord Redmayne; the Marquess of Salisbury; Lord Strathclyde; E. W. Swanton and the staff of *The Cricketer*; Peter Walker, M.P.; Sir Roy Welensky; Oliver Wright.

As always, the *sine qua non* has been my wife's advice and support. I am grateful, also, to Sir Max Aitken, Bt., and to Michael Geare, formerly of Messrs Dent, always enthusiasts for the project, and to my secretary, Miss P. J. King, for her devotion to the cause of producing a legible manuscript; and to William Blackwood & Sons Ltd for permission to quote from *Constructive Conservatism* by A. N. Skelton.

KENNETH YOUNG

Chart Sutton, Kent

1970

1. The Making of Alec: 1903 – 10

His birth in London. Charles and Lilian Dunglass. 'Naturalists from the start'. Homes, Douglases, Lambtons. Money and lands.

An heir to the ancient Scottish family of Douglas-Home was born on 2nd July 1903, in a rented house in London. It was not that the family lacked houses of their own. The baby's grandfather, the Earl of Home, had two castles and half a dozen other residences, as well as 100,000 acres of Scotland and £60,000 a year; and the parents themselves occupied a comfortable dower house on the banks of the Tweed, near Coldstream in Berwickshire.

In those days, however, the Scottish nobility, for reasons lost in the mists of history, liked their heirs to have a London birth certificate. So the baby's father, Lord Dunglass—a courtesy title long borne by eldest sons of the Earls of Home—rented No. 28 South Street, Mayfair, for his wife's first lying-in. The house had a fashionable address yet stood conveniently out of earshot of the clip-clopping carriage-and-pairs and the still rare but raucous motor cars clattering down Park Lane.

The blue-eyed baby had a fine, large head already tufted with the sandy Home hair. He looked healthy. Nevertheless the doctors examined him with special attention. They could find no trace of the tuberculosis from which his grandmother, a Grey by birth, was suffering and which had been described as 'the fatal scourge' also of his mother's ancestors, the Lambton family of the Earls of Durham.

A few weeks after the birth, Lord and Lady Dunglass took their first-born across the Border to Springhill House, a six-bedroomed, Georgian stone building surrounded by gardens and lawns, a short distance out of Coldstream and looking south east towards the Tweed and the Cheviots. This was to be his home for his first sixteen years and again later when he married.

The baby was named Alexander Frederick, though no one ever

called him anything but Alec, and he bore the family surname of Douglas-Home, the latter word being traditionally pronounced 'hume'. Names were always to be a slight bother to him and even more so to his biographer. He was Alec Douglas-Home for the first fifteen years of his life. When his father succeeded to the earldom, he was called Lord Dunglass. After thirty years of Dunglass he in turn inherited the earldom and became the Earl of Home. The name-changing should have stopped there. It did not. As the result of a chain of circumstances, as inconceivable in 1903 as putting a man on the moon, the Earl of Home at sixty turned itno Sir Alec Douglas-Home, Knight of the Thistle. There is no certainty that he will remain that.

Alec's mother, Lilian Dunglass, was twenty-seven when he was born, a tall, dark and beautiful woman with a mind of her own. She was knowledgeable, and a practical Christian. Her father, from whom Alec took his second name, Frederick, and who later became the fourth Earl of Durham, was an M.P. on the Liberal side. All the Lambtons had been interested in politics ever since the first Earl, known as 'Radical Jack', had fought for the Reform Acts and had won Dominion status for Canada in the middle of the nineteenth century. Lilian Dunglass, too, her son remembered, 'was a bit of a radical—not really interested in practical politics but her turn of mind was radical'.

The first Earl of Durham, 'Radical Jack', was also known as 'the dictator' and his great grand-daughter, although regarded as delicate, grew into a formidable manager, firm with her increasing brood of children, knowing exactly what she liked and disliked. 'We used to have splendid cooks,' Alec plaintively recalled, 'but after a fortnight my mother turned them into what she called good, plain cooks.' In old age she became withdrawn and sometimes abrupt.

By the time Alec was sitting up and taking notice, gazing alertly at his world from deep-set eyes,[1] 'Mama' was preoccupied with new babies—Bridget first and then five more—and soon he was promoted from the nursery to his own small bedroom over the front door of Springhill. As he learned to toddle, then to walk and could run through the gardens and shrubbery, 'Papa' began to dominate his horizon.

Between the two parents there could scarcely have been a greater contrast. Lord Dunglass, christened Charles Cospatrick Alexander, was a simple, kindly man with certain unexpected characteristics. Educated at Eton, he had gone on to Christ Church, taking with him

[1] See picture, facing p. 116.

a groom and half-a-dozen horses which he hunted to the detriment of his studies, receiving only a fourth in his final Schools.

At home he rode to hounds five days a week. He was a fisherman of renown and on one November day at Birgham Dub in 1903 landed sixteen salmon weighing 342 lb., an average of 21⅜ lb. He shot with skill and assiduity. For politics he had an unconcealed contempt, resulting from an early, unsatisfactory brush at a local by-election.

Charles Dunglass was, however, no hard-riding, hard-drinking, obtuse laird. His love of the countryside went deeper than killing its wild life. He had an extensive knowledge of its flora and fauna: 'He was a countryman, a naturalist, and he kept us out of doors all the time,' Alec recalled. 'He was quite a good bird man—Henry really inherited that.[1] We were naturalists from the start—flowers, butterflies, trees. . . . The secret of one's interest lies out of doors.'

So from early boyhood, Alec kept a nature-book and started a butterfly collection; he learned the names and particularities of flowers, shrubs and trees; and throughout his life he found solace in pruning roses and arranging fine blooms in large bowls.

He was never a horseman. Though he learned to fish and shoot and tear through the woods with his butterfly net, he had no stomach for riding or hunting: 'I was cured quite early on because I was made to do too much of it. My second brother Henry was fiendishly keen. Broke himself up into bits riding. I was never keen. I had rather too much of it when I was young.'

Of Alec's early horsemanship his brother Henry relates:

One day Father took Alec riding in the sunshine of a June morning. All was peaceful—Father leading through the grass rides. After some time he addressed Alec over his shoulder, and, on getting no reply, turned in his saddle. His eldest son was not there, and the riderless horse was ambling quietly on its own. Some way back, the heir of the Homes was sitting disconsolately in a patch of nettles, having managed to fall off a walking horse.

But, adds Henry, Alec made up for it by becoming an ardent racegoer and student of form.[2]

Alec was never a hearty, boisterous boy, never 'wild', his mother

[1] Alec's eldest brother, Henry Montagu Douglas-Home, b. 1907, became the 'Birdman' of B.B.C. programmes and a regular Army officer.

[2] Broadcast in the B.B.C. General Overseas Service, reprinted in *London Calling*, 10th November 1955.

recalled, but shy and retiring, obedient, seldom given to boyish pranks. Games he loved and one in particular that was never very popular in Scotland: 'Long before my brother went to school he was efficient both with bat and ball after hours of practice on the lawns at home,' Henry recalled. Cricket became a passion with Alec. It was not a 'Home' game though his mother's Lambton brothers played and so, history records, did 'Radical Jack', the first Earl of Durham.

Charles Dunglass, delighted that his first-born should share at least some of his own interests, was an indulgent father, yet he never for a moment forgot that a Home had duties as well as privileges: 'My father used to din into my head week in and week out that the purpose of life was to give service to other people.' He underlined the point by example as well as precept. Caring nothing for precedence and less for pomp, Charles Dunglass worked hard for the Boys' Brigade and later for Toc H and the Scottish League of Nations Union. He held a territorial commission in the Lanarkshire Yeomanry, and as their Colonel served in Gallipoli and Palestine in the first world war, sending home drawings of exotic birds. He opened bazaars and supported charities. Above all, he did innumerable quiet acts of kindness to those in need so that when he was an old man there were many who regarded him as a saint.

He was too a sincere believer in Christ and the Commandments, particularly in the 'eleventh' which bids men love their neighbours. His faith was simple and unostentatious; he was humble, finding it easier to commiserate than to condemn, more natural to be compassionate than to be critical.

These beliefs and attitudes, impressed so strongly in his boyhood, Alec made his own. They were and are part of his character. In his case, however, they were weathered by relationships with all sorts and conditions of men in a wider world than his father ever knew. Charles Dunglass in later life developed unchecked into a character of rare simplicity, so rare indeed that to the outsider he might appear eccentric, to the cynic a subject for jest. His third son, William, wrote:

There never was a man so humble as my father was. He was for ever thanking people. He would thank an Edinburgh taxi-driver for accepting a generous tip. He would thank the restaurant car attendant on the Flying Scotsman for dropping a potato in his lap. He would thank the actors in my plays for drawing a salary infinitely greater than my own. And, above all, he would thank God for every happiness as well as every tragedy that came his way.

4

His humility was not an act; it was as genuine as it was unconscious. He was innocently unaware of the impression he might be making and to him other men's motives were as simple and straightforward as his own:

He would go into Church in Coldstream, greet all his friends in a loud voice, read the First Lesson in an exquisitely natural style, come down the aisle to give a cheerful rendering of the Te Deum, and then return to dispose of the Second Lesson, just as though he were at home. In fact, he was at home. He was at home everywhere, with everybody, but above all in Church. Like a snail, he took his home with him wherever he went. Unlike a snail, he never shut himself up, selfishly, inside it.

He had, too, infinite compassion. When thieves broke into Douglas Castle, shortly before he ordered its destruction to allow a coal seam to be worked beneath his centuries-old home, he asked the police what they had wanted. 'Old clothes, my lord,' said the sergeant. 'Why the devil didn't they ring the bell?' was the reply.

He thought ill of no man and hated none, not even Hitler:

I remember once, when I was home on leave in the war, he picked up a copy of the *Sunday Graphic* to look at a photograph of Hitler, prancing along between two German generals. And all he said was this. 'Poor little devil. He's got his Sam Browne over the wrong shoulder and nobody dares tell him to put it right.' He could not hate. He could not presume to judge his fellow-men. Even though the war brought him his greatest tragedy, in the loss of his youngest son, he did not lose his saintliness. To him, Hitler was not a fiend incarnate but a 'poor little devil'.

Charles Dunglass, considerate and greatly loved by all who knew him from Border Dukes to his tenants' wives, was of course an oddity. He really did take pot-shots at rabbits from his drawing-room window when he saw them eating his begonias, just as 'Lord Lister' did in William Douglas-Home's play *The Chiltern Hundreds*. His children accepted it all as part of the natural order of things. But he was in no sense 'daft', and if the children were sometimes tempted to take a rise out of him he would quietly out-manœuvre them.

Once at the end of a family sojourn at Brown's Hotel in London, Lord Dunglass summoned the servants to receive their tips, which he dispensed from an envelope his solicitors had filled with the necessary money before he left home. As the servants lined up, his two eldest sons tagged on at the end of the queue and were tipped like the rest by their apparently oblivious father. Only when they were on the train and anxious for luncheon did their father discover he was short of money—and borrowed £5 from them.

Four miles north east of Alec's boyhood home stood the Hirsel where his grandparents, the Earl and Countess of Home, spent most of their time. It was a long, three-storied building, part eighteenth-century, part Regency, built on to a much older tower and with a late Victorian extension. On the north side of the house his grandmother had installed a private chapel. Inside, there was a staff of some forty; thirty gardeners, foresters and farm-hands kept the 4,400 acre estate in good trim. Guests came and went, one of them, Louisa Countess of Antrim, a cousin of Lady Home, observing that at the Hirsel 'the Home establishment ran on wheels greased with gold'.[1]

Gold there was, some £60,000 a year in 1881 with ever-increasing royalties from extensive seams of coal worked beneath other Home lands in Lanarkshire.[2] But like his son and grandson, Charles, the bearded Earl was modest and unassuming. In his early years he had been A.D.C. to Queen Victoria, not however by personal predilection. He 'didn't like all that side of life much', his grandson recalled. 'His interests were local rather than national. He was Lord Lieutenant of Lanark and Lord Provost of Glasgow. He very much liked living at the Hirsel and doing his trees and fishing. He had a rather quiet disposition.'

Alec as a boy had no great intimacy with his grandparents: 'Children didn't see as much of their grandparents then. All were kept to different parts of the house, except at stated, formal hours—an after-breakfast session, again in the evening, otherwise you were rather kept quiet.'

Each August the Earl hired a train to transport his family and himself to Douglas Castle for the grouse-shooting. With them went Alec and his parents: 'There in August and September, we had a great time. My grandfather was always lively.'

But as Alec grew into his teens, what contact he had with the Earl decreased: 'Grandfather was blind for a time—not totally blind—but he could barely see for six years of his life. We were rather frightened of him in his oldest age—he became rather remote, and it was hard for us to make contact with him.'

[1] *Recollections of Louisa, Countess of Antrim* (*née Louisa Jane Grey*). Privately published, 1937.

[2] *The Complete Peerage*, London, 1926, vol. vi, 'Home'.

He was, according to Lady Antrim, 'an inadequate match' for his wife, Maria, always known as May. This, in Alec's words, 'very distinguished-looking' lady was a quarter Irish through her mother and, through her father, Captain Conrad Grey, R.N., connected with the Earl Grey family of Northumberland. 'Outwardly a model wife and mother, she found her real vocation in spiritual devotion,' wrote Lady Antrim; 'like a cloistered nun, her soul was steeped in a deep inward peace and content. May loved the Chapels she installed at Douglas and the Hirsel and derived great comfort from the services there.'[1]

She had need of spiritual comfort. She was for most of her long life tubercular, suffering great pain and weakness and during one period became dependent on drugs. Nevertheless she did a great deal for the local villages, schools and the tenantry. Alec remembered that he 'used to enjoy being around with her, though she was often ill'. She outlived her husband by only a few months.

When Alec visited his grandparents at the Hirsel or went for his summer holidays to Douglas Castle, he was faced at every turn by portraits of earls and barons who were his ancestors, by Raeburns and Ramsays, jewellery and *objets d'art* which would one day be his, by a history of men bearing his name and stretching back to the remote past.

Homes were first recorded in a charter of 1138, taking their names from a place in Berwickshire, and their origins from the 'Earls' Cospatrick, collaterals of the Earl of Dunbar. They were Lowland Scots scarcely different in ethnic origin—a mixture of Celtic, Angle, Dane and Norman, with Norman predominating—from their English neighbours across the Tweed; and they spoke Northumbrian English not Gaelic.

The early Sir John or Alexander Homes, the Lord Homes of the Middle Ages, were no more than violent chieftains of savage bands. Their 'great halls' and castles were cold and often filthy dens piled with refuse and sewage. Ugly diseases were rife and even King Robert, a fourteenth-century Scottish monarch, was eaten away by leprosy. Lip-service was paid to Christian beliefs; but while heaven and hell were realities, 'love one another' was a forgotten commandment. It was a brutal world where men took what they wanted—including lives, wives

---

[1] *Recollections of Louisa, Countess of Antrim*, pp. 227-8. See note, p. 6 above.

and wealth—by superior muscle and bone. Sir Walter Scott, for all his medieval fancies, hardly concealed the brute facts:

> But war's the Borderer's game.
> Their gain, their glory, their delight,
> To sleep the day, maraud the night,
> O'er mountain, moss and moor. . . .[1]

Sometimes they fought farther afield but always against the English. One Home was killed in a battle against Henry Percy (Hotspur) at Verneuil in France in 1424 under the already 'auld alliance' of Scots with Frenchmen.

Nearer at hand was Flodden Field, a few miles south across the Tweed from the Home domain near Coldstream. On that drizzling wet day in September 1513 it was doubtless true, as Walter Scott wrote, that

> The Border slogan rent the sky!
> A Home! A Gordon! was the cry. . . .[2]

but the third Lord Home's actions on the battlefield were open to misinterpretation.

After an early successful skirmish against Lord Howard, Lord Home and his men retired from the field laden with spoils, leaving their King and hundreds of Scots to be slain and the battle lost. Home was severely criticized for running out. But did he? 'It is equally probable,' his descendant Alec claimed at the annual Flodden commemoration 450 years later, 'that having fought the skirmish, Home interpreted his duty as advance guard to press on and secure for the Scottish army the ford at Coldstream which would guarantee its safety.'[3]

Indisputable, however, is the fact that three years later, the third Lord Home and his brother were hanged and their heads displayed on the Tolbooth in Edinburgh. The feuding Scots wrought their vengeance in blood, their hatreds in destruction. In the time of Mary Queen of Scots, one of the Home castles that stood at Stichill, a few miles north west of the Hirsel, was 'destroyit', and then rebuilt as a rampart against the English, thanks to a gift of 2,000 livres from the King of France.

The sixth Lord Home, instead of fighting the English, embraced

[1] *Marmion*, 1808, canto v, verse iv.

[2] *Marmion*, canto v, verses xxv–xxvii.

[3] Speech on 8th August 1968. 'If the descendants of the slain had erected a war memorial in stone the names of the roll of honour would be our own,' he said.

them. King James VI of Scotland was his friend and with him in 1603 he travelled to London and the throne of England. Home became a Privy Councillor and in March 1604–5 was created an earl as well as Lord Dunglass and Baron of Jedburgh. *En deuxième noces*, he married a noble English girl, Marie Sutton, eldest daughter of the 9th Lord of Dudley, so putting the Scottish Homes firmly into the English aristocracy.

His grandson was not so lucky. He fought for the King in the Civil War and lost his estates to the Cromwellians. They were returned by Charles II in 1660 and the fourth Earl of Home became a member of his Privy Chamber, marrying Anne Sackville, daughter of one of the King's close friends, the Earl of Dorset.

Strangely enough, a later earl, the sixth, violently opposed the Act of Union of England and Scotland, and his son was suspected of Jacobitism. A contemporary described him as 'a tall slovenly man endowed with very good parts; is a firm countryman but never would acknowledge King William'.

The eighth Earl, however, was a thorough Hanoverian and a professional soldier. He fought against Bonnie Prince Charlie in the '45, and was rewarded by King George II with the Governorship of Gibraltar and the rank of Lieutenant-General. He was less lucky in love. He married a widow, daughter and heiress of a rich Jamaican; but deserted her within the year because, according to one account, 'she's a witch, a quean, an old cozening Quean'.[1]

Like many other Scots, the eighteenth-century Homes found, in Johnson's words, that the 'noblest prospect which a Scotchman ever sees is the high road that leads him to England'.[2] They had little choice, for the family fortunes were in decline and Alexander, the ninth Earl was a clergyman in the Church of England. The Rev. Earl, a much-married man, could do little for his son, who had to go into the Army and was killed in America fighting the insurgent colonists at the battle of Guildford in 1781.

In the nineteenth century the Homes had a turn for the better. It began with Alexander, the tenth Earl, who married a daughter of the Duke of Buccleuch and Queensbury, and inherited some money from his mother, who was the heiress of John Ramey of Yarmouth; in recognition of this, he altered his name by royal licence to Ramey-

[1] *The Merry Wives of Windsor*, IV. iii. 180.
[2] Boswell's *Life of Johnson*, vol. i, p. 425 (6th July 1763).

Home. But it was his son, Cospatrick Alex, the eleventh Earl, and the first of his line to go to Christ Church, Oxford—he matriculated in 1819—who really hit the jackpot.

The eleventh Earl—Alec's great-grandfather—after leaving Oxford, worked for his living as a précis-writer in the Foreign Office and as an attaché in St Petersburg. In 1828 he blossomed out as an under-secretary of State for Foreign Affairs under another Scottish peer, the 4th Earl of Aberdeen in the Duke of Wellington's Government—the only one of Alec's Home ancestors to become a government minister.

He retired from the Foreign Office and politics when he was 31, and in December 1832, married Lucy Elizabeth, the eldest daughter of the second and last Lord Montagu. It was the most significant event in Home history. Elizabeth's mother was the sister and co-heiress of the last Lord Douglas. In 1859 her mother died and Lady Home—'a notorious bore', Lady Antrim observed—inherited the wealth, vast properties, great estates and some of the best grouse moors in Scotland of the Douglases, bringing them—and their name—into her husband's family.

This lucky turn was the upshot of an extraordinary chain of events. The Dukes of Douglas were said to be the richest noblemen in eighteenth-century Scotland. But the family had been plagued by a dispute about the true heir. The case was fought through the courts and Parliament, and all England and Scotland followed it with interest, taking sides as though it were a Cup Final. Eventually, Archibald Steuart, son of Lady Jane Douglas, won the day, and the inheritance; but he was not made earl or duke and was denied the honours due to the chief of the Douglases. Was he in fact the Douglas chief, or merely the son of the 'glass-polisher of Paris'?[1] No one ever knew for certain.

The Douglas inheritance changed the Homes out of all recognition. They 'were always comparatively poor until they made the liaison with the Douglases', Alec Douglas-Home commented: 'They put up a good struggle before that, but once the Douglases came in there was a good deal of money.' There were also new titles and names. The eleventh Earl was created Baron Douglas of Douglas in the county of Lanarkshire in 1875; and his son—Alec's grandfather—added the surname to his own, becoming the first Douglas-Home. To the motto 'a Home, a Home, a Home' was added the Douglas 'Jamais arrière'. The arms were joined with the subscription 'True to the end'.

[1] Lillian de la Torre, *Heir of Douglas*, New York, 1952, p. 247.

As a boy Alec knew little of the detail of his inheritance which by the time he was ten in 1913 had increased to 134,000 acres and the gross annual rental to £93,035 with coal royalties on top of that. But he knew that one day he would be the 14th Earl of Home, Baron Douglas, and would have four other titles, and understood that he was a person singled out from birth to be above the ruck of humanity. If he had looked in Burke's Peerage or Debrett, he would have found his name already inscribed.

From this half-conscious awareness, acquired as imperceptibly as the ability to walk and talk, sprang a self-assurance, however shy, and a pride of ancestry, however concealed, that made him as sure of the future as he was certain of the past. Of his possessions, name, ancestry, he says only: 'I would passionately try to keep things together. That history has gone back such a long way. One would feel guilty if one had to liquidate it. . . . It's a question whether one can hang on.'

2. An Heir Educated: 1910 – 26

Miss Triplow, Ludgrove, Eton, Christ Church. Religion. Cricket. Touring South America.

At Springhill House, it was not all nature walks and bat and ball on the lawn. Alec could read and write quite early, and from the age of five spent some hours of the day in the schoolroom. His governess, Miss Triplow, 'a most splendid lady, very good', taught him sums, history and geography, the rudiments of French and Latin, and stimulated his interest in the world beyond the Tweed and Douglas Castle.

What an exciting world it was for a boy in the first decade of the century! Motor cars were still a novelty, and some brave men were already rising from the ground in a powered-vehicle which resembled a clumsy bird and was called an aeroplane. The *Boy's Own Paper* and the family magazine *Quiver* told of messages flashing across the Atlantic in a matter of seconds—and without a wire; of Peary and Amundsen reaching the North and South Poles for the first time; and of Younghusband penetrating to the secret city of Lhasa.

No less exciting were the story-books available in splendid abundance for Edwardian boys and so well wrought that they were still being read by Alec's son forty years later. G. A. Henty was still recounting episodes of history into which he mixed heroism and humour. Jules Verne stretched the mind with adventures in space and beneath the sea. New-minted were the *Just So* stories, *The Four Feathers*, *The Scarlet Pimpernel* and Sexton Blake.

Alec became a voracious reader. He still loved his butterflies and wild flowers which he pressed into albums, his summers with bat and ball, his fishing in the Tweed. But now he began what was to be a life-long habit of reading because he wanted to as well as because he must.

He grew tall. He would, his father accurately prophesied, become a six-footer, and he wore a miniature adult suit with long stockings and knickerbocker trousers.[1] With his large brow and prominent teeth, he was not classically handsome yet he had a calm, assured and thoughtful air that left no doubt either of his mental capacity or his character.

Both were now to be put to the test. At ten years old his destiny beckoned him and the great outer world came knocking on his door at Springhill. In September 1913 the halcyon days were left behind and his father took him away to his prep school, Ludgrove, at New Barnet in Hertfordshire. Nothing in later years is ever quite so disorientating, no new world ever so menacing, as the first week at a boarding-school for small boys.

For Alec—his mother's 'shy, retiring boy'—it must have been a traumatic experience. Homesickness, spartan conditions, the hostility of the 'old' boys to the new and the mutual distrust of the new are a sure recipe for unhappiness. Doubtless in the first few weeks Alec would have devoutly agreed with the words of his new school's song, written by a master called W. P. Blore, that 'we must all affirm, That we're longing for home and its leisure'—but thirteen long weeks came between.

If shock it was, it was buried too deep for recall half a century later. In any case, Alec was not long in acclimatizing to the life of dormitory, cold changing rooms, the smell of carbolic soap and chalky classrooms. He quickly found his feet as a footballer and when the summer term came his skill at cricket raised him out of the common run. Miss Triplow too had done well with her small pupil, a fact soon recognized by his teachers.

We had quite a lot of good teachers there. First of all they gave one one's keenness for games. A Scotsman's chances of learning cricket are not very good because the climate's so much against us up there. G. O. Smith was the head, an England footballer and a University cricketer.[2]

There was also a very good fellow who first taught me Greek and taught me to *enjoy* Greek. That was Mr Brown, a very good teacher—an old fellow with a stick-up collar. He was one of the austere old school but he did give one very good grounding in Greek.

This early predilection for Greek proved lasting; though his Latin was passable, it was always a grind.

As Alec rose through the school, his proficiency at cricket and foot-

[1] See picture, after p. 116.

[2] G. O. Smith, an Oxford blue for football, played twenty times for England between 1893 and 1901. He scored a century for Oxford against Cambridge at Lord's in 1896.

ball increased, and with it his popularity. This era was the bright day for sport and the hero-worship of sportsmen: Jack Hobbs, Sidney Barnes, George Hirst, C. B. Fry and Ranji were schoolboy idols. 'Googly' bowling had been perfected by the Oxford Blue, B. J. Bosanquet, and boys like Alec dreamed of playing for the school XI. As for football, soccer was played at prep schools such as Ludgrove—and at the major public schools—and amateurs, like Alec's headmaster, G. O. Smith, were still able to gain places alongside professionals; indeed if they were in the famous Corinthians as Smith had been they could sometimes beat even the cup-holders as Corinthians beat Bury in 1904.

By the time Alec became a senior boy—at thirteen—and was playing for both school XIs, his second brother, Henry, arrived at Ludgrove. Now during the holidays at Springhill, William their junior recalled, the house echoed to their lofty conversations about school which 'seemed to be peopled with inhabitants bearing strange names such as "The Bug", "Po", "Billy Bluff" and "Bunco Brown"'.[1] Such names bring an unmistakable whiff of Billy Bunter, Gussy 'the swell of St Jim's' and the 'bounder of the Remove', but whether life imitated art—if that is what the *Gem* and *Magnet* were—or art life, is uncertain.

It was 1917 when Alec left Ludgrove for Eton College, the school at which all the male Douglas-Homes had been educated from his grandfather's time. At fourteen he was a somewhat late entrant—Ludgrove had hung on to their best cricketer as long as they decently could—and he found the transition quite painless. This was, of course, wartime Eton where a preponderance of masters were near or over retiring age and where weekly lists were read out in chapel of Old Etonians killed in action. Diet was sparser than usual and there were fewer of the social occasions so much a feature of the school in normal times. Yet essentially it differed little from the Eton of Alec's father thirty years earlier, and Alec enjoyed it.

Like many who have achieved fame in later years and like Old Etonians generally, Alec Douglas-Home lightly shrugs off any suggestion that he actually worked at Eton: 'I was idle, I don't mind saying, at school and university, but at least one had the groundings on which one could build.'

It was not really true that he idled, though he may never have fully extended himself. Such school reports as survive suggest that he was

[1] W. D. Home, *Half Term Report*, London, 1954.

an intelligent, even painstaking worker. His history report for one summer term shows that he was given an alpha for his special study and was 'in some respects the most promising person in the Division [II]. He has worked well and taken trouble. He has plenty of ability and imagination and a very fair knowledge of history while his essays have been excellent especially those of a lighter kind'.

'His construing of Tacitus,' wrote the headmaster Dr C. A. Alington at the end of Alec's final term, July 1922, has 'been well and sensibly done.' His knowledge of French 'is very fair. He has taken pains and is always ready to help'. He gets β for a German composition and for a Latin unseen. His interest in naturalism is noted; indeed for his 'extra' he chose 'plant morphology . . . Work purely botanical'.

His feeling for Greek was further stimulated: 'I had a very exceptional Greek tutor who is still alive, Andrew Gow, now at Trinity, Cambridge.[1] Also an old classical tutor called Macnaghten who was well known, and C. H. K. Marten, one of the best historians of his time. Pretty good this lot.'

Latin he still found hard going but of undoubted benefit: 'I was made to do Latin verses against which I kicked quite a lot but which I slaved at for four years. It teaches you economy in words. I think there's nothing like the classics—in a way I wish I'd stuck to them— for disciplining your writing or your talking. I liked Greek better than Latin. But it's the Latin that teaches you the discipline of the language.'

It is, however, true that Alec's growing eminence at Eton sprang less from his work than from his out-of-class performances. Because he was good at sport—cricket, soccer, fives—he was elected early to Pop, the Eton élite group, and eventually became its president.

They wear bow ties and stick-up collars [his brother William wrote]. Coloured waistcoats of the fiercest hues and of the strangest materials —of velvet, silk or even crêpe de chine—sponge-bag trousers, rolled umbrellas, black patent-leather shoes, blue overcoats, spats if they so desire and, most eccentric of all, large seals on the centre of the top and fore and aft (below and above the brim) of their top hats—they stroll down the High Street at Eton linked arm in arm. They are, in fact, in that small world the Gods.[2]

[1] Andrew S. F. Gow, b. 1886, Porson prizeman at Cambridge in 1906 and 1907, was an assistant master at Eton, 1914-25. He edited the *Bucolici Graeci*, co-edited *Hellenistic Epigrams* (text and commentary), 2 vols., in 1965. He is a Fellow of Trinity College, Cambridge.

[2] *Half Term Report*, p. 35. See note, p. 14 above.

Members of Pop are the leaders of their juniors, the boys, and the advisers of their seniors, the masters. Among them Alec was effortlessly prominent, as a contemporary, Cyril Connolly, noted: 'He was a votary of the esoteric Eton religion, the kind of graceful, tolerant, sleepy boy who is showered with all the laurels, who is liked by the masters and admired by the boys without any apparent exertion on his part and without experiencing the ill-effects of success himself or arousing the pangs of envy in others. In the eighteenth century he would have become Prime Minister before he was 30: as it was he appeared honourably ineligible for the struggle of life.'[1] Less well-known are Alec Douglas-Home's views of Connolly at Eton: 'Very lazy and highly intelligent boy. Very clever and very amusing.' Honours remained even.

It was not his contemporaries alone who recognized his qualities— nor his unwillingness to make an effort before an effort was necessary. His housemaster, A. W. Whitworth—now ninety-five—wrote from Cotton Hall House to Alec's father in July 1922 that Alec had 'sound ability—quite enough to enable him with his other gifts to attain real success and power even in public life. But he is not at present ambitious and not inclined to go out and face storms from which he can stand aside'.

One 'storm' he did confront, and stubbornly. It was the custom for the President of Pop to lead in the annual procession of boats. To do so, it was required that he should be able to pass the swimming test. Alec and two of his friends, David Bowes-Lyon and William Hill-Wood, affected to regard this requirement as childish. So President Alec merely stood nonchalantly on the bank as the procession came in. He never learned to swim.

Nevertheless Alec lost no popularity. As captain of his house he was highly successful, and, his housemaster reported, 'not by going round and abusing people but by making attractive in his own person the right kind of action in all circumstances. I have never heard him grumble or harshly criticize anybody or anything'. He was just as 'unselfconscious and natural as when he was a lower boy', even though in a sense, as another master wrote, 'he had everything against him. He came to the front too early. He got into Pop too young and at a time when the atmosphere of Pop was not very good. But he has kept perfect simplicity and modesty'.

He was a natural leader, unassertively self-assured, cool and fair.

[1] *Enemies of Promise*, London, 1938, p. 294.

More than that. The Dean of Windsor, the Very Rev. Albert Baillie, told his father that Alec had done much to restore 'moral leadership among the older boys, the absence of which since the war has been one of the chief difficulties of the school'. Eton, like other schools after both wars, suffered from the aftermath of excitement and the excesses of patriotism. Adolescent cynics and glib revolutionaries abounded. Another of Alec's near-contemporaries at Eton, George Orwell, remembered Communist tracts being handed round in 1920 and 1921;[1] and boys of seventeen and eighteen, though still at school, were aware that codes of conduct were in the melting-pot, long-accepted beliefs under attack. Reflecting this, some of Alec's contemporaries talked of sexual freedom, of revolution—the Bolsheviks had just seized power in Russia—and professed to be atheists. Alec resisted the fashionable trend. He was, wrote the Dean, 'a real Christian in the best sense of the word with real thought in it. Conscientious, industrious and distinctly above the ordinary in intelligence with some quite rare intellectual gifts'.

Alec's firm Christianity derived from his parents; it was, and remained, an ethical rather than a speculative or mystical Christianity. But it had been developed and broadened by contact with the remarkable headmaster of Eton, Dr Cyril A. Alington, later the Dean of Durham: 'He preached the most remarkable sermons boys have ever heard,' Alec Douglas-Home recalled forty years later. 'He had a fine presence, classical features and a good voice. The effect on boys of my generation was profound.' On Alec it was life-long.

Alington, a fine scholar and theologian, was a man of many parts: he was a fluent and effective versifier; he wrote detective stories—unsuccessful because from conscience he eschewed murders and wrote only of more trivial crime; and he had a sense of humour. All these gifts, not least the last, went into his sermons, which were really conversational fables, as he indicated by the titles he gave them when they were collected and published—*Eton Fables, More Eton Fables*. Often they were subtle and always far removed from pompous 'blah'. One is a dialogue between Alington and his 'Uncle Richard' about science's claim that 'nothing can be true unless you understand it'. But surely, inquires Alington, 'we can say that some things couldn't possibly have happened?'

The crusty old uncle replies. '"Do you ever read Donne?" asked

[1] *Critical Essays*, London, 1946, p. 80.

my uncle, with apparent irrelevance. "No? I suppose you think him too old-fashioned. Well, if you did read him you'd find a good many suggestions as to the limits of our knowledge—

> 'Why grass is green and why blood is red
> Are mysteries that none have reached unto.'

No, don't talk to me about the spectroscope," he went on, fearing an interruption; "I've no doubt you can *talk* a lot of learned nonsense about it, but how much do you really know?"

'"I quite agree we don't know everything," said I, "but surely it's right to use what knowledge we've got?"

'"Of course it is," answered Uncle Richard, "but don't use it to bar out the possibility of more knowledge coming. I tell you the thing I'm really afraid of is being made to look a fool at the Day of Judgment. 'Why didn't you believe this?' they'll say to me, and I shall say, 'Oh, I didn't think it was possible.' 'And what do you know about possibilities?' they'll say, and I shouldn't know what to answer.'"

Alington's was neither muscular nor 'public school' Christianity. In a colloquy with a match, he says: '"You can't seriously want me to go and preach to a lot of Public School boys and tell them they're the finest specimens of their kind? Even if it were true it would be uncommonly bad for them; and that spirit of thinking they're the only class that counts is just the thing one wants to get out of their heads.'"

His Christianity led gently through morals towards the deeper mysteries of faith; it put good works into their proper place in the scheme of things but did not suggest that they were more than a part of religion.

Alec's faith, though it owed much to Alington, was intimately his own: 'Yes, I am a religious man in the sense that I couldn't do without it. I'm not sure I'm a very good practitioner, though I do go regularly to church. I have had no vivid religious experience except when I was ill and looked over the edge.[1] A glimpse of the infinite.'

In his last years at Eton, Alec came to know Alington personally but found him 'rather alarming, he never stopped talking—the boys were a little bit shy of him. He was a violent Conservative—what I would call a reactionary Conservative. She was the antidote to that'. *She* was Mrs Alington, formerly Hester Lyttelton and one of the famous cricketing-political family. Like Alec's mother, she was an evangelical

[1] He suffered from tuberculosis of the spine from 1940 to 1942: see below, p. 61, ff.

with a turn of mind still more radical. In fact she was 'a devoted Socialist always, and on the whole a Labour supporter.

'But she had a great sense of humour—she never thrust her politics down anyone's throat, or was too violent. She was very good with the boys.'

Mrs Alington talked politics when Alec, as President of Pop, took breakfast at the headmaster's house. But—alas for the biographer seeking intimations of the future—his interest was no more than polite. He took no part in the newly founded Eton Political Society which Mrs Alington patronized and to which she invited the left-wing politicians and thinkers of the day. In Alec, the father's contempt for politics had been transmuted into the son's indifference.

What really absorbed Alec was cricket, and whether he won or lost his battles on the playing fields of Eton it was there he spent much of his time and made friends for life. By this time he was an experienced player, good with both bat and ball—unlike his father who when he was at Eton played in a team 'which for obvious reasons went under the name of "Refuse"'.[1]

Alec had two years in the Eton first XI. In the trial game in May 1922, his last term, he captained one side, G. K. Cox, the Eton captain, another, and took one wicket, scoring 24 (out of 112). With the same teams a week later, he got 49 runs and one wicket. Later in the month he played for Eton against the Oxford University Authentics, among them such famous names as P. F. ('Plum') Warner, who was to play a considerable part in Alec's later cricketing, and A. D. G. Leveson-Gower. He took a wicket in a match against Scotland, and four wickets against the Incogniti.

The Etonian cricket world was now warming up towards the great game of the year against Harrow, but first there was the traditional match against Winchester, which began on 30th June. *The Cricketer*, pointing out that, although the result was a draw, Eton 'were much the stronger side', mentioned Alec as among Eton's best bowlers, and politely ignored what his brother, William, called 'the bodily contortions' of his run up. Alec did well as a batsman too, scoring 55 of Eton's 107 runs in the 1st innings and taking 3 wickets. His bowling analysis against Winchester was:

	Overs	Maidens	Runs	Wickets
1st innings	10.3	5	19	3
2nd innings	13	6	19	1

[1] *Half Term Report.* See note, p. 14 above.

Alec's swansong was the Eton and Harrow match at Lords, and it was a triumph. As always, there was a great crowd of spectators— 'And what spectators!' Sir Home Gordon, Bt, wrote in words of awe in *The Cricketer*: 'Cabinet Ministers, famous men in every walk of life, are foremost in the throng.' The Eton-Harrow match still drew the rich and fashionable, the parasolled ladies in silks and taffetas, their skirts still no more than half a foot above ground, the gentlemen in grey top-hats and Ascot dress. Among the 15,000 spectators were the entire Home family down from Coldstream, but not Alec's grandfather. He had died in 1918 and Alec was now Lord Dunglass.

Unfortunately the first day of the match, Friday, was washed out, but play began, still under a lowering sky, on Saturday morning. Tall and cool, Alec Dunglass went in with E. W. Dawson, and scored 66, while the pair between them put on a century. 'Lord Dunglass, less stiff than last year, though no great stylist, displayed the greater initiative. The way in which he and his comrade ran short runs showed ripe judgment and priceless service,' *The Cricketer* observed. He had hit three fours and five threes. At 190 for nine Eton declared and Lord Dunglass, who had carried his bat, was cheered all the way back to the pavilion.

Nor was that the end of it. He was on top too of his bowling form, taking 4 for 37 and clean bowling Cosmo Crawley, the Harrow player and later his friend, for 53. Harrow were all out for 184. Alec Dunglass's bowling analysis ran: 18, 9, 37, 4.

So in 1922, with cheering crowds and a prestigious halo, his Eton career neared its end: 'He is,' wrote his housemaster, 'a great person among us.' But what had Eton given him? The main thing, he believed, was 'learning to live with other people. And of course we were taught supremely well. You had a lot of freedom and you had a lot of people of all sorts to knock about with'.

Thirty-five years after leaving Eton, at an Eton Ramblers cricket dinner, he put it more formally, even arrogantly: 'Life is service and the foundation of service is integrity and it is because Eton teaches integrity to her sons that we hold the proud conceit that as Eton flourishes so too does the country.'

Cricket continued to dominate his life and thoughts when in October 1922 he arrived at Christ Church, Oxford, to read history. Yet his tutors never had cause to complain of his work. Though he had a sense of fun and a delight in practical jokes, he never fell foul of the authorities —unlike his father, rusticated for a jape obscurely involving window-boxes. He was no less popular with those set in authority over him than he had been with his Eton masters. With two of his tutors, J. C. Masterman, later Sir John, and Keith Feiling [1] he entered upon a life-long friendship; in Sir John he was still confiding his doubts and inner feelings as late as 1965 when he was making up his mind to retire from the Conservative leadership.

Masterman's first impressions of the nineteen-year-old Lord Dunglass were of a lively mind in a tall, rather frail, body. He would, he felt, take on the chin whatever disappointments or disaster came, merely giving a wide, toothy grin. He was, thought Masterman, modest even to excess.

Among his contemporaries he was equally popular and was one of the 'Peck gang', so called because they lived in Peck Quad at Christ Church; the gang had a *penchant* for practical jokes, fully shared by Alec Dunglass. Among his contemporaries, exact or near, were Alan Lennox-Boyd (Lord Boyd of Merton), A. L. Rowse, Roger Makins (Lord Sherfield), Col. Peter Acland and Godfrey Nicholson (now a knighted M.P.).

Despite later assertions of 'idleness', Alec Dunglass read widely in seventeenth- and eighteenth-century European history and got, he admitted, 'a knowledge of history in consecutive form'. His special period was the reign of William and Mary which involved the constitutional developments leading to the Act of Union of England and Scotland—so bitterly opposed by his ancestor the 7th Earl. He continued to study French, though he gave up Greek, which he later regretted. Masterman's tutor's book, detailing his pupils' progress from start to finish of their Oxford career, shows that his marks for terminal Collections never fell below a middle second (ranging from $\beta\gamma$ to $\beta+$).

Nevertheless in 1925 in his final Schools he achieved only a third, without even the inverted glory of his father's fourth. For this, illness in part accounts. Masterman's book shows that in 1924 he missed the last quarter of Michaelmas term, and in 1925 half the Hilary and Trinity terms. What illness? He recalled only that 'before the Schools I had some frightful internal sort of upset'.

Had it not been for Alec Dunglass's illnesses he would, Masterman is sure, have got the second to which his 'very good intelligence' would have entitled him. Masterman could have recommended him to wait another year before taking his finals—and would have done so if he

[1] Now Professor Sir Keith Feiling.

had thought that Dunglass would need a degree to earn his living. He did not: a degree, he thought, was not necessary for a man destined, it then seemed, to be a laird and landowner.

Illness apart, while he had certainly not been idle Sir Keith Feiling is probably correct in suggesting that at Oxford Alec Dunglass was not, academically speaking, fully exerting himself: 'I should have guessed,' he writes, 'that he began to work really hard after being elected to the House of Commons.'

At Oxford, as at Eton, however, politics still lacked much interest for Dunglass. He took little or no part in debates in the Union, then passing through a period of unpopularity. He did join the Oxford Carlton Club, recently founded by such elder contemporaries as Charles Petrie (Sir Charles Petrie), David Maxwell Fyfe (Lord Kilmuir) and Ralph Assheton (Lord Clitheroe).

Assheton—later a Minister and Chairman of the Conservative Party Organization—was the great prophet of Toryism in the Christ Church of his time, and 'in so far as politics came into my life at all at University I should think it probably was through Ralph. I always felt he was a pure Tory from birth, a convinced one and a very good expositor of the Conservative case'. Alec Dunglass, however, viewed party politics with some detachment. He regarded himself as a Tory and gave the matter no further thought. A left-wing undergraduate of the time told Masterman that if all Tories were like Lord Dunglass he would support the retention of the House of Lords.

His main effort, in addition to growing a moustache, was still put into sport, a little soccer—he played on the left wing—but mainly cricket. Apart from joining such *ad hoc* teams as Christ Church's 'Warrigalls', which toured the local villages, he played in the Oxford Seniors, which meant he was under consideration for the University XI but, so luxuriant was the cricketing talent at the university in those years, he never got his blue. He did, however, get a Harlequin. Occasionally he played for Middlesex, for which his birth in London, arranged with such foresight by his parents, qualified him. In May 1925 he scored 19 and took a wicket for the Middlesex club against Oxford University.

He was never quite a 'top-liner' but he was tremendously keen and a good team player—good enough to be invited at the end of 1926 to join an M.C.C. team under P. F. Warner in a three-months' tour of South America. He leaped at the chance. Curiously enough, he had never been abroad; his family holidayed on their various estates or occasionally on the coast at Dunbar or Bamburgh. They did not believe they would care for 'abroad'.

So for Alec Dunglass, this 20,000-mile tour by sea and land was an exciting prospect. It did not, however, start well. The voyage was excessively slow because the coal strike was on in Britain and the liner had to make do with coal that, in Warner's words, was 'German (and bad)'. Alec Dunglass discovered he was not a natural sailor, and during his first three weeks in the steaming heat of the Argentine he was, reported P. F. Warner, quite ill, though the sufferer afterwards ascribed this to a grumbling appendix.

He perked up later and quite enjoyed the balls and dances, endless hospitality from the British communities, then still large in number, the meetings with presidents and local luminaries: 'we were treated like Royalty', wrote Warner. As for cricket, Alec Dunglass took four wickets for 26 in the first match against Montevideo but was again unfit in several games against the Argentine, Concordia, and Rosario (where his place was taken by V. A. L. Mallet, the British *chargé d'affaires*, later Sir Victor). In January 1927 he recovered and 'made some splendid hits' against an Argentine team. At the end of the tour he came ninth in the M.C.C. team's batting averages; his bowling was overs 25.4; maidens 6; runs 86; wickets 8; average 10·75.

Summing up his performance, Warner wrote: 'As a batsman he is quick on his feet and hits hard, is a very fair medium right-handed bowler, and an excellent silly-point.'[1] His brother Henry, who kept wicket to him for many years in club cricket in Scotland, puts his bowling more precisely: 'I always maintain that for the first few overs with a new ball he is a most dangerous opponent. He can make the ball swing very late, and he is quicker off the pitch than many a fast bowler.'[2]

There are, it is said, two sorts of cricket-lovers: the one who loves the romance of long afternoons on the village green and beer at the local in the evening; the other who knows that the ball is hard. Alec Dunglass knew that the ball was hard.

The game remained an absorbing pastime throughout the years; he played with the Eton Ramblers, Coldstream and other clubs until well into his fifties, and in his sixties became President of the M.C.C.

[1] The above account is based on 'Over the Andes with M.C.C.' by P. F. Warner in *The Cricketer Spring Annual, 1927*.

[2] B.B.C. Overseas Broadcast. See note, p. 3 above.

The South American tour, however, ended whatever dreams he may have had of a gentlemanly career in first-class cricket, and, in ending them, brought him face to face with the future. In the spring of 1927, he went home to think about it.

3. Dunglass's Discontent: 1927 – 31

At the Hirsel. Lanarkshire: 'Terrible unemployment'. Lloyd George and Noel Skelton. 'A hopeless fight'. Success at Lanark.

For Alec Dunglass, home now was the Hirsel, the brownish-grey freestone mansion on a gentle rise at the end of a mile-long drive through woods and fields north-east of Coldstream. His mother and father had moved there after the twelfth Earl's death in 1918, bringing with them their children and the fun and laughter absent in latter years from the stately, somewhat sombre, rooms.

By this time the family fortunes had suffered certain setbacks. The twelfth Earl in middle age had spent rather lavishly on pictures and furniture, particularly at Douglas Castle, and more recently had given his friends presents of land. When he died, Strathearn and Blair, the family lawyers since the eighteenth century, took fright at debts and death duties and as the Homes had never had any income other than that derived from land, the new Earl had to sell practically all the contents, pictures and French furniture, of Douglas Castle, which was left largely bare. Large acreages in Jedforest, Whelphill and Little Clyde went and so did the London house in Grosvenor Square.

Nevertheless income was not greatly reduced and life continued much as it had always done. The household still went to the Lanarkshire estates for the shooting, staying in what had been the factor's house, Castlemains; for the season a house was rented in London. And for some months, the tall, slender young man joined with easy assurance in the time-honoured routine, though preferring to slope off to Lord's rather than to dance till dawn, to chase butterflies rather than to follow hounds.

At the Hirsel, he undertook all his father—and the neighbourhood —expected of the heir to the earldom. 'My father made me do a lot of local things in those two years when I was perforce comparatively idle, 1926–8. Boys' Brigade—I used to do quite a lot for that,[1] Burns' Clubs, Literary Societies and the local activities which abound in the country.' He also joined his father's old regiment, the Lanarkshire Yeomanry, as a Territorial officer. He knew he was born to lead and from the start had an unflinching sense that it was his duty to do so.

He studied the management of the estates, but 'we always had professional agents, though it wasn't so professional in those days; estates then were run much more for amenity than for profit. Nevertheless we had estate agents who were qualified and devoted.'

His father, indeed, thought that this should be Alec's full-time occupation, for much needed to be done with the estates. To his mind, 'one had plenty with which to occupy oneself'. It would certainly 'have been the *natural* thing to do' in a family which had for generations been content with the duties and pleasures of the landowning aristocracy.

Alec Dunglass was not and he knew it after the first few weeks back at the Hirsel: 'I was always rather discontented with this role and felt it wasn't going to be enough.' Those who knew him well caught a gleam of bright intelligence beyond his laughing, casual manner. The deep-set blue eyes were sometimes abstracted, like those of a scholar; the wide lips had a firmness that bespoke purpose. For this young man, the life of his father and his ancestors would never suffice. He looked for a broader horizon.

But where was it to be found? The Army, the Church attracted him not at all, and a business career for the heir to an earldom was not then a practicable proposition even if he had wanted it. Diplomacy was a possibility but he had no desire to cut himself off completely from the country life he loved so much.

Almost involuntarily his thoughts turned to politics, to which at Eton and Oxford he had, as we saw, been indifferent. The more he thought of it the greater its advantages appeared. Politics could provide an active, useful life, which would easily combine with country pursuits. He began to make his plans. There was, however, one serious snag: 'My father didn't want to encourage the idea very much; it was a profession he didn't like. My mother was quite in favour. I was sure of it myself.'

There was no great family clash. His father merely jibbed at the

[1] He was president of the West of Scotland district, 1934–9. His father was national president, 1933–47.

proposition, his mother rather liked it. Her eldest son was, after all, half Lambton as well as half Home, and it was natural for Lambtons to think of politics. Alec Dunglass had read the life of John Lambton, 1st Earl of Durham. He did not consciously think of emulating him— 'I think it was more his blood in my veins'—but he found himself 'fascinated' by him. Durham, like his own mother and Mrs Alington, was a radical. He could be awkward, spiky, independent: 'He was such a nuisance in Melbourne's government that M. did almost anything to get rid of him. That rather attracted me, too. He must have been a man of independent mind.'

Alec Dunglass, indifferent to and bored by theory and party and the quietist Establishment figures of his time, could see himself in the role of a fighter against odds to wipe out some crying evil and to improve the condition of fellow human beings. He could apply the principle of service to others, 'dinned in' to him by his father, beyond the Home domains.

As for the crying evil, it was close at hand. He saw it for himself every time he visited his father's Lanarkshire lands—the 'terrible state of unemployment in steel and coal'. This was what, he said later, 'really influenced me to go into politics in the 1920s. There were many thousands unemployed in the Lanarkshire burghs and some of the men had been out of work continuously for ten years and more. I was a positive supporter of anything that would improve the industrial well-being of the country'.

Where, however, did the key lie? 'The first thing that really attracted my attention was Lloyd George's "Safeguarding of Industry" Act (1921)—a very minor form of protection.[1] It seemed a good way of stimulating home production and creating home markets big enough to employ the modern production techniques.'

Alec Dunglass later asserted in public that had it not been for Lloyd George and his appeal to the new generation to look at things with new eyes, he would not have gone into politics at all.[2] That was not the whole truth. Nevertheless Lloyd George provided a convenient spur as well as a suitable excuse.

Was he, then, to seek a Liberal ticket? The prospect was unpromising. Lloyd George, the great war leader, was out of office and in many

[1] The Act protected key industries from foreign dumping. It was repudiated by Lloyd George in 1923 when he was out of office.
[2] Maiden speech in the House of Commons, 15th February 1932.

eyes discredited. Asquith was dead and the future of the Liberals seemed doubtful and was to prove non-existent. The Labour Party was a possible alternative but, though it represented many of the unemployed, it had acted feebly during its first brief term of office in 1924, its economic policy was undefined, and some of its members were pledged to the so-called 'dictatorship of the proletariat'.

In the end, it had to be the Conservative Party. Dunglass's own belief in protection to stimulate home production and hence employment 'fitted in pretty well with Conservative philosophy and policies. I thought Tories had the better idea how to deal with this. When I had studied the Conservative policy a bit more I came to the conclusion that we had a better chance than any other party of solving the industrial troubles and unemployment. Which indeed we began to do—under the name of a National Government [i.e. from 1930–5], but nevertheless it was 80 per cent Conservative.'

So Alec Dunglass sought a Tory seat. He spoke at local Party meetings in Scotland, and for the Junior Imperial League, the Primrose League and other Tory groups. He made himself known as a would-be candidate to Scottish M.P.s such as Sir John Gilmour, a Home family friend and at that time Secretary of State for Scotland, and to Archibald Noel Skelton, then Tory M.P. for Perth.

Skelton, an Edinburgh barrister, was one of the thinkers in the Conservative Party in a decade when thinkers were thin on the ground and ill-regarded by the Party as a whole. A friend of Anthony Eden— M.P. for Warwick and Leamington since 1923 when he was twenty-six—Skelton put his impress on several generations of young Conservatives, largely through his brief essay *Constructive Conservatism*, which appeared at first as a series in *The Spectator* and was printed in book form in 1924.[1] It was still being heartily recommended to Tory neophytes by R. A. Butler twenty years later when he was in charge of the Conservative Research Department after the second world war.

To Alec Dunglass, Skelton was 'a very able, thoughtful Conservative,' and he studied his work with care: 'It was a good start to one's political philosophy.' Skelton knocked the Establishment hard: Conservatism, he wrote, had become 'a bloodless, rigid, paralysed habit of mind . . . which has often imposed what would have been an intoler-

[1] With an introduction by Sir Robert Horne. William Blackwood, Edinburgh and London.

28

able strain on any loyalty less patient and less profound than is that of the people of Britain to the underlying truths of Conservatism'.

Yet, he believed, only Conservatives could release 'the best energies of the country.' While Socialism had plenty of force, fire and energy, its doctrines could lead only to 'economic disaster and moral despair,' to 'the omnipotent State, the kept citizen, responsibility checked, initiative crippled, character in cold-storage, wealth squandered . . .'

Now Conservatism must apply 'its active principles to the deeper troubles of the new era'. It must explain itself because democracy, he quoted Balfour as saying, 'is government by explanation.' Alec Dunglass never forgot the point; when he became Prime Minister nearly forty years later he announced to the nation that he would explain policies, plainly and clearly.

Politics, Skelton insisted, was no longer merely a matter of who was to administer the country's affairs. That might satisfy 'the prosperous, peach-fed classes'. They, after all, had many other interests in life and means of enjoying it—'fastidious living, beautiful homes, the enjoyment of literature, art, travel, the closeness and variety of their points of contact with human culture and civilization'.

It was not enough for the new generations. Conservatives must understand that universal education had altered the English habit of mind. Once, and traditionally, it had been 'prone to be sluggish and prejudiced'. Now the English were alert and receptive—and therefore wide open to the Socialist 'who comes disguised as an educator and teacher'. Conservatives must, therefore, take the trouble to expound their view of life; otherwise their case would go by default, with grievous consequences. Another thing: in the new, educated democracy 'if the British people do not now take their pleasure sadly, they certainly take their politics seriously'.

Skelton turned to unemployment, housing, the agricultural emergency, the financial burdens of the State, and found an underlying 'master-problem'. The fact was that for wage-earners 'political status and educational status have out-stripped economic status'. In short, they had the vote and free education but too little money.

They were unable to buy their own homes. Yet a chief principle of Conservatism was that 'the character and economic freedom of the individual citizen' depended on his personal ownership of property. Citizens knew this perfectly well. It was the reason why they gave their money to the Friendly Societies, Savings Banks, Trades Unions (on

29

their benefits side), War Savings certificates and Co-operative Societies.

Socialists, however, sought to persuade them that 'ownership by the State is ownership by the people, implying that that means a property-owning democracy. In fact, of course, it does not. What everybody owns nobody owns . . . We have yet to hear of the man who, in the Great War, rushed to arms to preserve his share in the L.C.C. tramways or in Battersea Park'.

The getting and then the using of private property were good for human character—the exercise of thrift, control, increased responsibility, a medium to express moral and intellectual qualities—and for the stability of the State, without which life could not be enjoyed or each individual develop.

Everything that weakened individual character was 'anathema to the Conservative', which is why action by the State should be limited to 'helping the individual to help himself'. Direct intervention by the State was second best though, Skelton admitted, 'essential in many cases, to sustain, shelter and support those who have failed in health or occupation'.

All citizens 'should possess something of their own'; but how was this possible for the wage-earner? He 'has only the economic status of a machine, for his wages as such are, and can only be, part of the costs of production, occupying the same position as the expenses of running the machines of the factory or workshop in which he is employed'.

This could have been lifted bodily from Engels. To the Conservative Establishment it was an over-bold admission—and what in any case was Skelton's answer? He offered a tripartite plan: workers should be given co-partnership in industries, 'or its halfway house, profit-sharing'. For the man who rented or leased his farm there should be ownership as part of a co-operative; 'for the rural world as a whole, agricultural co-operation' should be the aim. Such changes would give real incentives to workers; their interest would be identified with that of the owners. As a consequence, Skelton claimed, strikes would decrease, and employee and employer alike would agree on the need for 'tariff reform' which would mean increased prosperity for both. The Socialist Trade Union leaders might denounce the idea but, Skelton made plain, 'battle has to be joined with them in any case'.

Alec Dunglass was greatly taken by Skelton's arguments. His

thinking, like that of many Tories during the middle decades of the century, was rooted in *Constructive Conservatism*. One only of Skelton's chief ideas he did not accept. This was his belief in the need to use the referendum, that is, for Parliament to put important issues to the vote of the country at large.

The mechanism, Skelton believed, was 'needed now to protect democracy. For if democracy, faced in the new era by Socialism as its scarcely disguised enemy, is, from a constitutional point of view, to be made stable and safe, if its property and liberty are to be preserved, the people in the last resort, must directly and for themselves decide their own fate'.

Skelton was writing at a time when there was general alarm that Socialist-Communism—'Bolshevism' it was termed—was spreading from its source in Russia. The first Labour Government contained many admirers of the 'workers' state', and a letter, forgery though it may have been, was published from Zinoviev, President of the Communist International, giving the British Communist Party instructions for seditious activities. It seemed possible that a Socialist Government would pass radical legislation for which it had no electoral mandate (as, in the 1960s, one such Government did).

Alec Dunglass did not doubt the undemocratic aims of Socialism. He simply disbelieved in the efficacy of the referendum as a defence against them. Skelton 'had a bee in his bonnet about referenda. He was always very keen on the idea! Sir Robert Menzies once told me we ought to have the Australian system, the alternative vote: better than a referendum but I prefer the system we know.

'Skelton never convinced me. The questions have to be so over-simplified. Gibraltar *is* a simple case—do you want to stay with Britain or do you not?[1] With more difficult and complex questions I don't see how it's possible to frame the questions: you remember the Peace Ballot in the 1930s: are you in favour of peace or war?'

By 1928 Alec Dunglass, fortified by Skelton and backed by the Scottish Unionist Party, took the plunge and was adopted as Conservative candidate for Coatbridge and Airdrie—east of Glasgow. It was very obviously going to be a practice run. Although Labour had won the

---

[1] In the 1960s the Spanish Government applied pressure to take Gibraltar from British suzerainty. They were supported by the U.N. General Assembly's sub-committee on colonialism. In 1968, a referendum was held and almost 100 per cent of Gibraltarians opted to remain British.

seat by only 57 votes in 1924, since then Conservative chances had slumped appallingly. Coatbridge, once a boom town producing almost one-third of all Britain's pig-iron, was suffering from short time, unemployment and poverty. In Westminster, the Conservative Government under Stanley Baldwin had lost whatever steam it had started with, and the Chancellor of the Exchequer, Winston Churchill, had proved much less than successful.

When the election came in May 1929 the Conservatives were on the defensive and Dunglass found it 'a hopeless fight'. He lost by over 7,000 votes to the Labour member (9,210 to 16,789), though putting the Liberal into third place. Nationally, also, the Conservatives lost, and Ramsay MacDonald's second Labour Government came to power, though that power was at the mercy of fifty-nine Liberal M.P.s.

Alec Dunglass was not unduly cast down. He had won golden opinions from his supporters. Nevertheless the prospect of waiting another five years before trying again was daunting. Perhaps, like the peer's son in *The Chiltern Hundreds* who was defeated at an election, he hesitated, pondering that: 'Landowning's a full-time job. When Father's agent dies, I'll take his job and run the good old place.' Certainly his father would have welcomed the idea.

But then came a 'tremendous piece of luck'. The former Unionist M.P. for the Lanark Division, Mitchell, having been defeated in 1929, retired and in late 1930 Lord Dunglass was adopted in his place. The 'luck' was personal as well as political. The Lanark constituency was on the family's home ground, the Douglas estates, and if elected Alec Dunglass would be representing many Home tenants and workers. This, to the Earl, was perfectly proper—'he was quite happy about that'—and he withdrew his objections to his eldest son's ambitions.

Nor was a new General Election long delayed. The Great Depression spread from America to Europe. In Britain, unemployment bounded upwards. The Budget appeared unbalanceable, and the Labour Government, plagued by many mutually inconsistent policies, was visibly unable to cope. The Cabinet split and a National Government was formed, still led by the Labour Prime Minister, J. Ramsay MacDonald but including Conservatives and Liberals. Large cuts were made in all salaries paid by the State; the gold standard was suspended and the pound fell by a quarter on the foreign exchange.

During these alarming events, Alec Dunglass had been working hard in his constituency, but he did not always follow the official,

Baldwin party line, which seemed to him unimaginative. Instead in the early months of Socialist government, he spoke in favour of the Empire Free Trade doctrine, powerfully propagated by Lord Beaverbrook: 'We must develop the Empire where the markets, instead of being hostile and static and diminishing, are certain to develop and extend with the growth of the Colonies', Dunglass told the Scottish Unionist Conference at Edinburgh on 14th December 1929. 'What more natural than that the party which has always supported the Empire should advocate an Empire policy? Let us put Empire development in the forefront of our policy for the next General Election. May I ask the women throughout Scotland and the country to remember the Empire and to spend Imperially?'

By the middle of 1931 Empire Free Trade on Beaverbrook lines was a dead duck. Instead of exhortations to 'spend Imperially', the cry was now for economy, and Dunglass changed his tune. He bluntly told a Glasgow meeting on 20th November 1930 that when the Unionists returned to power there would be no new schemes of social service. Expenditure of public money had to be reduced. The party had to stand for capital because the more wealth brought into the country the more trade was stimulated; the more wealth circulated the better conditions became. The Socialists believed in capital, despite their disclaimers, just as much as he did; but their levelling-down policies would bring the clever down to the level of the dull, the thrifty to the level of the spendthrift.

Such talk was cold comfort for the Lanarkshire unemployed, and Alec Dunglass had some rough meetings: at least once, he was obliged to leave a hall through a window. Yet in those months of confusion few politicians in or out of Government had anything better to offer— except for Sir Oswald Mosley, a junior Labour Minister whose ideas were rejected by his Party but were 'a blueprint for most of the constructive advances in economic policy to the present day.'[1] To Alec Dunglass then as now it was obvious only that: 'If we went on taking more out of the pot than we put in, we should be in trouble.'

Nevertheless, if he was to win, he had to gain a proportion of the miners' votes; support from the agricultural areas would not be enough. He was lucky again. The Labour Party was split down the middle and the ordinary voter did not know any longer where his loyalty lay: was

[1] A. J. P. Taylor, The Oxford History of England, English History, 1914–45, Oxford, 1965, p. 285.

it to MacDonald, Snowden, J. H. Thomas—all strong and famous Labourites—who were with the Tories in the National Government, or to the Labour rump led by 'Uncle Arthur' Henderson, always a somewhat remote figure? Dunglass, standing as a National Unionist candidate, insisted in all his speeches that he was completely in support of MacDonald, who had put the nation before party.

Parliament was dissolved on 6th October 1931, and a General Election took place on 27th October. The contending parties were the National Coalition and the rumps of the Labour and Liberal parties. The result in the country at large was a foregone conclusion but not in Lanark.

Alec Dunglass was third time lucky. His Labour opponent, J. Gibson, frightened away a number of middle-of-the-road voters by introducing on to his platform such violently Leftist Independent Labour Party M.P.s as James Maxton, David Kirkwood and George Buchanan—the 'Clydesiders' who were bogeymen to the burgesses of Lanarkshire.

Luck, certainly, was with him and so was the national 'swing'. Far more decisive, however, in this difficult constituency were his own sincerity and good nature. He obviously hated unemployment, would do his utmost for the poor of the constituency, and had the drive and intelligence that were needed. This was no 'wet' sprig of an effete aristocracy. He was adept in the smiling riposte to the angry heckler; awkward questions he answered fully and frankly, baulking at nothing.

It came as no surprise to those who had watched his electioneering when on 27th October 1931 he won by an overwhelming majority, 20,675 votes to 11,815. His supporters carried him on their shoulders through the streets of Lanark, accompanied by a brass band and torch-bearers.

A week later, on 3rd November, a tall, sandy-haired figure, one hand casually in trouser-pocket, strolled across Palace Yard and into the House. Though no one, least of all himself, realized it, a new star had risen on the political horizon.

4. Wooing and Winning: 1931–6

In the Commons. Maxton and 'the nice, kind old things'. P.P.S. to Chancellor Chamberlain. Marriage to Elizabeth Alington. League of Nations. Paganism and permissiveness.

At Westminster in the autumn of 1931, Alec Dunglass was not merely a new boy in an old school. The 'school' itself was in an abnormal condition. Parliament and Government were on a wartime footing and nearly all M.P.s were on the same side. No less than 521 Conservatives, Labour and Liberals had dovetailed their differences to form a National Coalition Government. The Opposition consisted of 85 dissident remnants of the Labour and Liberal Parties.

The Prime Minister was the Labour leader, Ramsay MacDonald, who had once thrilled the multitude with his vibrant voice and romantic appearance but was, thought Dunglass, 'past his best'. The real power rested with the former Conservative Prime Minister, Stanley Baldwin, the deceptively placid master-manager, now Lord President of the Council. At the Exchequer for a few weeks remained Philip Snowden—'an acidulated, precise performer. I don't think he would ever arouse any emotions at all'. When he retired to the Lords, he was succeeded by the tall, saturnine Neville Chamberlain, later to play so prominent a part in the political life of Alec Dunglass.

The slender Opposition was led by George Lansbury: 'He was the nicest possible character but totally ineffective in Parliament. He was there I think only because he voiced the passionate peace pledge philosophy of the time.' Supporting Lansbury were Stafford Cripps—'people were very much attracted by him'—and C. R. Attlee. Attlee later became Leader of the Labour Party and after the war twice Prime Minister. 'At that time the House would scarcely have marked him down as a future leader, though he was always in his place. He never tried to make an effect; his speeches were the shortest he could possibly contrive but always very much to point.'

Lloyd George, 'the man who won the war' and Alec Dunglass's early inspirer, still sat in the Commons beneath his mane of white hair, though his support had sadly shrunk to a few members of his own family. Scarcely more regarded was the frowning figure of Winston Churchill who 'made his brilliant speeches from the corner of the back bench'. Few took them or him seriously. In Dunglass's early days in the Commons he was occupied by his opposition to the Bill giving independence to India, 'but the majority judged that things had gone too far to give India a longer time to mature her politics', and Dunglass believed that the majority were right.

Alec Dunglass had small acquaintance with the great ones and less with the embryonic great, Harold Macmillan, R. A. Butler, Anthony Eden, Oliver Stanley, Lord Cranborne. But he did not lack for friends in the House, particularly among the Scots. One of his family's intimates, Sir John Gilmour, was Minister of Agriculture and later Home Secretary. At the Scottish Office under Sir Archibald Sinclair was Noel Skelton. From the start Skelton attached Dunglass to the Scottish Office as an assistant Parliamentary Private Secretary. This was an unofficial and unspecific post and did not prevent him from taking part in debate.

With proper maiden modesty Alec Dunglass allowed three months to elapse before his maiden speech, which he made on 15th February 1932. This was the fourth day of the second reading of the Imports Bill, one of the chief weapons by which Neville Chamberlain meant to restore the British economy. The Bill provided for a duty of between 10 and 20 per cent to be put on about half the goods Britian imported, though for the time being Empire goods, raw materials and nearly all foodstuffs were exempt.

Objections came, naturally, from the free traders on the Government side and, more particularly, from the Scottish Labour M.P.s, among them the 'Clydesiders', who believed tariffs must raise the cost of living which inevitably would most seriously affect the unemployed whom they represented.

In his light voice, occasionally shushing his s's, sometimes plosive with emphasis, Dunglass boldly claimed to be himself a Clydesider. He recognized their sincerity and said that there was no one on the Government side who would not drop the Bill if he thought it was going to add to the burden already on the shoulders of the poor. But in reality it was the goods made by cheap labour abroad and dumped in Britain which were a 'danger to the standard of life of the working people of this country'.

Moreover the revenue from the import duties could be used to relieve the heavy taxation crippling industry; until industry was flourishing no real reduction in unemployed could be made. There could be no payment of wages and no employment unless the products of industry were marketable at a profit or at any rate not at a loss.

In Scotland, he said, his own country, 27 per cent of the working population were unemployed; in Lanarkshire it was as high as 32 per cent.[1] The fact had to be faced that many of those in shipbuilding, the main employment on the Clyde, would never get jobs in the industry again. The unemployed must, therefore, be diverted to agriculture, not merely to arable farming but milk and milk products, fruit, bacon and poultry, or be absorbed by new industry in new places.

Dunglass, though he spoke with assurance, was saying nothing new, nothing indeed with which the Chancellor of the Exchequer, Neville Chamberlain, would have disagreed. These were the orthodox economics of the time, and by applying them firmly Chamberlain gradually righted the national economy, so that by 1937 both production and employment reached record heights.

All the same, some young Conservatives, prominent among them Harold Macmillan, distrusted orthodox economics and were mentally edging towards a planned economy. Dunglass became aware of these ideas and the Keynesian theory generally though economic theory was never his *métier*: 'We were all interested in economics—I rather shirked them as "the most inexact of sciences".' Macmillan and his followers were well versed in theory and were thought to be good people to deal with such things, to be put in charge of the economy. The economy was running fairly smoothly at that time, until the inflationary period of war production in 1936. Then the inflation began to hit.

'Everyone was attracted by the Keynesian theory but few know how to put it into practice. It is easy to prime the pump in depression but hard to control the boom. Macmillan, later on, was right when he produced the analogy of driving a motor car; the driver presses the accelerator or the brake with the least possible disturbance to the passenger. But even now no one has got the pressures right.'

[1] The peak of unemployment, including those who had ceased to register, was reached in Britain as a whole in September 1932 with 3¾ million. It fell by a million in 1933.

Alec Dunglass was never part of the Macmillan group—his extra-Chamber activities being confined to the Scottish Members' group and to a discussion-dining club led by Lieut.-Col. the Rt Hon. H. H. Spender-Clay, who had married one of the Astors. But he came to know Macmillan, and what has been called 'the stimulating fringes', at K. Tennant's Westminster house where Macmillan, Noel Skelton, Archibald Sinclair, Robert Bernays and Thomas Dugdale met.[1]

Neither economic nor political theory attracted Dunglass. He had a more practical turn of mind. He wanted to do something immediate for that hard core of unemployed who remained, particularly in his own constituency, long after the general 'upturn' in the economy. So he hammered away at schemes such as large-scale migration from industrially dead villages, and the re-training of men under thirty-five in trades for which there was a future.

With the wholesale fervour of youth, he demanded that what could never be mended should be ended, that villages with no industrial future should be 'wiped off the map'. He did not believe that industry could or ought to be moved into the stricken areas where, he said, 'gaunt and monstrous skeletons meet the prospective employer when he comes to look at these depressed areas'.

Alec Dunglass took part in most of the debates of the time on the bitter subject of unemployment. But never did he so arouse the wrath of the Scottish Labour M.P.s as when he defended the 'means test': 'I believe our people realize that when an unemployed man falls out of the insurance and comes on to public assistance and has therefore to be kept at the public charge, information as regards his resources is essential.' There was uproar in the Commons and one Clydesider, James McGovern (I.L.P. Member for Shettleston), was removed from the Chamber by the Serjeant-at-Arms.

Dunglass was, strictly speaking, right: if public assistance is given, whether in the form of family allowance or otherwise, the need for it must be established, otherwise public funds will be 'milked'. In the context of the mid 1930s he was wrong. Better then that the public should have been swindled on occasion rather than that the authorities should have been seen to be cheese-paring to a small section of the nation who, generally through no fault of their own—and in part through the ineptitude of their leaders—had become unemployable.

[1] Colin R. Coote, *A Companion of Honour: the story of Walter Elliot*, London, 1965, p. 148. Kathleen Tennant became wife of Col. Walter Elliot, M.P.

The means test victimized the provident. Thus the bitterness of the days of mass unemployment—with their hunger marches, public demonstrations, coffins carried to Whitehall—was kept alive, and carefully fed by Socialist propaganda. It contributed to the Conservative *débâcle* of 1945.

Even though his speeches enraged the Socialists, most of them could not bring themselves to dislike their author. Dunglass, indeed, was generally approved by the House of Commons, even by his most savage opponents. 'Alec,' the Clydesider James Maxton said to him in the tea-room, 'I had been thinking that, come the revolution, I'll have you strung up on a lamp-post, but I think instead I'll offer you a cup of tea.' Alec delightedly accepted and in debate observed:

'When I came into this House, I thought that Members opposite were ogres. I have begun to realize that they are nice, kind old things and that any revolution they bring about would be so kindly that everybody's profit would probably be three times what it was before.... Their threats are only the theoretical ramblings of genial idealists.'[1]

It was not unemployment alone which agitated the Commons and the country in the mid 1930s. The threat of war and the need for defence against a resurgent Germany evoked bitter debates. Foreign affairs came back into the limelight. Japan invaded Manchuria, Mussolini threatened—and later invaded—Abyssinia, and Britain could do little to enforce 'collective security' since her armed forces had been run down every year from 1925 when the Locarno Treaty was signed. In 1935 the Royal Air Force ranked only fifth in Europe; nine cavalry regiments, sixty-one batteries and twenty-one battalions of infantry had been disbanded; and the Navy had not been lower in numbers for forty years.

Yet Alec Dunglass never opened his mouth in the Commons on either defence or foreign affairs—a strange fact in view of his future role which was to be, almost exclusively, concerned with these matters. The explanation is that in these years he thought of little outside the needs of his constituents; for this, indeed, he had gone into politics in the first place. On unemployment and schemes to help the unemployed he had the facts at his finger-tips. Foreign affairs were as yet a closed book to him.

He knew, of course, that rearmament was a vital necessity and that Baldwin was afraid of the subject. The propaganda of the League of

[1] 21st November 1934. Debate on the Address.

Nations Union and the Peace Ballot had its effect and, as always, Baldwin was sensitive to the national mood. Dunglass observed also the extraordinary illogicalities of the Socialists who demanded war against aggressors but resolutely rejected any idea that Britain should be made capable of fighting.

At the hustings before the 1935 election, Dunglass did indeed venture a comment on the subject. Taking his line from Chamberlain, Chancellor of the Exchequer, who had spoken delicately of 'filling the gaps' in defence, he emphasized that there was going to be no rearmament, and then talked in circumlocutions of a 're-equipment' of the Navy and protection against air attack: 'Any Government which asks less of its people today would be deliberately gambling with the lives of the people,'[1] he cautiously observed. 'We had,' he reflected thirty years later, in relation to the public mood, 'to tread warily to get anything done at all.'

He retained his Lanark seat on 14th November 1935, with a drop in his majority partly due to the fact that Labour and I.L.P. put up candidates, but he still polled 17,759, a majority of 6,809 over his Labour opponent. In the Commons as a whole, though the Conservative numbers were down, the Government kept an overall majority of 247; the Cabinet itself had 15 Conservatives out of 22. It was still a National coalition but now preponderantly Conservative.

For Alec Dunglass the new Parliament opened brightly. His devotion to the cause of his constituents and his knowledgeableness on the subject of employment had not gone unnoticed; and he was invited to become a P.P.S. to the Ministry of Labour. He accepted with alacrity and began work for the Parliamentary Secretary, Lieut.-Col. Anthony Muirhead.

A few months later came another happy surprise. David Margesson, the Chief Whip, asked whether he might recommend him as P.P.S. to Neville Chamberlain, the Chancellor of the Exchequer, and heir-apparent to the premiership when Baldwin should announce his expected retirement. This, indeed, was unforeseen preferment. It did not, however, spring primarily from Alec Dunglass's achievements as a parliamentarian.

Chamberlain, who was a very shy man, was out of touch with Members, especially younger ones, who translated his shyness as stand-offishness, his curt speech as disdain. Margesson thought that

[1] 3rd November 1935, speaking in his constituency.

Lord Dunglass, with his easy manner and the entrée everywhere, could humanize him:

'I imagine,' reflected Alec Dunglass many years later, 'that the Chief Whip wanted somebody he thought would keep Chamberlain in touch rather more socially with M.P.s. It was absolute murder trying to get him *in* to the smoking-room, or to talk out of school at all, he was so shy. He was charming to work for, in that he was most considerate to one as an individual, but was very difficult in the sense that he would never expand—never gossip. He made no effort to put himself across and no one could really do it for him.'

Scarcely had Dunglass accepted the post of P.P.S. than Parliament rose and his thoughts turned in quite another direction. He was going to get married. Over the years—he was now thirty-three—girls had come and girls had gone. He had never been a deb's delight but he liked female company and his smiling, natural charm was attractive to the opposite sex. On the other hand, he was discriminating. He did not fall on his knees before the first pretty face he saw. He looked for other qualities.

Three years earlier, during the Parliamentary vacation, his younger sister Rachel[1] had invited Elizabeth, one of the daughters of the Dean of Durham, to stay at the Hirsel. The Dean was none other than Dr Alington, formerly Alec Dunglass's headmaster at Eton. Alec did not recall Elizabeth Alington, nor she him, which was not surprising: Alec was nineteen when he left Eton, Elizabeth thirteen—and big boys of nineteen do not pay much attention to girls of thirteen.

It was not love at first sight. They met occasionally—and usually spent the time composing crosswords. One of their joint efforts appeared in *The Times* on 13th October 1933. But when Elizabeth came to London with her family Alec fell into the habit of taking her out—to parties, to the theatre, to dinners *à deux*, and for walks in the countryside.

Elizabeth was a shy girl, with soft brown hair and a sense of humour. She was a trained secretary and she worked voluntarily for such schemes as 'New Homes for Old' and the 'Personal Service League', which collected and distributed clothes to the unemployed mining families in County Durham. She had a deep personal, but unobtrusive, faith in God—and she was very attractive.

Early in 1936, Alec and Elizabeth went walking in the Dropmore

[1] Now Lady William Scott.

grounds in Buckinghamshire and he proposed to her. She accepted and the wedding day was fixed for 3rd October 1936, the place Durham Cathedral. The ceremony was to be performed by the Archbishop of York and by the bride's father the Dean.

Preparations went ahead for a large and fashionable wedding. All the Homes were coming and with them a large contingent of their estate employees—who gave the couple a mahogany writing desk, and were told by Alec that 'estates are not very fashionable these days but there is plenty of warrant in history and plenty of determination in the present for the carrying on of this estate in the best tradition of the past'.

The great day dawned and found Alec and Elizabeth breaking tradition. Quietly at 8 a.m. they met and went together to a small chapel where, alone, they were given Holy Communion. Then they parted to dress and meet again in the Cathedral.

There they sang a hymn, which Elizabeth already knew by heart, written for the occasion by her father. Its last verse was prophetic. It invoked the Holy Spirit to

> Be present in our hearts today,
> All powerful to bless, and give
> To these, Thy children, grace that they
> May love, and through their loving live.

Dr Alington's prayer did not go unanswered. The couple through the subsequent troubled decades, in sickness and in health, did truly 'through their loving live', being a perfect complement, and the exemplar of the blessings of a true Christian marriage.

For honeymoon they motored through the heart of Europe, via the Rhine and Switzerland into Italy—Alec Dunglass's first exploration of the Continent. On their return they set up house in Chester Square, London, and Lord Home presented them with Springhill House, where Alec had spent his boyhood.

In this fortunate year of 1936, even the small things which had sometimes divided father and son were finally dissipated. They were reconciled even in their views of the League of Nations. For long, Lord Home had firmly supported anything which had—or appeared to have—peace as its aim and he was chairman of the Eastern Borders council of the League of Nations Union. His son had reservations about the League, first because Britain was militarily too weak to support it if a real emergency came, and secondly because the United

States—obviously set to become the world's greatest power—had never been in it. He had yet deeper doubts; like others he found the moral implications of the Covenant repugnant and would have said, with Edward Grey, 'I do not like the idea of resorting to war to prevent war.'

Previously Lord Home had not agreed with him but the events of 1936, when sanctions were invoked against Italy who had invaded Abyssinia, alarmed him. If they had been successful short of war, that was one thing; they were not, partly because the United States had continued, even increased, her trade with Italy, while Russia (since 1934 a member of the League) had exported even more than her usual quantity of oil to Mussolini; and thirteen member states of the League refused to stop their imports from Italy. Britain alone had carried out her pledge and borne the economic brunt.

It was too much for the Earl. He resigned from his chairmanship and from the League not least because the Union had voted for a continuance of sanctions and, he said at a meeting: 'Their continuance could surely achieve nothing but the intense resentment of the Italian people and the embitterment of the hearts of the children of other nations—a tragic outlook for the future of those in Italy and elsewhere who are innocent of the sins of commission and omission of our time.'

This sad experience did not end the Earl's pursuit of peace—'a most democratic peer', a local Border paper called him—nor his belief in the power of Christian charity to solve the ills of the world. This was doubtless why, during the Spanish civil war in the late 1930s, he joined the United Christian Front, started by Capt. A. H. M. Ramsay, M.P. for Peebles, a distinguished soldier who lived at Kellie Castle in Angus and was detained with no charge preferred under Regulation 18b from 1940 to 1944.[1] Although Ramsay's motives in supporting the Franco side in Spain—it was also the Christian side—were understandable, he was violently attacked by the Communists. So was Dunglass. The *Daily Worker* pretended that it was he and not his father who belonged to the United Christian Front; although the error was pointed out, it was never corrected.

Alec Dunglass shared his father's—and Capt. Ramsay's—belief in the Christian message. He doubted, however, whether it was any longer getting through to young people. He blamed parsons and ministers who, he told the Church of Scotland Assembly on 27th May 1935, 'do nothing to attract young people today'.

[1] Ramsay remained M.P. for Peebles until 1945. He died in 1955.

This was the more serious because 'There is a pagan revival, stark and real. Paganism offers youth discipline, devotion to corporate action. It offers opportunities in the service of the State. It offers all these things with all the inducements which the modern propagandist can set forth.

'The modern pagan outlook is that if the State says "Let us prepare for war, then the State is right. Let us be freed from the fetters of Christianity and then we can get ahead."' (He was here referring to Communism rather than Nazism.)

He did not condemn young people. Indeed he spoke of the 'permissiveness' of the 1930s without evident disapproval: 'As a generation I think you will find that they are much less inclined to passive obedience to their elders than previous generations were.

'The "yes, Mama" of the Victorian age is replaced by the "why, Mama" of today. Parental authority, which is dying today, is dying with the permission of the parents of today.'

Young people would no longer drift to church because 'there is nothing else to do'. Instead they would go 'hiking'—that modish word of the 1930s for walking. Well and good: 'If the hiker won't go to the Church, the Church must go to the hiker.' The Church did. Open-air services with 'hikers' in shorts sitting on hillsides became a feature of the later 1930s. But soon the hiking gave way to the marching, while Lord Dunglass found himself, like Addison, involved in 'Superior toils, and heavier weight of cares'.

5. Appeasement's Victim: 1936 – 40

Prime Minister's P.P.S. Chamberlain's strategy. At Munich. Cliveden and von Trott. The dissidents. War. Impossible tasks.

Even so, when Parliament reassembled in late October 1936, Alec Dunglass was one of the happiest men in the House of Commons. He had an adorable wife and a stimulating if difficult job with a senior Minister in the Government. Life was good; happy, halcyon years seemed to open before him with no hint of disaster and every prospect of advancement in his chosen career.

It is well ordained by a beneficent providence that human beings have no prevision of the future. Alec Dunglass's zest for living might have evaporated like dew on the grass had he foreseen that within three years his political aspirations would be in ruins, possibly for ever damned, that within four years his new master would be dead, and he himself be lying desperately ill encased in plaster while the civilized world smashed itself to pieces with high explosive, starvation and psychological warfare whose true aim is the dissemination of lies and the induction of neurosis.

Blessedly unaware of the fate in store for him, Alec Dunglass sped into the corridors of power and was content. Participation 'at the centre of things' was for him the real attraction of politics. Of course his role as P.P.S. was humble and remained humble even after he and his master moved from No. 11 to No. 10 Downing Street. It has been knowledgeably said that

some P.P.S.'s are lazy, limiting themselves to arranging pairs for their Ministers and acting as hod-carriers between the front-bench and the Civil Service box in the House when Ministers are engaged in a debate. They never get anywhere. Others take an active part in the Minister's political life, working in the Ministry as a political aide, listening to criticisms, keeping the Minister informed of back-bench opinion, warning him, encouraging him and perhaps most important of all being used as a sounding board for his own ideas. It depends on ambition.[1]

Alec Dunglass was ambitious enough, ready for any amount of hard work. It was, however, a long time before he advanced from hod-carrying to becoming in any sense a warner or encourager of Chamberlain, though he did later do his part in seeking to influence M.P.s in his favour. He could not affect policy; he had no right to be present at Cabinet meetings where decisions were taken. He was 'on the fringe'.

Nor was his new master easy to get on with. Chamberlain was almost always aloof. Though his probity was total, though he had great intellectual gifts, and loved Shakespeare and chamber music, yet in personal relationships he was remote, even forbidding. 'I liked him. I think he liked me. But if one went in at the end of the day for a chat or gossip, he would be inclined to ask "What do you want?" He was a very difficult man to get to know. Few colleagues were at ease with him. Without his wife, he would never have faced social contacts.

'He was at his best relaxed with a small party after dinner, not more than half a dozen.' He had a 'nice quiet humour in after-dinner reminiscences but it broke down badly when he tried to amuse a crowd. Extracting his jokes from his speeches became a game among his secretaries'. His reserve never entirely disappeared except with his family circle.

Alec Dunglass, though at ease in most company, was a sensitive man, all too aware how incongruous it was for him, a junior M.P., to attempt to, as it were, launch into society a man twice his age who was also Prime Minister of Britain. He did his best but he was not cut out to be a public relations officer, and his success was limited: 'One evening Alec Douglas-Home (then Lord Dunglass) asked some of us to look into the smoking-room before dinner because he was bringing the P.M. in and wanted friendly souls to rally round. Alec . . . felt that the P.M. ought, like his predecessor [Baldwin], to meet informally more of the men whose Leader he was.

'About eight or ten of us gathered together and conversation admittedly dragged a bit, though we managed to get going to some extent on fly-fishing, which was Neville's great love. In spite of our efforts, however, it was not a great success and, as I was leaving the room, my Socialist friend James Maxton came up to me and said, "Ach,

[1] R. Bevins, *The Greasy Pole*, London, 1965, pp. 28–9.

Jimmy, ye'll have to do better than that. Anybody could see how un-happy ye all were."

'We certainly did not succeed in getting the new P.M. to frequent the friendly smoking-room.' [1]

Nevertheless through the agitated years leading up to the outbreak of war on 3rd September 1939, Alec Dunglass came to admire, then to feel warm affection,[2] and finally to pity and seek to protect Chamber-lain.[3] He began to understand that part of his aloofness, certainly a handicap in his political career, was due to the fact that in his formative years he had spent long periods of time in isolation managing his father's sisal plantations on Andros in the West Indies with only books and nature for companions; the habit of solitude never entirely left him. He was 'a rare, complex person, half of him hidden from the world'.

Alec Dunglass noted and sought to emulate the quickness of his working, the long hours he put in; he was 'a man of method, incapable of inaccuracy', his precision of thought and expression was 'uncanny'. Any slipshodness was 'mercilessly exposed. He was master of the art of marshalling facts, writing minutes and devising formulae'.

He was impressed, too, by Chamberlain's encyclopaedic knowledge and his prodigious memory. He recalled a dinner-table talk which turned on unusual names. Someone mentioned Wilhelmina Belcher; only Chamberlain knew that she was an obscure friend of Walter Scott.

Though Dunglass did not share his 'happiest taste in music and art', he found that Chamberlain's knowledge of natural history—birds, wild flowers, animals and insects—was 'professional' and when a few years later Chamberlain twice visited the Hirsel this brought the two men closer. Neither this nor anything else ever made them intimates.

As Chancellor of the Exchequer, Alec Dunglass recalled, Chamber-lain was orthodox, un-Keynesian, 'believing that the budget must be balanced annually, rather than over a number of years; he did not like leaving somebody else holding the baby'. He also believed that high

[1] James Stuart (Viscount Stuart of Findhorn), *Within the Fringe*, London, 1967, p. 83.

[2] Not, however, quite to the fulsome point of Sir Henry ('Chips') Channon who confided to his diary: 'I know now that I really love the P.M. and have great hero-worship for him—I want to embrace him: I trust I shall never be so foolish as to do so.' *Chips: the Diaries of Sir Henry Channon*, London, ed. R. R. James, 1967, p. 191.

[3] What follows is based on notes Lord Dunglass made a few years after Chamber-lain's death.

taxation could become the enemy of social progress. He was strongly in favour of protecting the home producer—'not an ideal system but inevitable in a world of varying costs and highly subsidized exports'.

He had been the main architect of empire preference; he had a passionate belief in Commonwealth and Empire as 'a living symbol of stability and peaceful progress in an unstable world'.

Chamberlain could, Dunglass recollected, be prejudiced in political relations. While admiring Lloyd George's energy he was shocked by his distortion of facts; he was fond of Baldwin but irritated by his laziness and indecision; and it was an exasperated Chamberlain who, so he claimed, drove Baldwin to the final decision on the abdication. But, thought Dunglass many years later, Chamberlain had been too impatient; Baldwin's timing had been right—he understood the pace of the public mind better than Chamberlain did and how to get his way with it: 'If he had forced the pace there would have been ructions and worse.'

Chamberlain *was* impatient. He could never let things slide, demanding direct, speedy action. For this reason, he discounted MacDonald as woolly-minded. It revealed much of Chamberlain, Dunglass thought, that he detested Disraeli for his flamboyance, his flirting with royalty, his appeal to the emotions.

Of Chamberlain's dealings with foreign affairs, with Nazi Germany and Fascist Italy, with which his name will always be linked, Alec Dunglass was a privileged observer and in the main a strong supporter. Chamberlain's chief objective, the pacification of Europe, he supported without reservation; it was, after all, Britain's age-old policy. Dunglass, like Chamberlain, condemned the Socialist demand simultaneously for war against the dictatorships (except Russia), and the reduction of British armaments.

He supported Chamberlain's search for peace while preparing for war. As early as 1934 Chamberlain wrote, 'For the old aphorism, "force is no remedy", I would substitute "the fear of force is the only remedy".' [1] Dunglass never forgot it, indeed almost echoed it when as Foreign Secretary a quarter of a century later he brusquely observed that the 'balance of power' was a cliché and substituted 'the balance of terror'.

Nor was Chamberlain ever in any doubt about the beastly brutality

[1] Keith Feiling, *The Life of Neville Chamberlain*, London, 1946, p. 252.

of the Nazis. 'Hitler's Germany is the bully of Europe; yet I don't despair.' Though he never took 'Hitler's peace professions at their face value' he was not prepared to allow him to bluster the world into war.

His strategic plan to deal with Hitler, Alec Dunglass remembered, was three-fold: direct contact to bring Hitler's grievances into the open, no question excluded; direct contact with Italy aimed at detaching her from the Axis and to give her a foot in the Anglo-French camp so 'that she might ultimately leave the spider's web; and the rearming of Britain as an insurance against the breakdown of these plans and against the ineffectiveness of collective security'. They were 'simple conceptions', applauded *nem. con.* when Chamberlain on becoming Prime Minister put them to a full, private meeting of the Parliamentary Party.

The snag was: time was short. Then, too, 'a cross-wind affected the course of history. I believe,' Dunglass wrote, 'that the outbreak of the Spanish civil war wrecked the chances of world peace and certainly destroyed the broad all-party consensus that a House of Commons tries to reach on Foreign affairs.

'Churchill and Eden agreed on neutrality—non-intervention. It was probably right, but in the end we had the worst of all worlds. We fell foul of Italy and Germany who backed Franco and of Russia who backed the Republicans. The Socialists here, for ideological reasons, backed Russia; their attacks on non-intervention were ceaseless. Chamberlain hit them and showed his contempt and they called him Fascist; the label stuck.'

Moreover because of Mussolini's participation in Spain, a year was lost for Chamberlain's hopes of negotiation with Italy and Germany. The Spanish affair 'left a deep rift in British politics', Dunglass reflected, and when negotiations did begin, the Opposition 'were determined to kill Chamberlain politically'.

Eden, the Foreign Secretary, resigned over Chamberlain's attempt to detach Italy from the Axis. Chamberlain wanted to sign a wide treaty with Italy before all Italian troops were withdrawn from Spain; Eden insisted that Italy's pledge to withdraw her troops be completely fulfilled first. Chamberlain prevailed and Italy stayed neutral until after the collapse of France. If France had held firm, Dunglass believed, Italy would have continued to be neutral.

There were other differences between Eden and Chamberlain but the real trouble was, Dunglass thought, 'Eden lived on his nerves and was

highly-strung. Chamberlain disliked emotional scenes. The two personalities never clicked and before long the friction became real. On
one occasion Chamberlain advised Eden to go away and take two
aspirins!'

It was no way to treat so sensitive a man as Eden and allowing him
to resign was politically a disaster for Chamberlain who already—
despite the efforts of Dunglass and others—had dissidents in his own
party. A certain group, who took their cue from Eden, claimed that
Hitler was bluffing, that his threats were hollow. Chamberlain believed
the opposite and he feared that Eden's appeals to the 'democracies' to
stand against Hitler would bring a line-up of countries which would
make war inevitable.

'Force is the only argument,' wrote Chamberlain in March 1938,
'that Germany understands.' He announced a fresh review of rearmament, and in May asked the Supply Board when Britain would be
ready to fight on more or less equal terms. 'In a year,' [1] came the reply.
Conciliation must, therefore, be the policy for at least the next twelve
months; and perhaps conciliation could stave off war indefinitely.

Meantime Hitler turned his attentions to Czechoslovakia, a country
to which Britain (unlike France and Russia) was not then pledged.
There was plenty of muddy water for him to stir. For some years the
Czech majority had imposed its will on the Germans, Slovaks, Hungarians, Ruthenes and Poles who together were numerically as large.
Masaryk's great dream of a 'sort of Switzerland' was dead; all the best
jobs went to Czechs, and the rest resented it.

On this matter, Britain stood on the sidelines. Chamberlain counselled the Czechs to make concessions and sought to dissuade Hitler
from overrunning their country. For, he observed, 'you have only to
look at the map to see that nothing that France or we could do could
possibly save Czechoslovakia.' [2] The French Government had, in any
case, made it quite clear to Chamberlain that they had no intention of
sacrificing ten million men to stop three million Germans in Czechoslovakia from joining the Reich; and the Dominions were loath to be
involved.

Political pressures, however, were put on him, particularly by the
British Left Wing because Czechoslovakia was allied with Russia. And
here, Dunglass thought, Chamberlain made a mistake. Bowing to

[1] Feiling, p. 350. See note, p. 48 above.

[2] Feiling, p. 347. See note, p. 48 above.

Socialist demands, he compromised and sent Lord Runciman to Prague as investigator and mediator: 'That was wrong because it identified Britain too much with Czechoslovakia. Her ally was France not us and France was able to remain in the background and let Britain carry the can.' The mission was a failure.

It was during August 1938 that Chamberlain privately began to think that no normal diplomatic procedures could save the peace. Without consulting anyone, least of all his P.P.S., he planned to make a face-to-face appeal to Hitler to cease his aggression for, he wrote privately, 'is it not positively horrible to think that the fate of hundreds of millions depends on one man and he is half mad?' For a man who shrank from publicity and who abhorred the spectacular, it was an extraordinary decision but he took it. On 15th September 1938 and again on 22nd September Chamberlain flew to meet Hitler at Berchtesgaden and then at Bad Godesberg. Dunglass did not accompany him but was afterwards told by Chamberlain that he found Hitler 'the most obstinate man, "an inhuman brute". He had little idea such a man could exist. He did not trust him for one moment because he found no element of morality or humanity in him'. The talks broke down.

Dunglass, like most M.P.s, was little more than a gravelled onlooker of these events, but in what followed he had, at least, two walking-on parts. Talks having failed, Chamberlain on 26th September 1938 reluctantly assured France of Britain's support if France went to war to fulfil her obligations to the Czechs. He also dispatched a civil servant, Sir Horace Wilson, his close adviser, to Berlin with a personal letter to Hitler, proposing direct negotiations between Germany and France with Britain present. In Britain, the armed forces were put on the alert and air-raid precautions begun.

Next evening, 27th September, Chamberlain got Hitler's reply. It was unsatisfactory but it left one small loophole for hope: 'I leave it to your judgement,' Hitler wrote, 'whether you consider you should continue your effort . . . to bring the Government in Prague to reason at the very last hour.'[1]

Chamberlain did two things: he appealed to Mussolini to intervene and, through the British ambassador in Berlin, Sir Nevile Henderson, put forward on the morning of 28th September the idea of an international conference to discuss arrangements to meet most of Hitler's demands on Czechoslovakia.

[1] *Documents on German Foreign Policy:* Series D, vol. ii, No. 635.

There was no immediate answer and Britain glumly girded herself for war.

That afternoon, 28th September, Chamberlain was due to review the international situation in the House of Commons. Still hoping against hope for a reply, he instructed Alec Dunglass to stand by in the Chamber. The hoped-for message would go first to the Earl of Halifax, the Foreign Secretary, who would be in the gallery. Dunglass was to await a signal from him, and then to collect the message and take it into the Chamber.

Chamberlain rose in a House packed to the doors. In the gallery sat Queen Mary, the Duke and Duchess of Kent, ambassadors and many peers. He began on a muted note and with his customary skill in marshalling facts detailed the events of the previous week.

Half an hour passed and Dunglass, peering up at Halifax in the gallery, received no sign. Then, a few minutes before four o'clock, he observed a slight flurry. Halifax was standing up and beckoning. Dunglass ran from the Chamber and up the stairs. In the corridor the tall, cadaverous earl gave him two sheets of paper.

Moments later, Dunglass returned, slipping in behind the Speaker's chair. He pressed the papers into the hand of Sir Samuel Hoare, the Home Secretary, who in turn passed them to the Chancellor of the Exchequer, Sir John Simon. Seconds later they were in front of Chamberlain, who paused to read them.

Then he broke the news: Hitler had invited him to a meeting in Munich next day. Mussolini would be there as well as Daladier, the French Prime Minister. Chamberlain would accept.

The Commons burst with relief, like champagne spurting from a bottle. They became an hysterical cheering mob, standing on their benches waving order papers and some attempting to sing; when later, accompanied by Dunglass and Mrs Chamberlain, the Prime Minister drove out of Palace Yard, M.P.s shouted themselves hoarse and, wrote Channon in his Diary, 'I felt sick with enthusiasm, longed to clutch him . . . I will always remember little Neville today, with his too long hair, greying at the sides, his smile, his amazing spirits and seeming lack of fatigue, as he stood there, alone, fighting the dogs of war single-handed and triumphant—he seemed the reincarnation of St George'.[1]

Dunglass had not been with Chamberlain on his previous flights to Germany and did not expect to accompany him to Munich. But at the

[1] *Chips*, pp. 171-2. See note, p. 47.

last moment—so late indeed that Dunglass had to borrow a clean shirt from his brother William's landlord—Chamberlain decided to take him. The party, which included Foreign Office advisers, flew off from Heston early on the morning of 29th September.

They were in Munich at noon: 'I remember when we got there these enormous crowds. Chamberlain was acclaimed though you can't pay much attention to that.'

Only Chamberlain and Sir Horace Wilson went into the conference room at the Fuehrerhaus in the Königsplatz. Alec Dunglass remained in the entrance hall: 'When we got into the building the chief thing I remember was the absolute contempt of the Germans for the Italians. This struck me very much. Openly in the passage they were insulting them, asking what are these fellows doing here? And the Italians were well aware of this. Goering strutted about, changing his uniform about three or four times that day. Ribbentrop was there. The only Nazi leaders not there, I think, were Goebbels and Himmler.'

The meeting went on with breaks for lunch and dinner throughout the day. An agreement was signed shortly before 2 a.m. on 30th September. But that was not the end. Chamberlain wanted—as, Dunglass recalled, it was 'a calculated piece of tactics'—a separate Anglo-German declaration of their mutually peaceful intentions. 'I remember Chamberlain at the breakfast table next morning. He had drafted the paper in anticipation of seeing Hitler again before leaving Munich.'

The draft said that the Fuehrer and Prime Minister regarded 'the agreement signed last night, and the Anglo-German naval agreement, as symbolic of the desire of our two peoples never to go to war with one another again'. There would be continuing efforts to remove possible sources of difference; the method was to be consultation.

Chamberlain took the paper to Hitler's flat—it was their last meeting—and Hitler signed it with 'suspicious alacrity'. Chamberlain's objective was, Dunglass recalled, simply to get an agreement which, whether Hitler kept it or not, would be 'a bull point with the United States' and public opinion generally. If Hitler broke it, it would show the world, without equivocation, that he was totally untrustworthy and that nothing was left but war. In a sense, the scrap of paper was window-dressing—'I will give it maximum publicity,' Chamberlain told Dunglass. The Prime Minister placed no faith in Hitler's signature; he had merely succeeded in gaining a tactical advantage.

Back in England, however, Chamberlain's 'calculation' forsook him.

In Downing Street, as vast crowds shouted and cheered, his *entourage* pressed him to appear at a window of No. 10, and one suggested he should say something about 'peace in our time'. He refused and then, partly to disperse the crowd, found himself on the balcony and the words came out: 'This is the second time in our history that there has come back from Germany to Downing Street peace with honour. I believe it is peace in our time.'

Chamberlain bitterly regretted his words, Dunglass remembered. They were 'totally out of character'. Within a week Chamberlain was asking the Commons not to read overmuch into words 'used in a moment of some emotion, after a long and exhausting day'.

Alec Dunglass himself, however, continued to echo the theme. War between Britain and Germany was more remote than it had been for years, he said at East Kilbride on 4th November 1938. 'A poor forecast,' he drily observed thirty years later.

The ink was scarcely dry on the Munich agreement, the plaudits had hardly ceased to echo, before Dunglass's services to his master were put under more intensive strain. While Chamberlain the peacemaker retained his popularity in the country—though it waned as Hitler's aggressions grew bolder—within Parliament itself he was faced not only by the hatred of the Opposition but by some thirty or forty critical Conservatives. The leaders of this Party cave were Churchill, Eden, Cranborne (later Lord Salisbury), L. S. Amery, and Duff Cooper who had resigned as First Lord of the Admiralty after the Munich agreement.

Dunglass, 'tall and thin with a slight stoop, charming manners, a mop of fair hair and a romantic appearance',[1] was to be seen in the lobbies trying to argue his master's case, to soothe the malcontents, to still the doubts of the waverers. 'Alec Dunglass and I,' Channon claimed, 'have woven a net around the P.M. whom we love and admire and want to protect from interfering, unimportant noodles.' He spoke of Dunglass as 'a miracle of tact, humour and sound sense', and even claimed that 'he admires Neville so much that he has even come to look like him', and had grown a moustache.[2]

Neither Channon's influence nor his relations with Dunglass were

---

[1] Or so he appeared to the London *Evening Standard*, 29th September 1938.

[2] *Chips*, pp. 198 and 194. See note p. 47 above. Any resemblance to Chamberlain was only in the eyes of Channon. Dunglass had sported a moustache since his Oxford days; it was quite unlike the Prime Minister's.

quite as close as he claimed: 'I knew him quite well. He was pleasant and agreeable to talk to and a good host for he kept open house. But he had a good deal of gush, and when he set his thoughts down he allowed his mind and emotions and desire for effect to run riot.'

Dunglass was sometimes dispatched long distances on Chamberlain's business. He turned up at the by-election at Kinross and West Perthshire—a seat he was himself to occupy from 1963—where the Conservative Member, the Duchess of Atholl, had been deposed by the Constituency Party for her pro-republican sentiments over Spain and her opposition to appeasement. She fought as an Independent with Labour and Liberal support against the official Conservative candidate. Whether or not it was due to Dunglass's intervention—he spoke twice after an overnight journey through a blizzard on 17th December 1938—the official candidate won, greatly to Chamberlain's relief.

The busy P.P.S. was by now known and well liked by the political world, and a few newspapers speculated on promotion for him. One said he was 'warmly tipped' for high office though, another commentator thought, his 'lack of showmanship' might hinder him. *Was* promotion on the cards? 'I might have got a job in the Scottish Office or in Agriculture at that time—it was more the line I'd been on in my early years in the House.'

Alec's chariot, however, was hitched to a falling star. The Prime Minister was daily losing ground and his policies were obviously failing. Hitler had not stopped at the Sudetenland; all Czechoslovakia would soon be his and 'peace in our time' appeared to many to be the cynical remark of a fatuous old man.

Certainly Chamberlain's usually good judgment deserted him when he pledged Britain's support to the threatened Poles, a mutual assistance pact being signed on 25th August. Even Dunglass doubted its wisdom: 'I'm not sure that the guarantee to Poland was a very wise choice as a *casus belli*. It was hastily given.' Poland was if anything even less defensible by British forces than Czechoslovakia; the only army that could come to its aid was the Russian, and Chamberlain knew from Intelligence reports that the Soviet Army's capability of offensive action was doubtful. At some point, however, Hitler's ambitions had to be halted.

But then Chamberlain had another—and no less dubious—plan in mind. In reply to a Russian proposal for a tripartite alliance of Britain, Russia and France, but excluding the threatened Poles, he broached the idea of a pact of mutual assistance between Poland, Russia, France and Britain. The Poles, however, refused any contact with the Russians, whom they had good reason to hate. The Russians dallied, suspecting a trick, and then, seeing a possible advantage, agreed to talks.

A delegation led by William Strang (later Lord Strang), an Assistant Under-Secretary at the Foreign Office, soon found that the price of the alliance was Britain's agreement to Russia's forcible absorption of Latvia, Lithuania and Estonia into the U.S.S.R. Chamberlain refused. It was later revealed that almost simultaneously with the talks the Russians were negotiating with the Germans; late in August a Russo-Nazi non-aggression pact was signed.

It was afterwards said that the reason why the Anglo-Russian talks failed was that the delegation was led by a Foreign Office official not a Minister: 'That excuse was always used, but I've never thought there was anything in this at all. The Russians were said to have taken offence. But I think it was total nonsense. If they'd wanted an agreement they would have come to one. They didn't want one; it wouldn't have mattered if Eden himself had gone.[1] Everything known about the Russians later confirmed this judgment.'

During the summer months of 1939, Alec Dunglass and his wife were occasional week-end visitors to the Astors' house, Cliveden, in Buckinghamshire, along with the Prime Minister, many members of the Government, Lords, M.P.s and distinguished figures outside politics. Sometime in June, the guests included a young German, Adam von Trott du Solz, a former Rhodes scholar and friend of David Astor.

Von Trott claimed to have had a conversation with Dunglass and reported it to Walter Hewel, liaison officer in Berlin between Hitler and Ambassador Ribbentrop in London. Von Trott stated that he discussed with Dunglass Germany's dislike of the British 'encirclement policy' and that Dunglass agreed to influence Oliver Stanley, then President of the Board of Trade. Later 'Stanley', von Trott wrote, 'spoke in Parliament in favour of a more practically accommodating attitude towards Germany'.[2]

Dunglass did not recall meeting von Trott but 'in so far as the Germans thought they were being encircled, I might easily have said that I would tell Oliver Stanley to correct this impression. Nobody was

[1] Eden, then on the back benches, had proposed himself as negotiator.
[2] *Documents on German Foreign Policy*, D, vol. vi, No. 497; quoted by M. Gilbert and R. Gott in *The Appeasers*, London, 1963, p. 216.

trying to encircle Germany. Hitler made it a point of propaganda. Without being an appeaser, this was a perfectly legitimate, indeed necessary, thing to say.'

Most Britons, except the out-and-out warmongers, still hoped in the summer of 1939 that some rapprochement with Germany might still be achieved. Some believed that Hitler had no desire to fight Britain and would eventually be obliged to tackle Russia, whose Communism at that time was thought to be the antithesis of Nazism. They kept their spirits up by a vague belief that some sort of a deal could be done to preserve the peace in Western Europe.

On 25th August Hitler himself proposed that he should guarantee the existence of the British Empire wherever such guarantee might be required, and he would regard Germany's western frontiers as final. His conditions were that Germany's colonial demands should be met and her special obligations to Italy recognized. But Britain must also accept Hitler's 'refusal ever to fight Russia'. The proposal was rejected flatly by the British Government on 28th August.[1]

Dunglass dismissed the idea. 'No such deal was on. In any case, our historic fear of a militant power dominating the Continent was too strong for us to be tempted.'

Two days after the Government had rejected Hitler's proposals, on Friday 1st September the Germans invaded Poland. Still, a small hope lingered. On 2nd September Mussolini tried for an armistice and a conference. Dunglass told Channon that 'some sort of a *démarche* might be made through an intermediary which would move the Germans to retire from Poland'.[2] There were extended meetings of the Cabinet, but Chamberlain rejected Mussolini's proposals unless Hitler withdrew from Poland. He would not.

There was no more to be done. On 2nd September Chamberlain dispatched a two-hour ultimatum to Germany. There was no answer, and on Sunday, 3rd September, he announced that Britain was at war with Germany. The House met and dispersed; the air-raid sirens sounded, though nothing happened; and Britain retired behind the *News of the World*.

After lunch on that sunny Sunday, Alec Dunglass telephoned his brother Henry: 'What are you doing this afternoon?' he inquired.

[1] Alan Bullock, *Hitler: a study in Tyranny* (revised ed. London, 1964), pp. 533 and 542.

[2] *Chips*, see note on p. 47 above, p. 211.

'Let's drive out to the Downs and look for some Chalk Blues. It's no good sitting here brooding.' Under stress, Dunglass instinctively sought the solace of nature, returning to the earliest pleasures of his life, just as in later days when things went wrong he would find calm in the savage pruning of roses or the arrangement of flowers in vases.

He had much to reflect on. Now that war had come and the Army was mobilizing, his first impulse was to join the Lanarkshire Yeomanry, of which he had been a Territorial officer for a dozen years. But conscience pricked. Ought he to leave the Prime Minister at the moment when his hopes were shattered? Dunglass was fond of the shy, unhappy man—never more so than when he saw him open a letter from which a white feather fluttered and heard him drily observe: 'Some people don't mind wasting stamps.'

He decided to stay: 'I was told he was lonely and that I was the fellow who knew him best. But I would like to have cut out of it. I should not have stayed. I made a mistake there for I missed the comradeship of soldiers.'

A mistake it was in more ways than one. Nor was it even true that Dunglass 'knew him best': Sir Horace Wilson, his Civil Service adviser, was closer to him and so was R. A. Butler, the Foreign Under Secretary.[1]

Politically it was a mistake. Dunglass was tying himself to a man who had made the cardinal error of staying in office once his policies had failed ignominiously. Though he brought Churchill and Eden into the Government, he had so evident a loathing of war and lacked the will to pursue it that he would inevitably be driven out and those in his orbit would share his obloquy. To stay was a credit to Dunglass's heart but not to his head.

Moreover he began to be set doubtful as well as impossible tasks. For example, he took a request from the Prime Minister to Duff Cooper who was about to depart on a lecture tour of the United States. Chamberlain requested that, while there, he should refrain from anything that might be considered British propaganda. This with Britain at war was too much. 'I cannot remember with what assurances I sent away the P.P.S.,' Duff Cooper wrote. 'If they satisfied him they must have been disingenuous. I was not going to America to talk about history or literature.'[2]

[1] 'The P.M. still feels more mentally at home with RAB than with anyone else.' *Chips*, see note, p. 47 above, p. 193.
[2] Sir Duff Cooper, *Old Men Forget*, London, 1953, p. 267.

During December 1939, while the war in France was static, Dunglass went with Chamberlain to visit the British Expeditionary Force. They saw the Maginot line—an incomplete series of strong-points—and called on General Gamelin, the Commander-in-Chief of the Allied forces. ('Neville got a very poor opinion of Gamelin, and thought his exposition at the Supreme War Council was unconvincing.') To assembled journalists, who found the 'twilight' war un-newsworthy, Chamberlain remarked 'better to be bored than bombed'.

But Dunglass's most difficult task was to keep large sections of the Prime Minister's own party quiet. Several groups of Tory M.P.s were determined to force his resignation and did nothing to defend him when the Opposition began to tear him to pieces.

Dunglass did his best, sometimes notching a success, more often a failure. One of Chamberlain's most vociferous Tory critics, L. S. Amery, pictures him at work: 'Quite separately from the group with which I was associated another group, numbering, I was told, some thirty or forty, led by Herbert Williams, had announced their intention of voting against the Government. Lord Dunglass, the P.M.'s P.P.S., succeeded in persuading them to hold their hand by a promise that Chamberlain would meet them next day to tell them of his plans for a drastic reconstruction of the Government.

'A similar approach to Emrys-Evans, acting secretary of our group, met with a frank negative which was later endorsed by the rest of us at an emergency meeting.'[1]

By the beginning of May 1940, it was clearly all up with Chamberlain. Dismally, Dunglass and a few more went on canvassing support for his continuing premiership. When no support was forthcoming, he took the side of those who preferred Lord Halifax to Winston Churchill as Chamberlain's successor. His side lost.

On 10th May it was over, and Chamberlain resigned the premiership though he remained in the Cabinet as Lord President. A triumphant Churchill sat in the chair of Dunglass's old master.

There was no reason now for Dunglass to stay. He bade farewell to Chamberlain—whom he never saw again, for in November he died—and cleared his drawer at No. 10. Then he went for a drink with the ubiquitous Channon: 'We were all sad, angry, and felt cheated and out-witted. Alec who, more than any other, has been with the Prime Minister these past few weeks, and knows his words and actions by

[1] L. S. Amery, *My Political Life*, London, 1955, vol. 3, p. 366.

heart, let himself go. I opened a bottle of champagne and we four loyal adherents of Mr Chamberlain drank "To the King over the water".'[1]

For Dunglass, the three years that had begun with such radiant promise had ended in near-disaster. True, he had learned much of the inner workings of the British political system, and the ways of Government. He had also learned—and would never forget—that a militarily weak Britain could have no effective foreign policy:'Munich—I have some reason to recollect it—was the result of negotiation from weakness,' he said a decade later.[2] Nor, too, would he ever forget that some of the responsibility for Britain's weakness must be carried by the Socialists and those who mounted such specious exercises as the Peace Ballot.

The other lesson was more personally hurtful. Chamberlain's unremitting search for peace had seemed to Dunglass both honourable and laudable. Now it was regarded as despicable, almost as treason. 'Appeasement', a respectable aim of British foreign policy since the nineteenth century, had become by 1940 a dirty word. With that word the name of Dunglass was inescapably associated, but he never sought to deny his belief that Chamberlain's policy was essentially right. He has since often stated that to carry a democracy united into war a leader has to go to the brink of appeasement. Chamberlain was judged to have gone over the edge.

'It was,' wrote one shrewd observer, 'rather hard luck on Lord Dunglass. A P.P.S. is forced to say ditto to his minister and there is no reason to think that echoing Neville was a great strain on Lord Dunglass, who supported appeasement with some enthusiasm. I speak of his "hard luck" because it was unlucky to be so closely associated with a policy, proved to be such a calamitous failure, at the outset of a political career.'[3]

Alec Dunglass was to ride out the opprobrium-by-association of his years with Chamberlain. But in May 1940 he did not know it. He was grievously disappointed, and saw his career in apparently irretrievable ruin.

His feelings showed in his face, which was drawn and pale. He was sleeping badly and had lost a stone and more in eighteen months. Nor did his departure from Westminster improve his health. In fact he was very seriously ill.

[1] *Chips*, see note on p. 47 above, p. 211.
[2] House of Commons, 29th November 1950.
[3] *Editorial: The Memoirs of Colin R. Coote*, London, 1965, pp. 260–1.

6. The Plaster Sarcophagus : 1940 – 5

Bleak months. Communism studied. Return to Westminster. Churchill interrupted: a prophetic speech. Defeat at Lanark.

'I wasn't well, at least I imagined I wasn't well. I'd felt pretty awful for some years before that, very much off colour.' Dunglass, however, had no pain or other sign of acute illness, merely a sense of weakness and malaise.

He left Westminster for Scotland, intending to join his regiment, the Lanarkshire Yeomanry. He was only thirty-six but, disconcertingly, an Army medical board rejected him as unfit, and did so again a few weeks later. Only then did he consult specialists in Edinburgh.

Eventually they gave their verdict: he had a tubercular hole in his spine possibly, they thought, due to a knock he told them he had received while gardening two years before. More likely, to use metaphor, he had carried too much for his back to bear and the general disfavour which had come to 'appeasers' was the last straw which broke it. He fell back on a weakness present in two branches of his forbears. He could fight no more and lay supine through the worst years of the war.

In 1940 it seemed as though he might be supine for ever. The doctors, recommending an operation to replace the diseased spinal bone with chippings from his shin, offered only a fifty-fifty chance of his walking again. In any case, he would have to spend two years encased in plaster from head to foot. If he decided against the operation, he would after perhaps six months never walk again unaided.

Without hesitating, Alec Dunglass chose the operation and it was carried out by Sir John Fraser in Edinburgh in late September 1940. As an operation it was successful. The doctors were more optimistic. They could not, however, yet guarantee that, after the long months in plaster, he would emerge fit.

He was taken home to Springhill where, as disaster after disaster fell upon British arms and the British people, Alec Dunglass lay in a sort of living death encased in a plaster sarcophagus and facing the possibility of being a permanent cripple. He could scarcely move his head nor, in the early days, was he able to read. It was then that he 'looked over the edge and had a glimpse of the infinite. If one feels one might be a gonner, the mind travels fast'.

He was surrounded by loving care. His wife Elizabeth, shortly to give birth to their third daughter, devoted to him both her affection and her intelligence. Ingenious methods were used to lighten the monotony of his life—he was moved into a downstair room whence he could see the Tweed, and later into a summer-house with a revolving base in which, lying snug through winter snowfalls, he was able to change the panorama at will, looking now on the Cheviots of his boyhood, now towards the woods concealing the Hirsel.

Despite the war and the disfavour in which the man and the policy he had worked for were regarded, Dunglass was not quite forgotten by the world of politics. He even received a warmly sympathetic paragraph in the *Manchester Guardian*: 'Much regret will be felt among all members of the House of Commons of whatever party, at the illness that has struck Lord Dunglass down . . . This delicate, earnest Scottish aristocrat was deeply attached to Mr Chamberlain and the friendship was plainly reciprocated . . . All who know him will wish him the quickest possible recovery and an early return to the House of Commons.'[1]

He managed to keep up some correspondence, though his wife did the writing for him. With his old tutor at Oxford, J. C. Masterman, he was often in touch. Shortly after Chamberlain's death in November 1940, Dunglass wrote: 'Neville's death is a great loss, but I am sure people will begin to appreciate his work very soon. There are signs of it now and the tributes which were paid to him rang true. The Americans, too, can understand better how naked we were in 1938.'

As for himself: 'I have to lie flat on my back in a plaster "shell" for a year, but a month of that has already gone and what with washing and eating and children etc., the days move along pretty fast. The doctors promise a full recovery, though I am doubtful whether my classic bowling action will be seen again—certainly not as it was.' The doctors, in fact, had not promised 'full recovery'.

[1] *Manchester Guardian*, 13th October 1940.

There were dark hours of despair. But there was faith. There was also his blessed sense of humour which, though sorely tried, was not extinguished. He often needed it for if he did not laugh he might cry.

He took up embroidery and worked sufficient *petit point* for eight dining-room chairs. But his greatest joy was when he was able to read again and turn the pages for himself. During his years with Chamberlain he had had little time for anything other than official documents. Now he turned voraciously to history, biography and detective stories, changing from one *genre* to the other as the mood took him.

Occupied with thoughts of what the world might be like after the war, he paid much attention to the study of Communism and of Russia. Though he never got very far into Marx's works—who ever did?— he read a number of studies of Marx, Lenin, Engels and others. He had shared Chamberlain's deep distrust of Russian intentions which the pact with the Nazis had confirmed. The distrust was not ideological. He regarded the Russians simply as casuists. He was not astonished by the German invasion of Russia: *realpolitik* was common to both dictatorships just as it had been to their Czarist and *junker* forbears.

His mind was clear of cant. When pressure was put on Churchill to open a 'second front now' to aid the Russian ally, he coolly examined the practical possibilities. To Masterman he wrote on 3rd October 1941:

'I cannot see where we could make any effective diversion with the forces which we have at our disposal here in this country. I should have thought they were clearly too few to put on the Continent where anything but a large force would be bound to be outflanked even by the depleted divisions which Germany has in the West. I suppose it is conceivable that we might make a front in Brittany, but except perhaps for cutting off Brest this would not seem to gain very much.

'I had thought that Norway—both because of the obvious unrest there and because of the country which lends itself to the employment of highly-organized bands of guerillas—might have given us an opportunity, but then of course Germany would not hesitate to violate Swedish neutrality and is already in Finland, and so would get behind us again.

'I rather think, therefore, that the historian will say that as long as we were compelled to keep large forces in the Middle East, it was not possible for us to create a Continental diversion to help the Russians.

Of course American man-power would alter the whole situation but it is unlikely that that will be forthcoming yet.'

So passed the bleak months. Fewer visitors came from the outside world to Springhill. Travel was difficult and more and more old friends were absorbed into the struggle against Germany. All four of his brothers and his brother-in-law were away at the war. The news became grimmer. In August 1942 the 8th Army was in retreat, the Germans were triumphant in the Crimea, and the British CIGS, Sir Alan Brooke, confided to his diary that 'we have already lost a high proportion of the British Empire and are on the high road to lose a great deal more'.[1]

It was during this low ebb for the nation that for Alec the tide began to turn. He was stripped of his old plaster case and a smaller one fitted to cover his trunk alone. For the first time for two years he was carried to a chair and discovered that his legs would bear him. He stumbled to the telephone and rang his father with the good news.

A few months later he was walking and even cycling in the estate. Grateful to his surgeon and doctors, he joked: 'You have achieved the impossible; you have put backbone into a politician.'

His interest in politics never lapsed, even in the darkest days. He saw himself as a politician, and indeed remained M.P. for Lanark.[2] During his convalescence he speculated on his future, unhesitatingly thinking of himself as a future Minister:

'I wonder what politics will hold after this? [i.e. after his illness]. Some of the Government Departments, and probably more as time goes on, will be huge administrative concerns where one will be immersed in a mass of detail and unable to think of anything but scales of returns and rations and the like. I feel that I ought to have been serving that dreary apprenticeship now, but there are compensations and I have had time to think, which is given to few nowadays. At any rate there is always something to be said for skipping the 2nd XI.'

No longer was he primarily concerned with domestic affairs; unemployment was a topic wiped out by war. Foreign affairs dominated his thoughts. His close connection with Chamberlain had begun it. The

[1] Arthur Bryant, *The Turn of the Tide, 1939–43*, London, 1957; paperback 1965, p. 286.

[2] It was agreed that M.P.s on active service should retain their seats and also that in case of an M.P.'s dying or resigning his seat, a member of the same party should not be opposed at a by-election. No Tory sought to replace Lord Dunglass, though he was neither in the Forces nor dead; Labour accepted the so-called 'party truce'.

war itself, ramifying into places scarcely more than a name before it began, broadened his horizons and compelled him to consider Britain's future place in the world:

'What problems there are and how easy it will be to go wrong! The regulation of our relationship with the Empire and the Empire's with the outside world will be one of the biggest.

'Australia seems bound to swing more and more into the American orbit; South Africa will surely be a trouble when another Smuts comes along. While India will have gained some more independence and will probably be misusing it.

'The answer to a lot would seem to be the closest co-operation with America, but how far can we merge with her without losing our identity and our world influence?' [1]

In late 1942 these were shrewd anticipations of the future.

Alec Dunglass ventured back to London in late 1943—almost four years since he had departed downcast and ill. He was forty years old, leaner than ever, the bones of his face more prominent, while his sandy thatch of hair, now flecked with grey, had retreated to reveal a high, wide brow. At first he was a listener in the Commons—he could not stand for long—feeling his way into the strange wartime atmosphere of Parliament. He had not lost his interest in social and economic affairs; he was one of the twenty-five original members of the Progress Trust, a non-party research project into socio-political subjects founded in 1943, a time when the Beveridge and Barlow reports were in prospect.

But when his doctors finally thought him capable of standing up long enough to make a speech, his subject was foreign not domestic. It was on 24th May 1944 that he rose to make what was almost a second maiden speech. He had butterflies inside but he spoke boldly and toughly.

Victory, he said, was approaching, but victory over Hitler would by no means bring security in Europe. There would be suspicion and civil war. There was no certainty that Britain, Russia and the United States would be able to live in peace with each other.

The time was coming when Britain, even with the Empire, would be unable to meet an attack from a first-class power; and it was uncertain whether an international organization backed with power would come into existence. He hoped—but was not sure—that America would integrate her defence with our own, absolutely.

Letter to J. C. Masterman.

Therefore Britain must form a security system, cemented by specific military treaties—not by federation—with Norway, Denmark, Belgium, Holland and France. It was the only way that we could be strong enough. Would Russia object? Not, he believed, if we took a strong line on moral issues and made absolutely clear where our vital interests lay.

Dunglass's speech, heard with attention, was based on reading and reflection—as he said himself, 'For the last four years I have had very little to do but study these problems, and I cannot say that the lessons of history are particularly encouraging.'

It also harked back to the bitter experience of Chamberlain. He wanted a strong system of alliances in Europe, with the Americans in if possible (as happened with NATO) but then, as now, he did not want federation (the federal idea had been current before the war, put forward strongly in the works of Clarence B. Streit). 'I have never been able to visualize a Europe federated as in the United States,' he reflected in 1969. 'I believe that the institutional forms adopted on the Continent will be of a different pattern. That will follow from the story of Europe and the long history of the nation states. It will be necessary to do certain things which are judged to be jointly advantageous and where necessary institutions will be set up to do them.'

Then as now he saw that only by close co-operation in Europe could Britain deploy sufficient power for the future, both militarily and economically. His opinion did not change over the next quarter of a century.

On 29th September 1944 Dunglass made what an historian has called 'one of the most important speeches in the House of Commons of the second world war; and it was the first true expression of the post-war era.' [1] The subject was what was to happen to those countries 'liberated' by the Russians and particularly Poland, on whose account Britain had entered the war.

Earlier in the day Churchill, who was to leave in a fortnight for talks in Moscow, hinted that Russia was going in general to get her way, and in particular there would have to be territorial changes in Poland 'because it is the Russian armies alone which can deliver Poland from the German talons'. Glancing round the House he added he hoped there would be 'no intemperate language' about this.

[1] Brian Gardner, *Churchill in His Time: a study of a reputation, 1939–45*, London, 1968, pp. 255–6.

Far from deterring Dunglass, this roused his ire, and he rounded on the great leader. It is a psychological curiosity that Dunglass returned to active politics with an attack on his fallen master's successor, the man who put bite into Britain's war effort. He said firmly:

'If after the defeat of Germany this gallant but unhappy people [the Poles] are left in bondage and if this country has failed to do anything that we ought to have done, then our national conscience will be uneasy for generations.'

Britain had gone to war because she had guaranteed Poland's independence. The Anglo-Polish treaty of mutual assistance, signed on 25th August 1939 still held. We *must* intervene: Russia must not be allowed to settle matters as she wished. We must honour our legal and moral commitments to restore a Poland as nearly as possible equivalent in territory, economic resources and international status to the Poland of 1939. Russia must be faced; there must be plain speaking to which alone Russia responded—otherwise 'we shall look down a long vista of political misunderstanding'.

This speech—though it sounded the keynote for the future—did not create much stir. Most Conservatives were still honeymooning with Russia despite much evidence of her intentions. Among them was a young M.P., Quintin Hogg, who suggested that Dunglass had long been hostile to the Soviet Union: 'I think that if we owe the Russians nothing else in this war it is to put the most favourable construction on everything they may do.' The one person who knew best how right Dunglass was was the Prime Minister himself.

It was a strange line for Dunglass to have taken. He knew little about the Poles except what he learned from one of his frequent visitors during his illness, Count Paul Stavzenski, who had been private secretary to Beck, the Polish Foreign Minister; the Count was in the Polish armoured division stationed at Douglas Castle. Apart from this, Dunglass's interest was confined to the fact that Polish independence had been guaranteed, however hastily, by his old, revered master. Moreover, as events were to show, Dunglass seldom stuck his neck out. He was no 'last ditcher' and usually accepted the majority view.

Yet here he was undoubtedly right not to do so. It was not simply Poland that he feared was being betrayed: it was Britain. Here lay the true significance of his outburst. He suspected, correctly as events showed, that Churchill's timidity sprang from his knowledge that

67

Britain was falling into the position of a second-class power who could not insist, against the super-powers, that her commitments be honoured. 'I had begun the process,' he recalled, 'of suspecting that the Russian menace would get worse and we should have to deal with it. If ever the time was ripe it was then when we and the Americans had the power. What were we *capable* of doing afterwards? The answer was "very little," and it has been the same ever since.'

When Churchill returned from Yalta on 27th February 1945, and asked the Commons to approve the joint declaration, it became clear that the Polish pass had been sold. Churchill, crushed between the upper and nether millstones of Russian demands and American acquiescence, had accepted Soviet nominees as the provisional government of Poland 'with the inclusion of democratic leaders from Poland itself and from Poles abroad'.

As he was narrating these arrangements, Dunglass jumped to his feet: 'I am sorry to interrupt the Prime Minister, but this point is highly important: is there going to be some kind of international supervision of the elections?'

Prime Minister: 'I should certainly like that, but we have to wait and see until the new Polish Government is set up and see what proposals are made.'

No such arrangements had been or were to be made. Dunglass was anxious too about Russian control of Germany. 'I never knew why Churchill didn't exert more influence on Stalin about this. He was the most dominating person at Yalta. I suppose he couldn't. But why before the final strategy for the Allied armies was deployed he didn't say to himself "Look, if the Russians get to Berlin there will be hell to pay", I don't know.'

Later in the debate Dunglass pointed out that Poland was the first test case 'in the relationship between a great power wielding great military might and her smaller and weaker neighbour'. The Prime Minister, he continued, said he accepted as 'an act of justice' that whatever the Russians had taken they would keep. He, Dunglass, had a fundamentally opposite view. He accepted it as a fact of power, but could not be asked to underwrite it as an act of justice.

We should, he said, be seen to preserve our moral standards in international behaviour. Our plenipotentiaries signed agreements as representatives of a great Christian people.

Elections in Poland must be truly free. We, the Russians, and the

Americans, with the possible addition of certain other nations, should join in supervising not only the elections in Poland but also in Yugoslavia or Greece or elsewhere.

In reply the Foreign Secretary, Anthony Eden, gave some generalized assurances which scarcely satisfied Dunglass. Nevertheless—though a junior Minister, Henry Strauss (Lord Conesford), resigned on the issue—he did not vote against the Government: 'In wartime,' he said later, 'I think one should give an anti-vote only if one was prepared to bring the Government down. So I decided not to do it. Nevertheless Yalta was a disaster'.

It took Churchill only three months to come to the same conclusion. In his victory broadcast on 13th May 1945, he said: 'On the continent of Europe we have yet to make sure that the simple and honourable purposes for which we entered the war are not brushed aside or overlooked in the months following our success . . . There would be little use in punishing the Hitlerites for their crimes if law and justice did not rule, and if totalitarian or police governments were to take the place of the German invaders.'

Lord Dunglass, Gardner comments, could certainly not have expressed it better.[1]

At the time of the debate, however, Churchill did not like Dunglass's intervention 'but he was very forgiving'.

So forgiving—and forgetful perhaps of Dunglass's pre-war allegiances—that he made him joint Under-Secretary for foreign affairs in the Conservative caretaker government that ruled for the six weeks between Labour's decision to leave the Coalition Cabinet in May and the elections in early July.[2]

Others were neither so forgiving nor forgetful. The Communists and the fellow-travellers launched an attack on Dunglass: 'There is amazement and concern in London progressive political circles,' the *Daily Worker* alleged on 28th May 1945 (in one of the earliest recorded uses of 'progressive' as meaning Communist), at the appointment.

'He has been a bitter critic of the Yalta agreement's "injustice" to Poland, spicing his criticisms with reckless accusations against the Soviet Government', and asserting that the Soviet Union was seeking to 'draw into its orbit a whole range of the smaller countries in Europe

[1] *Churchill in his Time*, p. 293. See note, p. 66 above.

[2] The result was delayed until 26th July to collect the servicemen's postal ballot from abroad.

by a mixture of military pressure from without and political disruption from within'.

Such statements were not surprising, the *Daily Worker* thought, coming from the former P.P.S. to Chamberlain and a member—the old lie was repeated—of the 'sinister United Christian Front whose chairman was Capt. A. H. M. Ramsay, the traitor M.P. for Peebles'. The Socialist *Daily Herald* repeated the lie a fortnight later on 7th June and added that Dunglass's appointment 'will make Stalin wonder . . .'

These and more slanderous accusations were bruited abroad during Dunglass's election campaign in July. He even had to deny whispers that he was pro-Nazi, a member of the proscribed *Link* founded by Admiral Sir Barry Domville, and that while he was said to be lying ill, he was, in reality off on some discreditable mission. He received telephone threats of personal violence. It was, he was reported as saying, 'the dirtiest election I have ever fought in'. Some members of the Communist Party were active in support of the Labour candidate, Thomas Steele, a former stationmaster who, as we shall see later, thanked them for the 'magnificent part' they had played.[1]

Dunglass lost the election, his comfortable 6,809 majority of 1935 becoming a minority of 1,884. His disappointment was, however, submerged beneath the greater shock caused to the Tory Party by the failure of the great war leader to carry them to victory. No less than 397 Socialists—shouting 'we are the masters now'—assembled in the Commons and sang 'The Red Flag': opposite sat a subdued remnant of 213.

Dunglass had no intention of giving up. He even thought of finding another constituency: 'I had hoped to hold Lanark,' he wrote to J. C. Masterman, 'but I had failed to foresee the extent of the *débâcle* and with so many miners voting in a bloc my chance was gone.

'Being naturally idle I never guessed a holiday could be so distasteful but it is profitless to lick one's wounds and I am turning to repair the many gaps in my political armour so as to take and make full use of any opportunity that may come. My trouble is that so few constituencies are appropriate to my geographical position and unless I am to wait for the next general election a by-election will have to be well placed.'

No such opportunity arose. The fact was that no constituency wanted him badly enough. He was on the political scrap-heap, possibly for

[1] Steele was afterwards M.P. for West Dunbartonshire.

good. Inertia, and auld lang syne allowed him to remain prospective Conservative candidate for Lanark Division but after the Labour Party's resounding win in 1945 his chances of regaining the seat seemed negligible.

He was philosophical about the Socialist victory, even finding in it certain consolations: 'If the Socialists had to come to power there is much to be said for the present. If they had lost they would have been sullen, resentful and out to queer the pitch of the Conservatives in foreign and domestic affairs. There might well have been a degree of violence which would have been very bad for us all.'[1]

Alec Dunglass, now forty-two, had endured a strange war in which he had come nearer to death than many combatants. Yet he lacked the experiences which brought a post-war *camaraderie*, an unspoken understanding of ways of thought, between those who had been in the forces. His brothers had all served and the youngest, George, a twenty-one-year-old Flying Officer, had been killed. So, too, had his wife's younger brother Patrick.

More bizarrely, his brother William had been court-martialled for refusing to obey an order which went against his conscience, and had been incarcerated in Wormwood Scrubs and later Wakefield Gaol. Dunglass had to apply for a permit to visit him.[2] William's was an honourable, if scarcely shrewd, reason for being gaoled. His escapade seems to have been little embarrassment to the family.

A happier wartime event had occurred in November 1943: after three daughters Elizabeth bore a son and heir, David, the future 15th Earl of Home. The family became a happy sextet, Springhill full of children's chatter and games. His father, now 72, still presided at the Hirsel; though Douglas Castle had long been demolished, and the coal royalties were soon to disappear by nationalization, some 80,000 acres remained.

Despite his physical tribulations and electoral defeat, Alec Dunglass had much for which to thank God.

---

[1] Letter to J. C. Masterman.
[2] The story is told in *Half Term Report*. See note, p. 14 above.

7. 'I Believe in God': 1945 – 50

Speech to youth leaders. Scottish politics. 'Progress Trust'. Communists at Lanark. A narrow victory.

If Alec Dunglass had much to thank God for, he did thank Him not only privately but publicly, and he worked to bring the knowledge of God to others. He supported Christian campaigns directed to the young people of Scotland, and took a close interest in youth organizations.

'Why I Believe in God' was his subject at an Edinburgh conference of youth leaders on 21st September 1946. His address was more a self-inquiry than a credo. Few men, he said, had a blind faith in God. They wanted to find out about Him for themselves. *Did* God create the world? One could speak of chemical reactions, life could spring from inanimate matter. Yet what did this mean? That 'the earth tired, so to speak, of its own passivity created its own audience?' He found less strain on his credulity in believing in a Supreme Being, a God.

Even so, if one did believe that God created the earth there were problems. He must also have made sorrow, 'if pleasure, pain; if trust, treachery; if love, hatred. Why did not an all-powerful God create a perfect world in which there was no pain, no cruelty, no evil?' Are 'we just the sports and playthings in a huge experiment in power?'

Evil was an obstacle to belief in God. Knowledge of evil, however, came only to those with a mind to choose—to man: 'Unlike the lion he need not eat his neighbour, he can choose whether he will be a Cannibal or a Christian—he can choose between good and evil.'

If men, alone, knew evil, they alone knew good: 'Love, kindness, sympathy, all these men show, and they are certainly no part of his animal inheritance.'

The fact that men alone had minds divided them from the rest of nature; the creation of minds in men was the first sign of a divine purpose in creation: 'Today the swallows are leaving Edinburgh, tomorrow they will be over Europe and Africa, but of the human drama beneath them they will know nothing. They are ignorant of the colour problem, or of El Alamein, the Roman Empire or even M. Molotov. "Poor beasts," we say, "unless ignorance is bliss".

'But we can sit in our chairs and can embrace the world in our minds, while with very little effort we learn what there is to know of its secrets.'

Since no compass could be set to the power of the mind, which was unique in nature, was it credible that this part of man should die? He was certain that 'the mind is the passport to immortality and that man is the instrument through which God will achieve the purpose of creation'.

Alec Dunglass could see no real dilemma between science and religion. The fact that science could operate only in a world of order, in which one thing is consequential on another, was an argument for the existence of a God since the more wonders science reveals, the more difficult it is to believe in chance.

He spoke of those who because 'they cannot comprehend, therefore do not believe'. Yet 'I can stand within inches of the jellyfish, but unless I impinge upon his sense of touch, he is quite unconscious of my presence. I can see nothing improbable in the existence of states of being of which man tied to earth by his body and with his limited senses is unaware.'

Of the traditional ideas of God and his heaven, 'When I see some of them I have sympathy with the dying man who, being comforted with the conventional condolences and pictures of the next world, summoned his strength and said, "Yes; doubtless I shall inherit eternal bliss, but do not let us talk of anything so depressing!"'

There are, indeed, 'gaps which only faith can bridge'. For himself, Dunglass concluded, 'I believe in God the maker of Heaven and Earth and in God the maker of man, the giver of man's mind, and I believe in a Christian God who sent Christ into the world to give man the promise that the purpose of creation was Good'.

It was a noble but precise affirmation of faith. Alec Dunglass was no theologian and he refused to go beyond his own experience; he would never parade beliefs he had not tested on his pulses. He was as fastidious in his wording as his distinguished predecessor, Arthur James Balfour, though lacking the philosophical niceties Balfour so elegantly deployed in *The Foundations of Belief* fifty years before.

Dunglass was almost alone among post-war politicians in declaring and discussing his Christian faith. He had, as we shall see, increasing doubts whether he was right in doing so.

During the years of Socialist Government, Dunglass's political life was largely confined to Scotland. He was chairman of the Eastern divisional council of the Scottish Unionists (by which name Conservatives are officially known in North Britain) and in 1948 President of the Party. He worked hard at Party organization and was on a Committee of Scottish M.P.s and peers which in 1949 issued a document entitled 'Scottish Control of Scottish Affairs', proposing a greater devolution of responsibility to Scotland particularly for the nationalized industries. The committee chairman was James Stuart, afterwards Chief Whip, a fact that was to have significance for Dunglass two years later.

He spoke at meetings up and down Scotland, but mainly in industrial areas, where he emphasized that State control was creating more petty tyrants in positions of authority than Britain had ever known—an attitude strikingly at variance with that of Tories such as Quintin Hogg, who had declared that the new Tory 'sees in the modern extra-political forms of public control a nationalization which has lost its terrors and in the larger joint-stock companies with limited liability a private enterprise which has lost its meaning'.[1]

Dunglass preached the Salisbury-Balfour doctrine: that it was easy enough to level down, the real aim must be to level up. The only way to greater prosperity for all was not the redistribution of existing wealth but the creation of new wealth. The idea was not in line with those of the new Tory reformers; one investigator of the time concluded that 'from an examination of the campaign literature officially provided by the headquarters of the parties, it was difficult to discover any basic conflicts separating the Left from the Right'.[2]

The era of 'centre-ism' was dawning. Though Dunglass's instincts were against most of its shared tenets, he took no public stand against it. He knew that the key to good government lay in compromise, 'the hallmark of the civilized and sensitive mind'.[3] In Dunglass compromise

---

[1] *One Year's Work*, London, 1944, p. 43-4.
[2] J. D. Hoffman, *The Conservative Party In Opposition, 1945-51*, London, 1964, p. 43.
[3] Ralph Harris, *Politics without Prejudice*, London, 1956, p. 117.

and tolerance were instinctive—he is no 'last ditcher'[1]; it was why he opposed Socialist dogma, knowing that it disguised the determination to impose, by compulsion if necessary, a way of life and thought on other men, and spelt death to tolerance.

Dunglass believed in the old virtues of truth, fair-dealing and keeping promises. The Labour Government, he wrote, came to power in 1945 with the declared determination to work with Russia. But Russia broke every treaty and agreement signed with Britain during the war; and the Government had found the price of co-operation was 'the sacrifice of the sovereignty and political freedom of independent countries'. He was quite clear that 'friendship can only grow from action based upon common moral and ethical principles, and so long as Communists direct Soviet foreign policy these are not there'.[2]

Alec Dunglass was largely isolated from the breeding-grounds of the new generation of Tory leaders. He did not belong to the One Nation Group in which Iain Macleod, Enoch Powell and Edward Heath were prominent. Unlike Macleod, Powell and Reginald Maudling, he had no job in the Conservative Research Department, presided over by R. A. Butler, whose reputation stood high. Butler had been the Minister responsible for the celebrated Education Act of 1944.

Dunglass had no intimacy with Churchill and little with his heir-apparent, Anthony Eden. His acquaintance with most of the younger Front Bench spokesmen was slight, and in any case more often social than political. The fact was that most of the Tory front-runners did not think him worth cultivating since he was obviously destined for the Lords, which is why his subsequent eminence shocked them.

He maintained his membership of the 'Progress Trust', to which belonged his Scottish friends, Major John Morrison, later Lord Margadale, and Thomas Galbraith, later Lord Strathclyde. By this time, the Progress Trust, Dunglass recalled, 'was a sort of working group for the Conservative party in Opposition when it was felt that Winston's idea of opposition was not methodical enough. The group was quite effective'. How effective? One critic wrote that Churchill was a near-disaster as Opposition leader: 'Sporadic appearances in the House,' one critic wrote, 'indifference to the consolidation of a *party* effort, and occasionally outright disregard for the views of his shadow

[1] Lord Salisbury, private communication.
[2] Letter to *The Times*, 5th March 1946.

cabinet colleagues imposed strains upon the Conservative party which from time to time seriously affected the quality of opposition.'[1]

Opposition was sorely needed. Under the Labour Government, Britain's affairs went from bad to worse. Austerities increased (bread was rationed for the first time in 1946); economic crisis and devaluation produced cuts in imports and of the meat ration; coal and fuel supplies failed and caused serious hardship in the severe winter of 1946-7; and the wartime Control of Employment order was brought back—a 'blank cheque for totalitarian Government', Churchill dubbed it. It was the era of snoek, 'drones', Sidney Stanley, and five-shilling dinners. Life had been made more tolerable for many by the Welfare State but it was a blanket, indiscriminate welfare, damning to both British character and British economy.

Abroad Russia's easy imperial gains had whetted her appetite and she threatened still more territories in Europe and Asia. In reply, America produced the Marshall plan which was to save Western Europe from Stalin's imperial lust—not however before Czechoslovakia had succumbed and Western Berlin been blockaded. As a result, NATO was formed in 1949 and the German Federal Republic was given a limited sovereignty. In 1947 British rule of India ended, Burma became independent in January 1948, and the United States attack on the Empire (under the cover of condemning the evils of imperialism and colonialism[2]) became more explicit. The dissolution of the British Empire—over which Churchill had declared he would not preside— was proceeding apace.

Dunglass itched to be back in the fray. No suitable local by-election had offered and, since a General Election was due by June 1950, he got down to active campaigning in his former constituency of Lanark. As it happened, the Labour Government had decided to make an issue of a subject of considerable importance to Lanark: the nationalization of the iron and steel industry. The Bill had passed the Commons. When the Lords used their delaying powers, the Government legislated to alter them, reducing the period by which the Lords could hold up a measure to two successive sessions and one year. The Iron and Steel Bill was passed. The Conservatives pledged themselves to repeal the Act.

[1] *The Conservative Party in Opposition, 1945–51*, pp. 268–9. See note, p. 74 above.
[2] Attlee, the Labour Prime Minister, was explicit on the matter in his memoirs, *As It Happened*, London, 1954, p. 180.

With these manœuvres as prelude, a General Election was set for 13th February 1950. Dunglass was ready. In Lanark he faced his old opponent, Thomas Steele, and he started his campaign with a bang. He circulated a leaflet which said: 'This letter was published on 8th August 1945. From Mr T. Steele, M.P., to the *Daily Worker*. I wish to pay compliment to the individual members of the Communist party for the magnificent part they played in the campaign. They *more than others* deserve the fullest credit.'[1]

Written in the days when Communism was respectable in the afterglow of the Russian alliance, it was damning in 1950, for by this time British Communism, at the behest of its Soviet masters, had become an arm of subversion and before long Communist spies were to be revealed in the Foreign Office itself.

Steele's solicitors demanded that the leaflet be withdrawn, and a complete and unqualified apology put in the newspapers. Dunglass refused. Steele had made no attempt during four years to deny the letter's authenticity: 'Lord Dunglass,' his agent replied, 'is sorry for Mr Steele in his dilemma but feels he cannot be expected to extricate him from a mess which is of his own or the *Daily Worker*'s making.'

In his electioneering speeches, Dunglass emphasized that the cost of living had risen because of the extension of State control. He painted gloomy pictures of the frustration for workers of having to deal with the remote authority of a nationalized board, rather than with a local employer.

The result on 13th February 1950 was close and there was a high poll. But Dunglass won with a majority of 685 (19,890 to 19,205). The Labour Government, however, survived, shakily, with an overall majority of only six. Life for all M.P.s was evidently going to be hard, but Alec Dunglass leaped joyfully on the London train.

[1] John Dickie, *The Uncommon Commoner; a study of Sir Alec Douglas-Home*, London, 1964, p. 82.

8. Our Man in Scotland: 1951 – 5

In the Commons again. The 14th Earl. Death duties. 'Home Sweet Home'.
Ministers of State. Attempts to 'poach' him. Lucid and debonair.

Dunglass quickly climbed back on the enchanted treadmill. He spoke on 9th March 1950—and was nine times interrupted—about iron and steel nationalization, condemning 'these monstrous State monopolies', and giving examples from his constituency of the inequities to employees caused by State ownership of railways and road haulage.

He returned to 'over-centralization and over control' on 7th November. Nearly two million people—about 11 per cent of all insured workers—were in nationalized industry, which would breed in them a mass psychology giving birth to mass reactions. Bad humour would pick on trifles as an excuse for big strikes. Even more trickily, one of these days nationalized workers would strike with good reason so that their strike could not be written off as Communist-inspired. What then would the Government do? Would they tolerate opposition from organized labour? Most likely, they would 'direct' labour and then Britain would slither towards the one-Party State and personal freedom would end.

The Korean War broke out in June 1950. Though both Parties officially agreed that Britain must support America and the Allied countries opposing the aggression, there were Socialist M.P.s ready for sophistry: 'It is always foolish to play the Communist game,' Dunglass told them, 'but when at this moment the life of every person in the free countries and of every Socialist on the benches opposite is preserved by American power, these speeches become positively indecent. . . .'

The old shadow still fell over him and he boldly put a searchlight on it: 'If, as honourable members opposite are so fond of saying, we are to have no more Munichs, then it is up to them to see that there is no more weakness.'

Communism's boot was also on Western Germany and Persia. Russia intended to stop 'the Western powers from getting the benefit from minerals and other raw materials from South-East Asia', he said to the Commons on 29th November 1950. 'Their second objective is the possession of Persian oil, the end of Turkish independence and a footing in, and control of, the Eastern Mediterranean. The third, above all, is the possession of Germany'.

The West might survive without the first two, 'but Western civilization is finished and the savages walk in if Russia should get control of Germany, and therefore of the Continent of Europe'.

What did his fellow M.P.s really think of Alec Dunglass? To the extreme Left he was a Communist-baiter, a lightweight scion of title and privilege: come the Revolution . . . Few of them, however, longed to put the cord round his neck and hoist him up the lamp-post. Most M.P.s who knew him liked him but, then, few knew him well even in his own Party. His friends were mainly Scottish M.P.s and peers. To the public outside the Westminster club, he was not even a name.

So when in the fullness of his years the 13th Earl of Home died on 11th July 1951, those parliamentarians who thought about it at all supposed that Alec Dunglass, now the 14th Earl, would either retire from politics or be given a junior post in the Lords by the next Tory Government, whence he would gradually fade away, like the smile on the Cheshire cat, and disappear beyond the Cheviots.

Either was possible. The new Lord Home was deeply affected by the death of that humble, kindly man, his father, and there were financial problems. The estates themselves had been made a limited company before the war. The former Earl's personal fortune, however, was less assured.

For years his solicitors urged him to make it over to a family trust to safeguard it from excessive death duties. He was evasive, saying that all taxes, even though they were unjust, should be paid in full. In August 1946, however, he finally agreed—and died just six weeks too soon for his heir to benefit from the five-year rule. Appeals were made without satisfactory result and during the following decade some 12,000 acres of land were sold.

Alec Home and his co-trustee, the Duke of Buccleuch, spent many months on these and other estate concerns. It became clear that, though the new Earl would not be a poor man, his income would be greatly reduced from his grandfather's £60,000 or so a year. It might be better, or even necessary, to give up politics and an expensive London life; and in those days peers were not paid for attending debates.

While Alec Home was in Scotland putting his affairs in order, the Labour Government was breaking up; there were ministerial resignations and tiring cat-and-mouse games with an Opposition rejuvenated by the prospect of power. The *coup de grâce* came in October 1951; and at the Election the Conservatives were returned with a small but workable majority. In Home's old Lanark seat, Patrick Maitland, the Master of Lauderdale, put on an increased majority.

The excitement of victory filtered through to the Hirsel. Though a peer is not allowed to play any part in a General Election, he can scarcely prevent his impassioned friends telephoning him with their tales of close-run-things and of opponents floored. The 14th Earl found himself as susceptible as ever to the whiff of Westminster. He realized too at the age of 48, just as he had done in his mid-twenties, that 'the role of territorial magnate was still not going to be enough'.

The Commons was no longer open to him; the Lords was. He would take his seat. He had small expectation of office. Winston Churchill, forming what was to be his last Ministry, had plenty of talent to choose from—Eden, Salisbury, Butler, Macmillan, Macleod, Lyttelton, Woolton—and indeed once confided that he could have formed a very good inner cabinet from the Lords alone.[1] Moreover, Churchill scarcely knew him; Alec Home had never been close to the men close to the Prime Minister—with one important exception. He had worked in Scottish Unionist affairs with James Stuart, M.P. for Moray and Nairn, who was Chief Whip from 1941 to 1948. Stuart had been Churchill's mainstay in his often difficult relations with Conservative M.P.s and had the Prime Minister's complete trust in a field he himself too frequently left uncultivated.

In the new Government, Stuart was to be Secretary of State for Scotland. Churchill, however, thought that the office should be strengthened by the addition for the first time of a Minister of State who would normally be resident in Edinburgh. There were two reasons behind his decision. He was impressed by the idea of a measure of devolution for Scotland put forward in the paper produced by Alec Home, Stuart and others, 'Scottish Control of Scottish Affairs', a *résumé* of which appeared in the 1950 Party manifesto 'This is the Road'. The other reason was that there was discontent in Scotland based on the

[1] *Memoirs of the Earl of Woolton*, London, 1959, p. 365.

feeling that industry there had been neglected. This discontent found vent in the demand for a Scottish parliament, spearheaded by the Scottish National Party and the Scottish Covenant.

These remote rumblings burst into national thunder when on Christmas morning 1950 the Stone of Scone was mysteriously spirited away from beneath the Coronation Chair in Westminster Abbey, and the Covenanters—claiming 3½ million signatures of support—pressed still harder their claim for Home Rule.

A Minister, then, there must be: whom, Churchill inquired of Stuart, would he like? 'Winston,' Stuart recalled, 'produced a half-sheet of paper with a few names on it, presumably supplied by the Chief Whip, representing those M.P.s and Peers thought suitable for me to have as my Minister of State (a new office) and Under-Secretaries. I did not like the look of parts of this document and said so . . . In the first place I asked for Lord Home as my Minister of State.'[1] '"Home Sweet Home" it shall be,' agreed Churchill.

Alec Home was delighted. Not only was it his first important job in Government but it was also a sort of benison on his work for the afflicted Scots of his constituency in the days of depression in the 1930s, an opportunity now to do what he could for all his fellow-countrymen.

His mandate was outlined by Churchill in the Commons on 21st November 1951: Lord Home 'will be concerned specially with the industry and development and the peculiar problems of the Highlands and Islands and aspects of local government, in addition to education matters. While he is not a member of the Cabinet he will, as necessary, be invited to attend meetings of the Cabinet on behalf of the Secretary of State'.

At a private briefing Churchill was more abrupt: 'Go up to Scotland and see if you can get rid of this embryo Scottish nationalist thing.' Doubtless that was a tactical objective. But that Churchill meant him to have a really constructive function is shown by the fact that he gave him a team of three Under-Secretaries—T. D. Galbraith, M.P. for Pollok, who was to concentrate on housing and health; W. McNair Snadden, M.P. for Kinross and W. Perthshire, to look after agriculture; Sir James Henderson-Stewart, M.P. for East Fife, to examine educational problems. Their headquarters was St Andrew's House in Edinburgh.

[1] James Stuart (Viscount Stuart of Findhorn), *Within the Fringe*, London, 1967, p. 162.

With them he worked as a committee in which he was merely *primus inter pares*. He did not seek the limelight, he lacked vanity, he was never bossy: he preferred the job to the kudos and at the job he became very good indeed.

On the question of Home Rule and nationalism he thought it well to make his views plain from the start: 'Nothing could be more disastrous for Scotland,' he said in the Lords, 'than that Scotsmen should try to take a narrow parochial view and try to confine their particular talents within their own margins, particularly in these days when power, both economic and military, is in large systems. It would seem to me that the prosperity, and indeed the survival, of both England and Scotland depends on close and trusting union.'

He saw clearly that the economics of the two countries were so closely interrelated that disentanglement was very nearly impossible. They were no less so eighteen years later when he presided over a Conservative Party inquiry into the same subject.[1] Nevertheless he believed that many functions of central government could well be handed down to Edinburgh. 'The right start' for it was to have a Minister in the Lords.

He was given a very free hand: ' James Stuart was a very good Chief because he let one do what one liked. He said "Provided you don't get me into trouble I don't care what you do".'

So Alec Home worked out a scheme for himself: 'The technique I adopted was to go round all the local authorities and all that kind of thing; I made myself available to listen and to visit them and speak to them at their dinners and other functions and generally to show interest in Scotland's special problems. I also took every opportunity to visit Scottish industry and consult the Scottish Development Council.

'At the same time, I went down to the Lords once a month on a fairly carefully-staged occasion to get the maximum publicity for Scottish affairs. This did the trick.'

Even if his four-year tenure is regarded only negatively—or in Churchill's private, blunt terms—it was a success: the extreme manifestations of the Covenanters disappeared from the front pages of the newspapers—to reappear only when excessive Socialist centralization had again left Scotland high and dry in the second half of the 1960s.

But was Home's role only an elaborate exercise in public relations?

---

[1] See p. 266 below. In the report *Scotland's Government* (Edinburgh, 1970) an elected 'Scottish Convention' was proposed.

On the contrary, he could point to solid and effective legislation. His Crofters (Scotland) Act of 1955 went a long way to arrest the decay of Highland farming by injecting capital in the form of grants and loans and ensuring that absentee tenants did not weaken the system. He provided grants also to encourage re-afforestation; a joint agricultural-forestry survey investigated local situations where farming and forestry interests clashed.

Electricity was spread to remoter agricultural places by the Hydro-Electric Development (Scotland) Act; and, tactfully urging his own priorities on the Minister of Transport—who was responsible for roads throughout the United Kingdom—he got money for Highland roads which, as he said, 'are literally life to the Highland communities'. He was, of course, from time to time frustrated by the Treasury.

In the Lords, where he introduced the often intricate legislation, he earned golden opinions and not from his own side alone. The Welshman Lord Ogmore, a Labour peer, envied Scotland in having so active a Minister who really got things done. Though Home appeared in the Lords only half a dozen times in the year, every appearance counted.

So successful was he that other Secretaries of State sought to 'poach' him from Stuart: 'I was certainly right in my choice of Alec Douglas-Home, as the P.M. also knew and probably realized even more fully when two or three years later both Lord Salisbury and Anthony Eden wanted him to leave me in order to strengthen their offices. The P.M. told me himself of these requests for Alec's services, adding "Your Home, Sweet Home seems to be doing well."' [1]

For Alec Home it was immensely useful experience. From his office in Edinburgh he had his fingers on all the public affairs of Scotland. He presided over committees ranging from health to finance, agriculture and education to civil defence. He also talked in his easy way to all kinds and conditions of men and women. Preferring personal meetings to official letters, he was constantly on the road and could have written a detailed guide-book to Scotland.

Always a very quick reader, he could run through a mass of official papers, picking out key points with a speedy skill. He learned the intricacies of administration and the Civil Service. In short, he learned how to handle the levers of power. His regret was only that he had nothing to do with foreign affairs, his interest in which had grown during the war and had not abated.

[1] *Within the Fringe*, p. 162. See note, p. 81 above.

At least, he could occasionally take time off to glance shrewdly at 'the British Socialist Party' and its holy, immutable doctrine of nationalization. 'It does not matter if the Labour Party has nothing to offer an island which has to live by competitive prices in foreign markets,' he told a Bradford audience on 27th January 1953. 'It does not matter if the coal industry's finance is in the red, and the Transport Commission has only one idea, which is to raise freights and fares. It is the Socialist theory—the public must swallow it.'

Then again—a reason more compelling: 'Nationalization is the only platform on which Mr Morrison, Dr Dalton, and Mr Bevan can meet on speaking terms. It is a shocking thing that in order to cement the widening cracks in the Socialist Party the community should have to pay.'

Wherever he went, Alec Home's lucidity pleased the thinking and his debonair manner charmed the ladies, seldom unsusceptible to the aura of an earl. He was no old-time orator, plying his audience with thunderbolts and moonshine and a radiant dawn coming up over the mountains. His voice was too light—and sometimes it cracked—and his sense of humour too uncontrollable. Exposition and cool analysis were the natural modes of his mind. He thought, he did not emote. And he thought practically rather than philosophically. He was by nature a 'doer'; the rest of the politician's accoutrements he acquired the hard way for, unlike his fellow-countryman Robert Louis Stevenson, he never believed that 'Politics is perhaps the only profession for which no preparation is thought necessary'.

9. The Commonwealth and Suez: 1955 – 6

Eden's choice. The impossible Nehru. Seretse Khama. Suez: 'I went along with the scheme'. Operation 'bungled'. The Commonwealth 'touch-and-go'.

One of the drawbacks to Scotland is that it buries politicians alive. Though Lord Home was a successful Minister of State, few of the Westminster political pundits, the newspaper correspondents and the 'well-informed' backbenchers, knew who he was or even if he was.

Great, therefore, was their surprise, not to say vaticinal chagrin, when Sir Anthony Eden, succeeding Churchill as Prime Minister in April 1955, announced that the new Secretary of State for the Commonwealth was to be the Earl of Home. 'Your old Home sweet Home can't be too bad,' Churchill observed to James Stuart. 'Anthony wants him at the Commonwealth Office.'

It was no pot-shot. Eden, an experienced judge of politicians, knew exactly what he was doing when he picked Home:

'When I came to form a government early in 1955, I wanted to select one or two men to bring into the Cabinet who had, as I thought, proved themselves in important subordinate offices and might be looked to to play leading parts in government and party in the future. The two I selected were Mr Selwyn Lloyd in the House of Commons, and Lord Home in the House of Lords. Mr Lloyd had had experience of defence problems as Minister of Supply, a difficult post which he had filled most ably, therefore I decided to appoint him Minister of Defence.

'Lord Home had had all-round experience at the Scottish Office. It was evident that he could one day become an effective and respected Secretary of State for Scotland. On the other hand, I suspected that he had significant diplomatic gifts and that there was much to be said for giving him a chance now to display them. Moreover, I thought that the time had come for a younger man at Commonwealth Relations.[1]

[1] The Earl of Swinton, Home's predecessor, was 71, Home 51.

85

'I knew most of the Dominions at first hand myself and I thought that their Governments would welcome a man like Lord Home as Secretary of State and that he would grow to fill the office with distinction. This, I felt, could lead to a future career for him in a wider sphere than administration, and so it proved.'[1]

To have detected 'diplomatic gifts' in Alec Home was remarkably perceptive. For more than three years he had been immersed in Scottish domestic matters and before that had made some far from diplomatic speeches on foreign affairs. He had never set foot in a Commonwealth country and if he was an 'Empire man' he had kept it to himself.

Nor were Eden and Home intimates: 'I always kept in close touch with Anthony during those trying years before the war. But I didn't see a terrible lot of him afterwards. I suppose he thought I had done quite well with people in Scotland. Certainly I hadn't been abroad very much, but he took the risk.'

To be Commonwealth Secretary was a big leap forward in Alec Home's political fortunes. It brought him into the Cabinet alongside such stars as R. A. Butler who, though only a few months his senior, had been Chancellor of the Exchequer since 1951; Harold Macmillan, nine years older; and Lord Salisbury, a decade older. Closer to his own age—and to his new office—was Alan Lennox-Boyd, the already experienced Secretary of State for the Colonies.

In 1955 Lennox-Boyd's office was the more important: it still controlled some forty-five governments. Independent Commonwealth countries numbered only eight, preponderantly white; as well as Britain they were Canada, Australia, New Zealand, South Africa, India, Pakistan and Ceylon.

By the time Home left the office five years later, the position was reversed. It was the era of 'independence' struggles, sometimes bloody; when the struggle was successful, the colony usually became a member of the Commonwealth. So that Home's responsibilities gradually increased, though the heat and burden of the day fell upon Lennox-Boyd.

Home had scarcely started his new job before Eden called a General Election, and the Tory majority rose to 59. In December 1955 the Prime Minister made a few changes in his government; Macmillan,

---

[1] The Earl of Avon to the author, 4th September 1969.

after only a few months at the Foreign Office,[1] was replaced by Selwyn Lloyd, and became Chancellor of the Exchequer, while Butler was made Lord Privy Seal and Leader of the House. Three other men, with whom Alec Home's political career was to be inextricably bound for the next decade, received promotion: Iain Macleod joined the Cabinet as Minister of Labour, Lord Hailsham—four years Home's junior at Eton and Christ Church—was given the Admiralty and Reginald Maudling the Ministry of Supply (later Aviation).

In addition to his Commonwealth responsibilities, Home became Deputy Government Leader in the Lords. His Leader was the prestigious fifth Marquess of Salisbury, a man whose talents fitted him for Prime Minister but whose ancient peerage was felt to disqualify any such promotion. Now Lord President, he had been Secretary of State successively for the Dominions, Colonies and Commonwealth Relations. His experience in Home's new field was deep and unrivalled. Like Eden, whom he had served as Under Secretary at the Foreign Office in Chamberlain's Government, he had resigned in protest against the then Prime Minister's policies. He was to do so again, with unexpected results for Home.

The new Eden administration started off sluggishly, becalmed beneath the long shadow left by the departed Churchill. The Prime Minister himself, kept waiting so long for his inheritance, was under strain personally and politically. He worried himself and his ministers, too. 'I got on very well with him,' Home recalled. 'He was a very active Prime Minister and if he had read something in the papers and thought "why haven't you done this or that or the other" he would be on the telephone early in the morning. Then one had to keep out of his way and get on with one's job!'

Home got out of Eden's way at once. To make up the considerable deficiency in his knowledge of the Commonwealth he served, he set out in September 1955 on a tour to Australia, New Zealand, Singapore, India, Pakistan and Ceylon—a 35,000-mile journey.

According to Anthony Sampson, *Macmillan*, London, 1967; paperback edn., 1968, p. 105, Macmillan after a few months at the Foreign Office 'seemed worn out by the exacting conditions of work—the travelling, the bombardment of telegrams, the 'phone calls from America in the middle of the night.' This has bearing on his subsequent remarks before and during Home's tenure of the Office that it was 'a killer'. Macmillan himself, in *Tides of Fortune, 1945–1955*, London, 1969, says that he was happy at the Foreign Office: 'Life although strenuous, was agreeable . . . I was sad indeed to leave.'

He was a great success in Australia where his impeccably polite, but total, candour, his easy humour, and lack of 'side' surprised and delighted all he met. He complimented the Australians on their wisdom in joining Britain and New Zealand in sending troops to strengthen the 'strategic reserve' in Malaya for 'the enemy must be held far from Australia's shores'. In due course, when law and order had been established, Malaya would have 'a form of self-government' but there would be permanent arrangements for her defence and that of Singapore.[1]

He saw the Snowy Mountains hydro-electric scheme, the Radium Hill uranium mine, a great many civic dignitaries at civic luncheons—and Sir Robert Menzies, the Prime Minister. Between them there was an immediate liking, mutual understanding, and a common addiction to cricket. This happy relationship was to prove of crucial importance during the next twelve months.

Some few awkwardnesses there were—about Anglo-Australian trade upon which fresh import restrictions were imposed during his visit, and about the indifferent quality of imports from Britain, their uncompetitive prices and badly kept delivery dates. This was in part a result of industrial disputes in Britain. Such disputes, Home told the Lords on 30th November 1955, did more harm to British prestige and influence abroad than anything else.

Delhi was different. President Nehru was living in cloud-cuckoo-land and very severe on those who would not join him there. He preached 'non-alignment' and 'peaceful co-existence' and put forth a five-point charter of neutrality; his five principles were 'perfectly acceptable—except that the Chinese took no notice of them', Home later observed. At the same time, he was ready to use force to prise from Pakistan her portion of Kashmir and encouraged the dismemberment by all available means of Britain's colonial Empire. These contradictions he camouflaged beneath an unceasing mystical, parapolitical disquisition.

'He was very much putting the pressure on us all the time to get out of the colonies as quick as we could. He took the lead in that, without really understanding the conditions in Africa,' Home recalled. Nehru preached international morality at Britain and the Western Alliance, implying that such military pacts were immoral while suggesting that but for these activities the Russians would be neighbourly and well behaved. This Home could not bear: 'So I deliberately made

[1] Sydney, 22nd September 1955.

a speech that was controversial to the Indian Council of World Affairs. I don't think he much liked it.'

Home thought that this lack of realism had to be exposed, and that it was dangerous for India. As to Nehru's entente with the Chinese, 'it stuck out a mile that he was being duped and he would not believe it. And non-alignment: the fact was that, at the back of his mind, he relied on us to come and help him, and would have been outraged if we had not given or offered any assistance.'

At this time, the Western world generally recognized that there was an element of humbug and selfishness in Nehru's attitudes. Home saw beyond this: 'one cannot deny that he was a very great man in his own country. He had an enormous hold over the Congress party; they liked his kind of mysticism, but his politics left India exposed and unprepared.'

The speech Nehru did not like was made on 23rd October. Reporting it, *The Times* observed that while other distinguished visitors to Delhi seemed willing only to please, Lord Home boldly presented another aspect of the world crisis.

Three times in half a century, he said, Britain has held out the olive branch of conciliation—to the Kaiser, to Hitler, to Stalin—'and the lessons we and our friends in Europe have learned in a bitter school is that weakness invites aggression and that neutrality has no meaning in the context of totalitarian ambition.

'To match strength with strength has been the policy of risk which to you in Asia might seem unnecessary and dangerous, but the North Atlantic Treaty corresponded to the instinctive and genuine need for self-preservation which was felt in Western Europe.'

These opinions were anathema to Nehru who, such was his democratic outlook, saw to it that they were not reported in the Indian press. 'No, I wasn't very popular in Delhi,' Alec Home recalled drily.

Just seven years after Home's warning, the Chinese crushed and humiliated India in one month, annexing the territory (Ladakh) they desired and then announcing their cease-fire proposals. Power, as Mao Tse-tung had informed the whole world, grows out of the barrel of a gun. Britain was the first to send military equipment; Russia sent nothing.

Plain-speaking, which was to become his trade mark, never lessened Alec Home's friendly buoyancy and sense of fun nor did he bear a grudge.

He travelled on to Pakistan where he felt more at home, although the meal of sheep's eyes on the Khyber Pass tested his natural courtesy. 'I hope,' said the Labour Commonwealth spokesman, Lord Ogmore, 'that they were as tender as his own Scottish mutton.'

Nor could Home forbear to inform their Lordships that, while excellent new universities were being started in the Commonwealth, 'I noticed that many young people were reading economics. But they will soon recover from that, as we have done.' [1]

In general, Home later thought, the tour was 'a successful one because one got to know a lot of people'. It was also successful because a lot of people got to know him and felt a fresh breeze of realism blowing out to them from Britain.

Alec Home had a quick mind and, like his old master Chamberlain, could swiftly extract the essentials out of the sometimes verbose documents the civil servants put before him. They liked him for it as they liked him for his lack of fuss and airs. But he was becoming very much his own man, thinking his own thoughts. There was, for example, the Seretse Khama affair. Seretse was the heir-apparent to his uncle, Tshekedi Khama, the ruler of the Bamangwato tribe of Bechuanaland. He had, however, married an English wife, and the former Labour Government's Commonwealth Relations Secretary, P. Gordon Walker, had 'exiled' him to England. The Churchill Government had confirmed Seretse's exclusion from the chieftainship.

Home was responsible for sending Seretse Khama back to Bechuanaland: 'There was a row about this. The Labour Party were too chicken-hearted for words because of a kind of inverted colour-consciousness. Because Seretse had a white wife they decided he must stay in Brighton for the rest of his life. They would not risk sending him back to Bechuanaland.

'I thought this was absurd and the chance must be taken. The man was terribly unhappy in Brighton and wasting a useful life. Now he's still alive. He has been a great success and his wife too in guiding his new country.'

It was an executive act early in his days as Commonwealth Secretary and, reportedly, against some advice. But it did something worth while for the people living in that part of Africa.

Home did more than that. He saw that if the three High Commission territories—Basutoland and Swaziland as well as Bechuanaland—were

[1] Parliamentary Reports. Lords, 30th November 1955, col. 194.

to survive they needed money for developing trade and providing social services. Somehow with the help of Lennox-Boyd he managed to get it for them. He also encouraged the territories in their desires for self-government (they became independent in 1967), and generally took them under his wing, particularly to shelter them from embodiment into South Africa. Their leaders remain touchingly grateful.

He had planned to visit the three territories and South Africa in the autumn of 1956. It was twelve years before he got there. More momentous matters intervened. They began sociably enough with a white-tie-and-tails dinner party which Home attended at No. 10 Downing Street on 26th July 1956. The dinner was in honour of King Feisal of Irak. But as the company relaxed over dessert, the host, Prime Minister Eden, was handed a note telling him that President Nasser of Egypt had just announced that he was going to nationalize the Suez Canal.

When the guests departed, Eden signalled Home and other Ministers to remain behind and an impromptu discussion began. Later the Chiefs of Staff, the French Ambassador and the American *chargé d'affaires* were called in. The threat to the Canal was serious enough. It carried much of western Europe's oil from Arabia, and in the company which operated it Britons were the biggest shareholders.

Far more serious to the minds of Home and the others round the table was the fact that Nasser, who had declared his intention of creating an Arab empire, was heavily backed by the Russians who had long been pouring military supplies, 'technicians' and money into Egypt. 'I was quite clear,' Home recalled, 'that Nasser's seizure of the Canal was part of a wider scheme in which the Russians were immensely interested. This was really the justification of what followed. If there was to be a general Middle East war, the point to stop it was on the Canal and at that time.'

Home was in and out of the intense diplomatic activity, the conferences and the planning which followed the Nasser declaration. The main decisions were taken—and not always communicated to the Cabinet as a whole—by Eden and a small inner Cabinet comprising Selwyn Lloyd; Macmillan, Chancellor of the Exchequer; and on occasion R. A. Butler, Lord Privy Seal and Leader of the House; Lord Salisbury; with the Defence Ministers attending as required.

Home's particular role was to keep the Commonwealth informed of the general trend of Government thinking—which until ordered to stop he did, and in turn to inform the Cabinet of Commonwealth reaction. He therefore knew that Eden, having failed to dissuade Nasser from his Canal nationalization, was contemplating military action: 'I went along with the scheme,' he said later. But he was obliged to report to Eden that, while Australia, New Zealand and South Africa agreed that Nasser must somehow be taught a lesson, Canada was cool, Pakistan was opposed (mainly on Moslem, co-religionist grounds), and Nehru of India was screaming with rage at the idea of the moribund lion swishing its tail.

Such considerations did not deflect Eden nor did Home believe they should. The problem really was not whether there should be military action but rather what form it should take. Home preferred a strike by British forces alone. Eden, however, knew that too much of the naval armament required was in mothballs, that no contingency plan existed for re-occupying the Canal Zone (evacuated by the British eighteen months before) and that alternative bases in Cyprus were not yet ready.

He preferred to act with the French who under their Prime Minister, Guy Mollet, execrated Nasser and his Russian friends, regarding them as the evil geniuses behind the Algerian uprising. An Anglo-French military planning team was set up early in August, and a few days later produced the blueprint for a joint landing at Alexandria and thence a direct advance on Cairo.

Eden hesitated. General Eisenhower, facing a presidential election, refused even his moral support; and it was obvious that, however unjust Nasser's theft of the Canal might be, the United Nations Security Council, in which sat Russia, the real instigator of the affair, would veto any action at all.

The French had another idea. Nasser was harassing the Israelis by sporadic raids into their territory; he threatened them with invasion and extinction. It was likely that the first-class Israeli Army, under General Moshe Dayan, would take reprisals. Would it not be well to encourage them to do so and then, under the pretext of restoring peace, follow them into Egypt and seize the Canal Zone?

To this plan, in its starkest form, Eden never agreed. He could not be seen to be encouraging the Israelis; there would be tremendous repercussions on Britain's economic and military relations with the rest of the Arab world. Yet if the Israelis did invade Egypt a contingency plan was necessary. It was right, Home reflected later, to try to prevent a war engulfing the whole of Arabia—'it was necessary to look ahead'.

It was by no means certain that the Israelis would invade Egypt. It was just as likely that they would strike against their other enemy, the Jordanians. However, if the Israelis did go for Egypt, the plan it now seems clear, was to stop them on the Canal by ultimatum and give the same ultimatum to Egypt. If the Egyptians did not obey, their air force would be destroyed, after which there would be ground landings to seize the key-points on the Canal. Thus, in theory, the Anglo-French objective would have been achieved as part of an operation to restore peace and without incurring the obloquy of the rest of the Arab world.

What Eden—ill during October with recurrent fevers—regarded as a contingency plan, the French took as being the British go-ahead to arrange a concerted attack with the Israelis on Egypt. The result was cross-purposes and distrust: the French appeared to be playing a devious game which would account for some of the gaps in forward-planning that were afterwards to appear obvious.

By mid-October, however, for the harassed Eden the contingency plan became the only plan. If the Israelis did *not* attack Egypt, the whole conception of a military operation against Nasser would have to be reconsidered, and probably dropped. Nasser's theft would go unpunished and Russian plans unchecked. The issue, it seemed, would turn almost on the spin of a coin in Tel Aviv: were the Israelis to attack Egypt or Jordan?

The coin duly spun. Tempted by the prospect of the destruction of Nasser's air force by the English and French, the Israelis decided on Egypt. In the greatest secrecy, the French conveyed the decision to the British; Selwyn Lloyd and Patrick Dean of the Foreign Office flew to Sèvres to concert the tripartite plan; and Eden imposed a security blackout so severe that only his inner cabinet knew exactly what was afoot.

The blackout included the Commonwealth countries: 'In those final hours I could not inform the Commonwealth. When a military emergency occurs, there must be absolute security. Eden was right to insist on it.' (Nevertheless, it has since emerged that the Australian Government knew of the operation in advance.) This puts a different complexion on what Randolph Churchill referred to as Lord Home's 'considerable culpability' for not warning the Commonwealth countries of the impending action.[1]

[1] *The Rise and Fall of Sir Anthony Eden*, London, 1959, p. 281.

On Monday, 29th October the Israelis invaded Sinai with their army and air force and supported by French supply planes. Their objectives were speedily secured. The full British Cabinet met next morning, 30th October, and solemnly gave Egypt and Israel a twelve-hour ultimatum to stop forthwith all warlike action on land, sea and air; and to withdraw all Israeli military forces to a distance of ten miles east of the Canal. Egypt was asked to agree that Anglo-French forces should move temporarily into key positions at Port Said, Ismailia and Suez. If Egypt refused, British and French forces would intervene immediately, and of course the Israelis would continue the battle.

In the afternoon it fell to Home, deputizing for Lord Salisbury, to announce the ultimatum in the Lords, and to state that Israeli troops had penetrated deep into Egyptian territory, 'not far from the banks of the Suez Canal' (in fact they did not reach the Canal zone until three days later). An immediate meeting of the Security Council was, he added, being sought by Britain, France and the United States.

The ultimatum expired at 4.30 a.m. next day. The Israelis accepted it, the Egyptians did not. Now was the time for the Anglo-French forces to invade. But where were they? It took British and French planes fifteen hours to go into action; thirty-six hours later they had 'taken out' the Egyptian air force, as promised. The main Anglo-French invasion forces were nowhere in sight. They were in fact still on the high seas. By a barely credible piece of folly the sea-borne troop invasion had been launched from Malta, 1,000 miles down the Mediterranean from Port Said, instead of from Cyprus, 250 miles away. They spent five days lumbering eastwards, shadowed by the American fleet, and arriving off Port Said on 5th November, six days after the ultimatum had expired. Not until this fleet was off Port Said were the Anglo-French parachutists, waiting on Cyprus, dropped near the Egyptian port.

'It was bungled, no doubt,' Home thought. In particular, the slow haul from Malta was 'catastrophic'. The French, indeed, had urged Eden to dispatch the invasion fleet a week before the Israelis attacked; but how could he since officially he knew nothing of Israeli plans? The reason why Malta rather than Cyprus was chosen as base was that hutments were not available for the troops though it is still unclear why they could not sleep in the open in the mild climate of the island.

What ought to have been a swift, sharp action became a cumbersome exercise though, once on the ground, the troops showed themselves

94

the masters not only of the enemy but of their own Chiefs of Staff and the politicians. Anthony Head, the Defence Minister, later left the Government. He had succeeded Walter Monckton in the post almost on the eve of the operation, though he had been concerned with planning in his previous post of War Minister. Home considered that Head could not be blamed.

With operations proceeding in the first week of November, all hell was let loose in the press and Parliament, though there was evidence that the man-in-the-street approved the Government's action. In the Lords—where hell is suitably muted—Home led for the Government in the debate of 1st November, Lord Salisbury being indisposed. Echoing Eden, he said that as regards Suez 'our life is at stake'. Nasser, whose speeches were reminiscent of Hitler's ranting, was bent on aggression and had repeatedly asserted that he was 'organizing Israel's destruction.'

The Government was criticized because it had not waited for an answer from the United Nations: 'Is it any use disguising from ourselves that the United Nations machinery has fatal defects in the case of an emergency like this? Time and again it has proved itself deliberate, slow and inconclusive, and time and again the Soviet veto has frustrated a decision.

'If the Communist nations, or their friends, decide to prevent the machinery of settlement from working, is there no collective redress for a member of the free world? If a dictator, seeking to dominate another country, does everything short of physical aggression to bring that country to its knees, are we merely to wait until it is strangled?' [1]

Moreover nothing in the United Nations charter absolved any Government from its duty to protect its own people, and property, or of upholding international treaties.

Home tackled the ticklish question of why the United States had proffered no support. There was, he delicately admitted, 'a different emphasis' in the policies of the two countries with regard to the Middle East. It was one of the very few areas of common concern 'where we do not see eye to eye with the United States and cannot always wait for the concurrence of the United States before we act.'

He had been accused as the Minister concerned with not having consulted the Commonwealth. 'I can truthfully say that up to the time of the Israel accusation and attack upon Egypt, there had been a con-

[1] Parliamentary Reports. Lords, 1st November 1956, cols. 1251–6.

tinuous flow of information and consultation . . . When the attack developed, there was simply no time for consultation, although the Commonwealth countries were informed before the Prime Minister's statement of what the British Government had in mind.' Mr Menzies had issued a statement to say that Britain was not at fault at all in not consulting other British countries in advance: the circumstances were those of great emergency.

The use of force, the Socialists complained, was 'shocking'. But 'it cannot be wrong to use force in the defence of law and justice, because without justice there is no life left for the free . . . Where would our reputation be if we failed to stand on the side of justice?'

The British action was 'a police action; an action of holding the pass: of keeping the peace pending a permanent settlement, which everybody hopes can be underwritten by a United Nations organization equipped in future to guarantee that justice shall rule the world.' [1]

Home made no comment on 'collusion', mentioned by a Socialist lord, though it was denied by Eden and Selwyn Lloyd in the Commons.

Home's main task during the week of crisis was to hold the Commonwealth together. He had said in his speech that 'it is too early to say what the final reaction of the Commonwealth countries will be.' That was to put it mildly: 'India and Pakistan very nearly left the Commonwealth. Canada was very critical. That was my main task, holding them in,' he remembered. 'But it was touch-and-go.'

Daily he saw the Commonwealth High Commissioners. Mrs Pandit,[2] with whom he had good relations, was extremely understanding, despite the shrillness of Nehru. The Pakistani High Commissioner, Mohammed Ikramullah, was too an able and discerning man, although the Moslem question was uppermost.

'I had to do a lot of retrieving,' Home recalled. 'After all the Commonwealth Office is above all things a diplomatic office. All you can do is to persuade because they are after all independent countries. My argument with them was that they could not wreck the Commonwealth on this issue, and that there was a very strong case for using force to stop a war which could have spread to the whole Arab world which would set the whole Moslem community, including Pakistan, on edge.

'In that emotional state, all one could do was to persuade and, in the

[1] Parliamentary Reports. Lords, col. 1257. See note, p. 95 above.

[2] Mrs Ranjit S. Pandit, Nehru's sister, was Indian High Commissioner in London, 1954–61.

end we did manage to get Pakistan and India to hold their hands.' Indeed, when the Commonwealth Prime Ministers' conference met in June–July next year, 1957, all was 'goodwill and friendly understanding'. Eden's intuition that Home possessed 'diplomatic gifts' was vindicated.

During the week of crisis, Eden needed every available crumb of comfort. Things were going disastrously wrong, and Eden was increasingly distraught. 'The situation at times seemed out of control,' Home wrote a few days later.[1] There were U.N. resolutions condemning the Suez operation and demanding an immediate cease-fire. There were threats from Bulganin, the Russian Prime Minister. American opposition became relentless and vindictive. Eden, wrote a junior Minister, was subjected to 'straight blackmail' from the American ambassador (Winthrop Aldrich);[2] and Selwyn Lloyd said that though not expecting American support, we never expected they 'would lead the pack against us.'[3] Macmillan saw in it 'this damned bug of anti-colonialism,'[4] which Home was later himself to encounter.

The final blow to the by now very ill Prime Minister was under the belt. A massive flight from the pound began and a withdrawal of capital from Britain. Macmillan, the Chancellor, was obliged to apply to the International Monetary Fund for an immediate loan of £300m. to avoid disaster. He was told that America would agree only if there was a cease-fire from midnight the same day. Macmillan, the strongest supporter of the Suez expedition, now 'white as a sheet', told Eden that it must be stopped. It was the wrong advice: the whole Canal area and Cairo too could have been in Anglo-French hands within three days. To the victors, the pound and the franc would have flown back roaring and rosy, as snobs at a party flock round the V.I.P.

But Eden retreated; his reserves of physical and nervous energy were almost exhausted. To his colleagues he put the situation fairly. Even though the military opinion was that the British troops would take only another day or two to reach the other end of the Canal, he counselled capitulation. Home and the Cabinet accepted his view. The crux was, Home recollected, that 'the pound was running out hour by hour. There were heavy pressures [i.e. American 'blackmail']. This was all

[1] Letter to Selwyn Lloyd, 9th November 1956.

[2] R. Bevins, *The Greasy Pole*, London, 1965.

[3] Randolph Churchill, pp. 293 and 301. See note, p. 93 above.

[4] Bevins, see note above.

because we had lost time and because the Americans were able to play up these pressures so strongly and affect British opinion.'

Time, indeed, had been lost, as the invasion forces rumbled across the Mediterranean long after the Israelis had invaded: if this was 'collusion' it was singularly ill organized and altogether too hesitant.

With Home, the American betrayal rankled. If the United Nations was unable to exercise its authority, he said on 12th December, the United States was unwilling to do so. 'I am not criticizing. I am simply saying that the United States, possibly for its own very good reasons, has never thought it need go so far in this area of the Middle East. A great many of our troubles, I am afraid, have flowed from that attitude.'[1]

Looking back Home thought that, apart from military bungling, 'the fault in the whole operation was that if one was going to do the thing at all one had to contemplate taking charge of the whole of Egypt. Supposing we had got to the other end of the Canal, we could not have stayed there long'. This important point seems to have been ignored by the political planners. Yet to secure the freedom of the Canal and to prevent the dispossession of the Company, it was essential to stay long enough to get Nasser replaced, and that was the prime object of the exercise.

There was, Home thought, one unsung political hero of the Suez period. Selwyn Lloyd, the Foreign Secretary, heaped with contumely by the Leftists, almost alone in the inner Cabinet kept his head. To him Home wrote two days after the cease-fire: 'Your skill and patience has been uncanny . . . your tolerance of your colleagues has amounted almost to saintliness. I feel certain that your sureness of touch will lead us through all this turmoil to better times. My admiration knows no bounds.'

He never ceased to defend the Suez operation, not simply out of loyalty to Eden but because he believed it to have been right, and found in it some benefits: 'When the Middle East was about to burst into flames—no sooner—but by no means too soon—the United Kingdom used her power. A general war has been stopped—a Communist plot has been forestalled. The United Nations has been compelled to shoulder its responsibilities.'[2] (A United Nations 'peace-keeping' force had been installed on the Canal.) 'We have galvanized

[1] Parliamentary Reports. Lords, 12th December 1956, cols. 1103-4.
[2] 26th November 1956, address to the Rhodesia and Nyasaland Club in London.

98

America to declare its support for the Baghdad Pact powers . . . If Russia could work out her policy of dominating the Middle East, Europe's fate would be sealed in a matter of months . . .'[1]

One of the best speeches of his career was made in the Lords debate on Egypt on 12th December 1956—or, at any rate, 'Jowitt told me that it was the best defence of Suez he had heard.[2] So I suppose it must have had some merit.'

Lord Attlee (former Socialist Prime Minister), Home said, 'all but, if not quite, dubs us aggressors.' Yet twice in a generation England had expended her wealth and many of her lives 'because we have known for certain that not to deal with a dictator who wishes to dominate mankind is a fatal policy.'

Russia's 'ruthless and unrelenting probing' was directed to extend her dominion, and one prong of this sustained attack was to deny Europe the oil of the Middle East: 'My lords, what a prize if Russia could bring that off, the destruction of an industrialized Europe, the outflanking of Turkey and Iran and Irak and Pakistan, and the opening up of the gateway to Africa!'

Yet one of Russia's tricks was to label others 'colonialist': 'I do hope,' said Home glancing over his spectacles at their Socialist lordships, 'that not many of our friends will "fall for" this Russian game.' Britain made independent free countries of her former colonies; the Russians 'preach co-existence and practise anarchy.'

Of course, he said, we have our 'watertight' system of international law: the only thing wrong with it was that 'the wicked will not obey it and the righteous will not enforce it. All it means is giving an open licence to the criminal.'

Over the Suez expedition, he agreed, 'there may have been mistakes. No Minister of a Government in this situation, when events have not been of our own timing, can claim, or would claim, that every action has been perfect.'

Home's speech marked a change of emphasis. No longer was Nasser the mad, Hitlerian dictator pictured by Eden who had to be removed at all costs—and in any case had not been: 'We did not intervene between Israel and Egypt in order to remove Colonel Nasser; we did not intervene in order to impose a settlement for the control of the Canal. We intervened to stop them. We intervened to stop the war growing. That

---

[1] 3rd December 1956, at London University.

[2] Earl Jowitt was Labour Lord Chancellor, 1945–51.

was not only a moral right but a moral duty because the first duty of a Government is to bring security to the life of its people.

'In the Middle East, Russian policy has had a setback which may have lasting consequences. I greatly welcome this opportunity to exorcise international Communism, which has been the curse of mankind . . . This may,' he concluded with optimism, 'be one of those turning points where the free world will live and breathe again.'[1]

Others saw the situation in starker terms. Suez was 'The final end of Britain as a world power. That had come about through the influence of Left-wing British intellectuals, American anti-colonialism and the weakness of Government.'[2] The humiliating end of the Suez expedition certainly lowered Britain's prestige in her remaining colonies and hastened the scuttle that followed for it sapped the will to rule, as Sandys later confessed.

Home, however, was of more sanguine, resilient temperament. 'We have shed a terrible lot of power,' he wrote privately in December 1963 when he had become Prime Minister, 'but it is useless to cry over spilt milk. In life I have always thought it best to cut a loss quickly and look for the next chance. Quite a lot of opportunities will open up for us if we have the sense to equip ourselves to seize them.'[3]

---

[1] Parliamentary Reports. Lords, 12th December 1956, cols. 1104–10.

[2] Bevins. See note, p. 97 above.

[3] Prime Minister's personal minute (M.48, H/63, 20th December 1963) to Sir Michael Fraser: see below, chapter 19.

10. A Lofty Perch: 1957 – 60

Macmillan's style. Leader in the Lords. Policy steering. 'Big bangs and small forces'. Pacifism. 'Precarious peace'.

Harold Macmillan, stylish and clever, full of ruses and usually 'unflappable', became Prime Minister on 9th January 1957. His way with his Ministerial colleagues was vintage port to Eden's fire-water.

Where Eden might telephone 'many times in a morning', Macmillan left it to his Ministers to get on with the job. Telephoning he disliked and 'to get his ear you had to go to him. He was always accessible'.

Macmillan ran his Cabinet meetings as he would run the board meetings of the distinguished publishing company of which he later became chairman. He was determined to bring back confidence to the nation and to his party. In March 1957, accompanied by the stalwart Selwyn Lloyd, he made peace with the Americans at a meeting with Eisenhower in Bermuda.

Soon after Macmillan took over, Home jumped several rungs up the ladder of status and influence. It came about almost accidentally. The Colony of Cyprus suffered outbreaks of terrorism and Archbishop Makarios, the leader of the revolt against British rule, was exiled to the Seychelles. By 1957 Cyprus was no longer thought of as a useful Middle East base, so there seemed little point in keeping Makarios exiled. To Lord Salisbury, the keeper of the Tory conscience, the decision to free the wily priest—though he was not to return to Cyprus—was a sign of 'scuttle' policy and he resigned from the Cabinet and the Leadership in the Lords.

Macmillan put Home in his place. As for the Makarios issue, Home agreed with Macmillan: 'Salisbury thought we ought not to deal with Makarios. He did not trust Makarios. But there was no one else to deal with if bloodshed was to be stopped.' Cyprus, though long independent, is scarcely settled yet (1970).

Home as Leader in the Lords—he was for a time Lord President of the Council as well as Commonwealth Secretary—was involved more closely with policy-making in the Cabinet, and in the Party itself. He was, for example, a member of a small steering committee, presided over by Macmillan, which prepared the Conservative Manifesto for the 1959 election. Butler, Lord Hailsham, then Chairman of the Party, Iain Macleod—Minister of Labour and assisting Butler on policy formation —and Edward Heath, Chief Whip, were the other original members, with Michael Fraser, Director of the Conservative Research Department as Secretary. Home was there to advise on Commonwealth and Scottish matters.

As Leader in the Lords, Home had to speak on a diversity of subjects. For example, he defended the new defence policy of 'big bangs and small forces'. Duncan Sandys, Minister of Defence, ended conscription, and his scheme over five years reduced the armed forces from 690,000 to 375,000. There were anguished cries from many quarters at home and abroad, one argument being that a nuclear deterrent could not be used for policing operations or local wars in the Empire or Commonwealth.

Home's own view was that conscription should be abolished. He has been constant in this view: 'The volunteer and professionally trained army is the right answer always providing you can get the recruits. The regulars hate conscription; they spend precious time training recruits for two years and then they lose them—a waste of potentially good soldiers. The regulars are much better occupied in training themselves as an efficient fighting force. The Territorial Army is different and a great asset. If a government of the future were faced with a total inability to attract recruits it could not let security go and it would have to face some kind of conscription. But, militarily, that is not desirable.'

As for the reduction of the forces, in 1957 he accepted the financial argument, underlined in August that year by a sudden run on the gold reserves and a rise in bank rate to 7 per cent. For the redundant servicemen there would, he told the Lords on 9th May, be a scheme of compensation 'seen to be fair by the man, the country and Parliament'.

The first British hydrogen bomb was exploded in 1957. Home never doubted that Britain must have up-to-date nuclear weapons: 'We are faced with a potential enemy who will stop at nothing and for whom the end justifies the means', he declared in the Lords on 9th May 1957. 'Russia has the capacity to wage total war, and will be deterred from delivering that knock-out blow which would give her world mastery only if she knows that her bases and country would be instantaneously subjected to the same kind of annihilation as she gives to other people.'

He admitted that it was 'one of those horrible decisions'. Nevertheless 'we must retain the deterrent and that deterrent must be produced in this country so that we have an adequate supply absolutely under our own control. We must have the nuclear bomb and test it, so that the world will know it is a real deterrent.'

To those who objected that if a dozen nuclear bombs were dropped, England would no longer exist, Home replied:

'It is certain that in some areas some people will survive. What Lord Nathan [1] is doing is throwing up the sponge. We are not prepared to do that.' (Macmillan had used the same metaphor: 'We must rely on the power of the nuclear deterrent or we must throw up the sponge.' [2])

For disarmament the Government would work with all their power, he said on 7th March 1958. There were three essentials: disarmament must increase the security of all nations and diminish the security of none; it should be controlled by international machinery; it should include conventional as well as nuclear forces. When a disarmament treaty was ratified the British Government would halt, under international supervision, the use of new fissile material, study measures to prevent a military use of outer space, limit the size of the armed forces and lay the country completely open for international inspection.

In these years Home was disturbed by the morale of British youth, by the Ban-the-bomb marches and 'the infection of the young, the pacifist feeling over again.' He began to sense that 'morale might run away as it had in 1936 and the young become pacifist.'

There was a mood in the country, he noted in the Lords on 7th March 1958, closely related to the Peace Ballot of some years ago which led Hitler to believe in his own mind that Britain could be conquered. There was no panic yet but it could easily degenerate into something like that.

Today, he said, under the impact of the hydrogen bomb people were bewildered. The young put up a brave façade but they could not conceal that their faith in the future and purpose of life was wavering. They did not know what to think, and therefore they did not know what to

[1] First Baron Nathan, a former Labour M.P. and Minister, d. 1963.
[2] Sampson, p. 133. See note, p. 87 above.

do. Was there such a convulsion of values that we had to rethink our whole historic attitude of opposition to tyranny? Were even freedom, liberty and justice worth the possible death of the whole nation?

In such a crisis of soul and mind, both Government and Opposition had a duty to guide. The cruel truth was that to submit to totalitarian government was not to escape death for ourselves or even for our children. Hungarians had found it better to fight with their bare hands than live tortured in body and soul under a totalitarian society. We could never rest under Communist rule.

Courage and hope would come when people knew that their goal was to end the cold war, and that the Government intended to do all they could to proceed with disarmament. The country's leaders took these risks and armed themselves with nuclear weapons to prevent war. At worst, since war and peace were not solely in our control, they knew that instantaneous retaliation could save millions of people, and at best these weapons would deter.

Home recognized the strength of the appeal of a United Nations organization. But he had no patience with those who mistook the U.N. as it was for that proposed by the authors of the Charter. Through the United Nations, he said in the Lords on 14th May 1957, we might pass from co-operation between nations to shared sovereignty. To this end, the Government wanted a review of the Charter but the Russians plainly indicated that they would veto such a proposal. The fact was that 'until international Communism was dead, world government could not be born'.

The idea of world government was not Home's alone. It was common currency in the late 1950s in both Tory and Labour parties. Sprung from sentimentality and the Socialist urge to dictatorship, it befogged real thought. To Home world government was, in reality, utopian and he insisted that it was impossible to arrive at even a modest degree of collective security unless the partners observed the Charter's rules of behaviour between sovereign states.

Dominated by Communists, world government would be a mockery and the greatest tyranny of all since it 'would be the ultimate, because inescapable, tyranny.'[1] As for giving 'teeth' to the U.N., which he was prepared to consider, events in the Congo in the early 1960s gave him pause for thought.

He took a more realistic line on another Socialist proposal: 'I do

[1] Brian Crozier, *The Masters of Power*, London 1969, p. 329.

not fancy the "other club" which will consist of the United States and Russia, as two powers with all the nuclear strength in their hands and none in the hands of any other nations', he said in the Lords on 13th July 1959.

And later: 'If we leave everything to the United States and the Soviet Union, I do not believe we shall salve our conscience, save our national soul or preserve peace.' We should expose ourselves to 'the fate of Hungary and the loss of the liberties we have gained over the centuries . . . We might well become a Soviet rocket base from which international Communism would threaten all who remained free' (11th February 1959).

'One other thing was always in my mind,' he remembered. 'When a nation has nuclear weapons it cannot allow another nation to decide when to push the button.' So, although Britain allocated her weapons to NATO, it was necessary to insist that if the country found itself in dire need they should be reclaimed for Britain's purposes. And in the Lords he said on 10th March 1959: 'We cannot, and no Government could, transfer any important section of our defence to another country however friendly.'

The Socialists repeatedly cast doubts whether the British deterrent could alone deter Russia. Home knew that it could. The plain fact is that the British deterrent, Home asserted in 1969, is 'based not so much on the destruction of Russian airfields as of Russian cities—one of the appalling facts of modern war. In itself [the British deterrent] would destroy a large number of Russia's biggest cities—not as good as the United States deterrent but enough to make an aggressor pause. Today [1969] this policy has not changed, though the V-bombers are falling out, and now it is Polaris.' [1]

Such a deterrent was also a symbol of power; with it, Britain would never, in Aneurin Bevan's striking words, go naked to the conference table. Moreover it ensured her a seat at the top table. Behind his thoughts on defence in the 1950s and now, there was the determination that Britain should never sit below the salt:

'To carry weight,' he wrote in a private communication, falling naturally into cricketing metaphor, 'we must be in the first XI and not only that but one of the four opening batsmen. It is fashionable to think that power can be discarded but those who think that way are moving unconsciously towards neutralism and there should be no such word

[1] See below, p. 204.

105

in the English vocabulary. It is not in the British character. We cannot lead from behind or from the middle ranks—we must be in front.' [1]

'Weakness,' he pointed out on 30th June 1960, 'had not saved the people of Hungary or Tibet, nor had neutralism saved the frontiers of India from invasion', and he remembered his warning to an irritated Nehru four years earlier.

Home had risen to a point of vantage in government. From his lofty perch as Leader of the Lords, his gaze swept across the ampler landscape of politics, a panorama of prime-ministerial dimension.

The Homeness of Home began to appear. He was a patriot by temperament for whom Britain came first; yet hopeful of co-operation with the rest of the world. He refused to part with trump cards for the sake of nebulous, impractical doctrine. Reconciliation, yes, but always strength. Negotiation and conciliation were second-nature to him. He would agree generally that 'Conservatism never is more admirable than when it accepts with good grace changes that it disapproves for the sake of a general conciliation.' [2] But where the security of the nation was concerned, the lines had to be drawn distinct and firm.

Left to him, the irresistible force would never be allowed to approach anywhere near the immovable object, which was the reason why he did not share Salisbury's intransigence over a position no longer tenable, nor Macmillan's enthusiasm for 'summit' meetings. His expectations were never pitched too high, so that when hopes were dashed he remained equable. Macmillan sank into despair, talking of the 'possible extinction of civilization' [3] when his 'summit' with the Russians collapsed in May 1960. Home nonchalantly observed that 'the world remains a dangerous place', and, after all: 'We should remember that we have lived with the nuclear deterrent, and over the last few years there has been peace.

'It may have been a precarious peace; but it has been peace.' The deterrent had worked.

---

[1] Prime Minister's Personal Minute, M.48, H/63, 30th December 1963, to Sir Michael Fraser.

[2] Russell Kirk, *The Conservative Mind*, London, 1954, p. 50.

[3] Sampson, p. 151. See note, p. 87 above.

11. Tantalizing Africa: 1957–60

Independence 'a problem of man'. Educational evangelist. Sir Roy Welensky. Monckton Commission. Iain Macleod. 'Wind of change' mystery.

To give way with good grace for the sake of general conciliation—an admirable Tory sentiment! But for the practising politician the vexatious question, as Home discovered, is always where and when to hold firm, where and when to let go and at what pace.

Giving independence to the colonies was not Home's business as Commonwealth Secretary. Only after they became independent did they come under his aegis. There was, however, one exception and it was to tantalize him for the rest of his political career. The Central African Federation, formed in 1953 out of Southern and Northern Rhodesia and Nyasaland, had semi-dominion status and its Prime Minister by convention was invited to the Commonwealth Prime Ministers' conference. The Federation's business was Home's business and so was that of the self-governing colony of Southern Rhodesia. Northern Rhodesia and Nyasaland, on the other hand, were the direct responsibility of the Colonial Office. To add to the tangle, while the Federal Government looked after the three territories' external affairs, economic and fiscal policies and law, each territory dealt with its own law-and-order, local government and taxes, labour, native affairs and housing. The division led to friction not between Home and Lennox-Boyd but between the officials in the two offices.

Throughout the Federation, which was pledged to multi-racialism, there were vociferous African independence movements, as elsewhere in Africa, though they were far more violent in the two Colonial Office-ruled territories of Northern Rhodesia and Nyasaland. In Southern Rhodesia government was largely in the hands of white men whose home it was and where for blacks and whites there were greater educational and economic opportunities.

Home had clear-cut views on the future of the Colonies. 'The goal of Colonial policy', he wrote in a paper for the Steering Committee, previously unpublished, 'is self-government.'[1] That is, the British Government intended to get rid of all colonies. Nevertheless British 'protection' could end only when the people of the colonies accepted the need to safeguard the political rights of minorities and of individuals. In short, no independence before political maturity, and maturity came largely as a result of public education and training: 'The quickest road to a date for self-government is complete co-operation on programmes of education and development,' Home wrote.

Progress to self-government was, Home asserted, not 'so much a problem of blueprints for constitutions or of systems as a problem of man'. Britain did not insist on 'any universal pattern' of constitution. Safeguards for minorities and individuals would be written into constitutions 'but the only real safeguard that a country will maintain stability within and follow the policy of the good neighbours without is when the leaders have enough maturity to recognize the absolute obligation to protect minority rights and to respect the individuals'.

In franchise matters 'the pace of advance to "one-man, one-vote"' would be variable since 'the complete universal suffrage is only meaningful when the individual voter can exercise a free and unfettered choice between parties and when voters in the aggregate have learned not to misuse the vast majorities which often emerge from free elections'.

In multiracial societies, responsible use of the franchise and tolerance were even more important. British policy aimed at a common roll of voters where any individual of any race might exercise his political right on a basis of complete equality.

But that could not come about overnight: 'As democracy can survive only in an educated society, there must be qualifications for the vote.' It took Britain 600 years to graduate from the qualified franchise to 'one-man, one-vote'. Education must 'underpin the franchise'.

Such were the humane and practical thoughts of Home in the early months of 1959. But even as he wrote his paper, the British Government was giving independence to violent minorities whose countrymen were as politically immature as they had been in the Stone Age; despite careful provision for the rights of minorities and individuals, there were massacre, starvation and the one-party State.

[1] SC 45. A paper for the Steering Committee, 23rd June 1959.

And who, really, could pin his faith to the panacea of education, that great, vacuous shibboleth of the twentieth century? The Germans in 1939 were as highly educated as any people on earth. It was evident too that in the dark continent the men who spurred and organized destruction and killing were the educated Africans. It was they who, as soon as the independence flag was run up, deleted what elsewhere Home called the 'very fabric and inspiration' of the Commonwealth:

'The new Commonwealth countries of Asia and Africa,' he wrote, 'who knew the impact of British administration all find virtue in the way of life which we in Britain have been at such pains to build up during centuries of trial and experience.

'They value and preserve parliaments where the representatives of the electors control the Executive—Law under which all men are equal—Justice which is impartial—Religious tolerance—respect for the dignity of individual man.'[1]

What a hope! Yet such a credo, fragile to the point of parody, explains some of the ambivalences that emerged in Home's attitudes towards particular Commonwealth issues. He learned the hard way, though he never wavered in his belief that in the end the secret of success for the modern Commonwealth was education. He became the evangelist of native education. At the Commonwealth Economic Conference in Montreal in 1958 what began as an effort to get capital moving to the newly independent countries developed under his missionary zeal into something he regarded as one of his positive achievements, though he modestly gave the praise elsewhere:

'It began with economics,' he remembered, 'but turned into an education exercise. At Montreal the Commonwealth education scheme was born which arranged for the training and exchange of teachers. This has since become quite an important feature in the modern Commonwealth.

'This was a surprise outcome of this conference. I was not responsible but we did take David Eccles with us [2] with this in mind—that we would inject education into the Commonwealth Conference because Derry Amory [3] and I and David were also keen on it. It was accepted

[1] SC 14, 2nd May 1958.

[2] Then President of the Board of Trade; earlier and later Minister of Education; a Viscount 1964.

[3] Derick Heathcoat Amory, Chancellor of the Exchequer, 1958–60. Later Viscount Amory, K.G.

eagerly by the Commonwealth countries who were greedy for the education without which their societies could not advance and could never narrow the gap between them and the "haves".'

Home did not stand on the sidelines of his African responsibilities. He took part in the game, paying his first visit to the Federation of Rhodesia and Nyasaland in October 1957. He was still sanguine that the multiracial experiment would work; he did not believe that 'most' Africans were against it—the reality was that 'most' of them had no clear idea of its meaning, purpose and achievement. He, therefore, deprecated as 'unhealthy' the excessive political controversy about the Federation.[1]

Home had old friends in the Federation, not least among them his Etonian contemporary, Sir Humphrey V. Gibbs, son of Baron Hunsdon, and shortly to become Governor of Rhodesia. Gibbs, a kindly expatriate 'Establishment' figure, had been farming in the Bulawayo area since the 1920s.

A new friend was the Federal Prime Minister, former railway worker and boxing champion, Sir Roy Welensky. The two found themselves in immediate rapport. The bluff, determined Welensky, Polish-Jewish-Afrikaner, found the slim, smiling Scottish aristocrat 'full of understanding' and believed that 'mutual trust' was established.

But, Welensky recalls, Home 'had a point of view and I was never left in doubt as to what it was'.[2] Home in fact was wondering just how multiracial the Federation really was, or could become. He saw that Africans played a considerable part in civil service and government (two junior ministers were African) and that the accepted policy was 'partnership'; as their education advanced—and the Federation took giant leaps—they were meant to take a major role. Yet, Home remembered:

'I had a very interesting African who went round with me at that time, Nathan Shamuyarira,[3] later editor of *The African Daily News*. He was a Federal African at that time, a convinced one, but he had never been enlisted as an ally by the Federal Leaders. That was a mistake.

[1] Lords, 7th November 1957.

[2] Welensky to the author.

[3] Shamuyarira was editor of *The African Daily News*, 1956–63, and joined ZANU, a terrorist group with Chinese links.

There were more of this kind. They lost a priceless opportunity.'[1]

Nevertheless Home recognized that the Federation had brought an economic transformation, visible in the Kariba hydro-electric dam and the new, multiracial University College in Salisbury. He saw with satisfaction that primary and secondary education for Africans was advancing with great strides. The Federation was eminently worth preserving though, he said on 28th October 1959, certain changes were required to build 'the framework of a working democracy into countries still largely primitive'.

He had no doubts about the terrorist aims of a minority of Africans. In Nyasaland there were outbreaks of violence and the Governor was obliged to declare a state of emergency. Home condemned this 'campaign of arson and murder', and characterized the terrorists' aim as 'the murder of moderation'.

The Federal Constitution was due for review in 1960, and during 1959 the form this review was to take was discussed by the British and Federal Governments. Welensky thought it should be a formal affair, the business only of constitutional lawyers. Macmillan, however, was facing a General Election and had, partly as a result of the Kenya *débâcle*, become sensitive to Left-wing clamour against Federation, which he seemed to think would become an election issue. Though a Labour Government had originated the Federal idea, Hugh Gaitskell succumbed to the extremists and fellow-travellers in his Party to save his position as leader: 'I am their leader, I must follow them,' as the Duke of Plaza Toro said.

Macmillan, therefore, sensed that the Federation was running into difficulties and sent Home to Salisbury in April 1959, in an attempt to persuade Welensky. Home explained that pressures were building up that could cause the Government to give Nyasaland the option of seceding from the Federation; it would then be difficult to avoid giving Northern Rhodesia the same option and the Federation would be at an end. The British Government, desiring to preserve the Federation, believed that a preliminary Advisory Commission, 'chosen among the right people and appointed before the General Election, would carry a great deal of weight—and in fact take the sting out of the Election, certainly on Federal issues'.[2]

[1] According to Sir Roy Welensky, efforts were made to recruit Shamuyarira but he 'sat on the fence' (Welensky to the author).

[2] Welensky to the author.

Neither Welensky nor his colleagues believed Federal matters were likely to influence a British General Election, nor did they. Home had to make a personal appeal to Welensky before he gave a reluctant assent to a visitation from an Advisory Commission. 'Because I respected and trusted Home, he did in fact more than anyone else to persuade me to accept the Monckton [1] Commission—something that Harold Macmillan could never have done.' Upon one matter, however, Welensky was adamant: such a Commission should have no right to consider the secession of any of the three territories comprising the Federation. Home agreed.

Home believed that if the Commission was to carry weight and give its imprimatur to the continuation of the Federation it must contain, among the other 'right people', some responsible African leaders, but most of all he wanted members of the Parliamentary Labour party, so that its recommendations, despite possible minority reports, should have an all-party, as well as a no-party, flavour. 'I didn't see much chance of settling this emotional issue except by agreement with the parties,' he reflected a decade later. 'I cannot imagine any greater disaster,' he said in the Lords on 28th October 1959, 'than if one party in this country attempted to identify itself with one racial group in Africa.'

The 'disaster' had already happened, and Gaitskell refused to have any part in the Commission, despite Home's personal appeal. 'I felt very strongly and I told him what I thought about the Labour Party not co-operating. He, I think, understood but faced by his Left Wing he refused. It was an opportunity thrown away for narrow political reasons though he was perfectly polite and seemly.' After this, Home decided that, as it was in his view a last hope, the Commission must be allowed to do its work; a last-minute appeal from Welensky to drop the Commission was refused.

Gaitskell's minimum price for co-operation was that the Commission should hear the African extremists' reasons for desiring their territories to secede; and that the Commission should make its recommendations on this issue. This Home refused. 'Had Macmillan or Home ever suggested,' says Welensky, 'that the Monckton Commission would have the power to recommend on this issue, then we would never have accepted the setting up of the Commission.' [2] Clearly there was mis-

[1] Viscount (formerly Sir Walter) Monckton was to be chairman of the Advisory Commission.

[2] Welensky to the author.

understanding. According to Welensky, Macmillan informed him that 'the British Government had no intention of making an extension of the Commission's terms of references to include secession; they had agreed them and they would stand by them. Every member of the Commission had, after all, accepted on this basis.' This was not exactly so. One of the Commissioners, Lord Molson, stated that 'When I was invited to serve by Lord Home I was assured that the possibility of secession was not excluded.' [1]

In reality Macmillan gave Monckton a free hand to interpret the terms of reference as he thought fit in the light of the situation as he found it when the Commission began work in the Federation on 15th February 1960. This 'free hand' stretched out like elastic. The Commission, Home said later, knew that they would listen to evidence on the question of secession, though they were not entitled to recommend it. [2] Recommend it, however, in due course they did.

Small wonder that Home should confess to the Lords on 3rd November 1959, that 'I wish it fell to my lot to be "dummy" more often in playing this controversial hand'.

Meanwhile, when in October 1959 the Macmillan Government went to the country in a General Election, the affairs of the Central African Federation—as Welensky forecast—were not an issue, and the Conservatives won a resounding victory, returning with an overall majority of 100; Gaitskell's Labour Party, tails between legs, slipped back to fill only 258 out of the 630 seats.

In the new administration, Home remained as Commonwealth Secretary but the man with whom he had worked so harmoniously, Alan Lennox-Boyd, left the Colonial Office and politics. [3] He was succeeded by Iain Macleod, formerly one of Butler's 'back-room boys' in the Conservative Research Department, and more lately Minister of Labour. An incisive speaker with a clever mind—too clever by half, Lord Salisbury dubbed him—he made his name in battles with Aneurin Bevan over national health; his political experience was confined to home affairs.

It soon appeared that Macleod had the job of dissolving the British African empire at top speed and by methods until then regarded as

[1] Welensky, *Welensky's 4,000 Days*, London, 1964, pp. 157–60.
[2] *Walter Monckton: The life of Viscount Monckton of Brenchley*, by the 2nd Earl of Birkenhead, London, 1969, pp. 342 and 343.
[3] He was created Viscount Boyd of Merton, 1960.

unorthodox. Instead of dealing with Governments or the Leaders of Parliamentary Oppositions, Macleod consulted Africans of minority groups and without official status. By juggling with complicated constitutions and 'fancy franchises' in Kenya, Nyasaland and Northern Rhodesia, he provided smoke-screens for retreat. He freed Banda in Nyasaland—though Macmillan gave the order—and outraged Welensky, who found him 'subtle and secretive'. Nor was Welensky alone in observing that Macleod 'if resisted or criticized tended to become bitterly angry . . . in face of rational, firm opposition he could not always control his own feelings.'[1]

Home, scarred by the results of earlier appeasement and temperamentally against sudden change, gave warning to the Lords—and by implication to Macleod—that the kind of 'racialism which claims Africa for the Africans can equally imply an attempt to dominate' (28th March 1960). It was possible to 'betray' by going either too fast or too slow.

In his official dealings with Macleod, the equable Home found it less easy to establish the understanding he had with Lennox-Boyd. He felt that every year gained before independence would bring the chance of stability nearer. There was a point where the concession had to be made; to talk of immediate independence fanned the extremists into violence and resulted in independence before the native peoples were fitted to manage their own affairs. Home felt that where Lennox-Boyd had got it right, Macleod went too far and too fast.

The impression that Britain was rapidly disengaging from her African responsibilities was reinforced by Macmillan's 'wind of change'[2] speech, delivered in the House of Assembly in Cape Town, in January 1960, when he spoke of the growth and 'strength of the African national consciousness', and told the South Africans that his Government could not give them 'support and encouragement' because of 'some aspects' of their policies.

Home had seen a draft of the speech. He did not think it would stir the kind of furore it did. Later he said, 'perhaps I ought to have twigged that it would stir things up'. There is some evidence that Macmillan worked on it further after he left London, with the help of the British High Commission in South Africa, and that the speech was different in some ways from what Home had been shown.

[1] Welensky, p. 187. See note, p. 113 above.
[2] The phrase was first used by Macmillan in Lagos during his tour of Africa.

Though widely taken as a sign of change of policy, 'really it was meant to have been much more a philosophical discourse, suggesting that the independence movement, started in India, would not *stop* at Africa. But of course the speech did stir things up. For Southern Rhodesia it made a difference in that it became progressively more difficult to hold', even though at that time Sir Edgar Whitehead's government was pro-Federation. As Kilmuir, then Lord Chancellor, wrote, 'Neither Macmillan nor his colleagues had any conception of the mine he had unwittingly exploded.' [1]

The speech still *reads* quite mildly but it certainly 'stirred things up'; it increased the pace of intimidation by African extremists of their fellow countrymen in the Federation and even in Southern Rhodesia; it gave seeming *carte blanche* to Macleod's rush down the slope. Nigeria was given independence and Tanganyika was demanding it. There was bitter opposition in Kenya from the Europeans.

Home talked to Sir Edgar Whitehead, Prime Minister of Southern Rhodesia who, seeing the wind blowing against the Federation, wanted to ensure that in the cataclysm his country should be its own master. Though Rhodesia was self-governing, Britain retained—on paper at any rate—extensive powers to veto certain classes of legislation particularly concerning Africans. A series of conferences began to alter the constitution so that Southern Rhodesia would be independent as soon as possible with the framework of the Federal Constitution. Progress was made, though there was the question of 'alternative safeguards'. Whitehead, despite, in Home's words, being 'a bit of a hermit', was understood by the Africans: 'Possibly because he *was* so blunt and firm and they knew where they were on the pace of multi-racial advance.'

On 11th October 1960 the Monckton Commission reported. It had in fact discussed secession and moreover recommended that all three countries forming the Federation should have the right to secede from it after a given number of years. It also recommended total, unqualified franchise, which Home in his paper for the Steering Committee had expressly opposed. The African extremists and their Socialist supporters hailed it as victory.

Home was disconcerted. He thought that Welensky who, believing himself betrayed, repudiated the Commission's findings with ferocity, had a genuine grievance and that the Commission ought to have con-

[1] *Political Adventure*, the Memoirs of the Earl of Kilmuir, London, 1964, p. 315.

tented themselves with noting evidence of the desire for secession and gone no further.[1]

Could the Federation have been saved? Could *Home* have done anything to save it? 'I always thought if Roy [Welensky] could have immediately said "snap" to the Monckton Commission's conclusions the day might have been saved. Some most responsible Africans signed it. But it had run an awful long way downhill and I came to the conclusion reluctantly that the Federation could be held together only by British troops. [2]

'But I had constantly warned my colleagues that it would be no solution to break up the Federation because the racial problem would be cornered in one part of it. And it *was* cornered—in Rhodesia.'

So Home was dissatisfied with his part in the affair and he was, of course, the Minister directly responsible for the Federation. He made his feelings known to Macmillan but never contemplated resignation. Instead, before the report was made public he was given a different portfolio. Nor would his resignation have altered the course upon which Macmillan and Macleod were embarked. British Ministers were deafened by the propagandist, and often subversive, clamour from the Leftish minority, distracted by the anti-Western bias of the United Nations, and inhibited perhaps by a feeling that the anti-colonialist 'bug' in the United States—which Macmillan had once condemned—must be appeased. It was, of course, Africans in their thousands who paid the price with their lives and sufferings for the policy of headlong, premature 'independence'. The British too, however, began to feel the effect of the precipitous retreats of the previous five years and the resultant financial decline. How to counter these largely self-inflicted wounds would preoccupy the Macmillan, and all subsequent, governments.

On one issue, however, Home and Macmillan stood firm together, opposing the attempt to drive South Africa out of the Commonwealth on the grounds of her *apartheid* policies. The newly joined coloured

[1] Birkenhead, p. 359. See note, p. 113 above.

[2] Welensky agrees: 'Harold Macmillan was well aware that the moment Monckton was allowed to exceed the terms of reference, and break the promises and assurances given to the Federal Government, by making secession recommendations, the Federation was dead.' But, Welensky adds, how could he have said 'snap' to the right to secede which was 'the death-knell of the Federation'? (Welensky to the author).

Above
A few weeks old,
Alexander Frederick Douglas-Home,
born 2nd July 1903, on his
mother's knees.

Sir Alec's father, the 13th Earl of
Home, painted by James Gunn:
at the Hirsel.

Alec, aged 4, 'gazing alertly at
his world'.

Left
Alec with his
grandfather, the
12th Earl of Home,
in Lord Lieutenant's
uniform, 1907.

and below
With two brothers
and two sisters at
Springhill, 1913: left
to right, Bridget,
Rachel, Henry,
William. Alec is on
the extreme right.

Right
Tall Etonian
cricketer, Lord
Dunglass, at the
wicket, 1921.

Last game at the
Oval, the Earl of
Home, 1951.

and below
Captain Lord
Dunglass, Lanark-
shire Yeomanry,
May 1939.

Sir Alec with
Lee Kuan Yew,
Prime Minister of
Singapore,
9th March 1970.

Lord Dunglass and his bride,
formerly Elizabeth Alington,
leaving Durham Cathedral,
3rd October 1936.

Below left
In peer's robes for the Coronation
of Queen Elizabeth II, with his son,
David (Lord Dunglass), 1953.

April 1956, the Earl of Home,
Commonwealth Secretary of State,
1955–60.

With President J. F. Kennedy at the White House, September 1963.

With Russian Prime Minister, Nikita Khrushchev, August 1963.

At Checkpoint Charlie,
January 1962,
gazing at the Berlin
Wall, Lord Home,
Foreign Secretary, and
Willy Brandt, Mayor of
West Berlin.

Below
On a visit to Lagos as
Prime Minister, Sir Alec
with the former Nigerian
Prime Minister, the late
Sir Abubakar Tafawa
Balewa, March 1964.

Sir Alec Douglas-Home, Prime Minister, with his wife (*left*) and Mrs Christopher Soames, electioneering, October 1964.

Electioneering at King's Lynn, Norfolk, September 1964.

On the Tweed at his favourite pursuit of salmon fishing, with his son David, 1964.

Sir Alec Douglas-Home on a shoot near Los Angeles, February 1970.

Commonwealth states were in league at the United Nations with the Communist countries who had long cast cupiditous eyes on the immense mineral riches of South Africa, and who had organized both subversion and propaganda there long before the rise of the Prime Minister, Dr Verwoerd.

Home knew that there would be a trial of strength at the Commonwealth Prime Ministers' Conference in May 1960. There was, and it was led by the Canadian Prime Minister, John Diefenbaker, whose anti-South African campaign was supported with the blandest hypocrisy by Nkrumah, whose own State, Ghana, was completely racialist. At preliminary meetings Home sought to keep the matter off the agenda, for by long-standing convention the domestic affairs of constituent countries were not discussed.

He was unsuccessful. Though the subject was not mentioned in the communiqué, it was clear that it would be raised again, with consequent damage to Britain's defence arrangements (the Simonstown agreement of 1954), her trade and to what Home described as 'this endless adventure of the expanding Commonwealth.' [1]

Nevertheless, reflecting nearly a decade later on his five years at the Commonwealth Office, Home could justifiably say: 'I think that at a time of precipitate change we did manage to hold the Commonwealth together fairly well for the five years, because they became an oddly assorted lot.'

There had been difficulties at which he hinted in a speech on 6th July 1960, his swan-song at the Commonwealth Office. A Commonwealth Secretary, he told the Lords, 'must secure that the Commonwealth aspect is appreciated by every other department in Whitehall both when they are taking their day-to-day decisions and in the framing of United Kingdom legislation; and he must be certain that the interests and views of Commonwealth governments are kept at all times before his colleagues in the Cabinet when they are framing United Kingdom policy.'

It was only after his departure that conflict between the Commonwealth and Colonial Office rose to such heights that a separate Central African Office had to be created, with a very senior Minister, R. A. Butler, in charge, something for which Sir Roy Welensky had asked long ago. As one historian delicately puts it: 'While responsibility was divided between the Commonwealth Secretary and the Colonial

[1] SC 14, Paper for Steering Committee, 2nd May 1958.

Secretary, the two ministers were apt to be regarded in some quarters as identified with conflicting sectional interests in the Federation . . .'[1]

Home had suffered from the conflict of the departments where each took sides. But he said nine years afterwards, 'it had been fairly quiet going in the Commonwealth Office as offices go. It isn't a spectacular office unless something like Suez or Rhodesia happens and Rhodesia hadn't happened by then.'

He did not mention the change in himself. Five years before he had never set foot in a Commonwealth country abroad and scarcely mentioned the subject in his speeches. By 1960 he was an enthusiast, and of the future of this 'partnership' had written: 'It is such a novel and exciting prospect that the written word can scarcely capture the spirit of the Commonwealth or its unity of purpose.'[2] The idealism remained, though severely dented.

'Politics did not so much engage him,' wrote Dr Johnson of George Lyttelton, 'as to withhold his thoughts from things of more importance.' In a sense, this was true of Alec Home. The centre of his private life was his family, in 1960 growing apace, and he was seldom parted from his wife even on duty journeys abroad. The focal points of this life were at the Hirsel or Castlemains in the long weeks of recess. Fishing, shooting, all the pursuits of laird and landowner occupied his still considerable leisure even though the red boxes of Whitehall pursued him. 'The secret of one's interests lies out of doors' was true of his middle age as of his childhood. There were cricket to be watched, butterflies to be chased, roses to be pruned, horses to be backed. He still found time for the local fête, the Conservative gala, for friends from the past from Eton, Oxford and the days of young manhood, and for reading on the old round of biography, history, thriller as the mood took him.

Unlike his master Macmillan, he was not spiritually drawn to either of his Alma Maters. He enjoyed fun with them, and a few in-jokes. A Wykehamist, he informed the annual dinner of the Eton Ramblers— the Old Etonian cricket team—on 12th November 1957, 'is, as you know, one who extends his adolescence to L.S.E.'. Even better was his joke about Harrovians: 'There was a riot in one of H.M. prisons but order was instantly restored when the Governor ordered "Forty years on" to be played over the loudspeaker system.'

[1] Hans Daalder, *Cabinet Reform in Britain, 1914–1963*, London, 1964, p. 129.
[2] SC 14, p. 5, para. 12. See note, p. 109 above.

Sometimes in London pent he would long to be in the Border country and he preferred speaking engagements in Scotland, where he felt at home and could enjoy a sense of throwing his cap over the moors. Yet Westminster still pulled him like a magnet:

'I don't think it's the exercise of power. I don't think I am particularly interested in power. It is—to use this awful modern word—participation at the centre of things.'

He wanted to be in on decision-making at the top, to be privy to the inmost secrets of the nation, to see what was in the red boxes, and to do something about the problems revealed. This was the real lure and a powerful one. So that while, in Johnson's words, politics did not 'withhold his thoughts from things of more importance,' politics as he defined them was a ruling passion to which, as Austen Chamberlain wrote of that other seemingly detached politician, Arthur Balfour, 'he was prepared to, and in fact did, subordinate all others'.

Nevertheless like Balfour with his love of philosophy, music and society, Home's other interests, not least his estates, gave him a balanced life, invaluable for a politician; unlike most of his contemporaries he could say with Balfour, 'I never think about politics in bed.'

The strange thing was that Home, 57 years old in 1960, a seasoned Minister, member of the Cabinet, Leader of the House of Lords, was still unknown, and not merely to the public at large, to whom at best he was an aristocratic name who spoke in the Lords on that dullest of subjects, the Commonwealth. Even experienced political correspondents still thought of him vaguely as a lightweight Lord, possibly a nominee of the Cecils, for whom Macmillan, with his often-noted *penchant* for the nobility, had found a job.

True, such correspondents as met him socially came away impressed by his grasp of his subject and his willingness to listen as well as talk. Nevertheless they regarded him as a man without a serious political future, barred by his earldom from the highest office. Admired by political intimates and his civil servants, he appeared insufficiently ambitious, and in a way not a political animal, for in penetrating the motives of this or that politician's move and counter-move he was a *naïf*.

Then one day at the end of July 1960, Harold Macmillan dropped the political equivalent of the Hiroshima bomb; and the Westminster world was never quite the same again.

12. Foreign Office Furore: 1960 – 2

Stupefaction and rage. Heath reluctant. Tough talk. 'Summitry' doubts.
Kennedy persuaded. Common Market enthusiast. Canon Collins. Berlin,
Spain, Portugal.

One of the best-liked men in the Cabinet, Derick Heathcoat Amory, Chancellor of the Exchequer, retired after the 1960 budget. Selwyn Lloyd was to be his successor, and Macmillan wanted R. A. Butler to succeed Lloyd in 'the cruel and gruelling position at the Foreign Office.'[1]

'Harold had thought really that Rab would make a good Foreign Secretary,' Home recalled, 'but Rab for some reason at that time did not want it. He was in the middle of some interesting work at the Home Office, so he was quite unexpectedly not interested.

'In any event, Harold came along and said would I do it. I hesitated a lot because I wasn't sure I *had* had enough experience to take it on. But I thought the Commonwealth Office was not a bad training. So I decided to say "yes". But there was all the criticism in the world and one had to live it down.'

Criticism was a mild word. In the Conservative Party itself, there was 'stupefaction', as Kilmuir put it,[2] when the Prime Minister's intention was conjectured by one newspaper and then officially confirmed. The Socialists were enraged. Who was this 'faceless earl'? 'Insufficiently distinguished', *The Times* loftily observed, and another newspaper wrote that the appointment was 'the most reckless since the Roman Emperor, Caligula, made his favourite horse a Consul'. Home, suggested one journalist, was to take part in 'a charade of ceremonial significance rather than to have a role in the real political drama.' More shrewdly he noted that 'probably the worst thing from the point of view of everybody was that it was a complete surprise'. Once more, as

[1] Parliamentary Reports. Commons, 28th July 1960, col. 627.
[2] *Political Adventure*, see note, p. 115 above.

with his Commonwealth appointment, the pundits were outraged. Deeper still perhaps was the feeling that the un-class image of the Tory party, so carefully furbished by Butler and his Party aides, had been splintered: Disraeli's 'two nations', then, still existed.

In the Commons, Gaitskell, Leader of the Opposition, taunted Home with Munich and Suez; Sir Harry Legge-Bourke thought he had never heard a cheaper speech, though Gaitskell added that 'I don't want to criticize him in terms of ability. He is courteous and conscientious. I do not doubt that.'

None of this Home in retrospect resented: 'His criticism was on general grounds—he just didn't think I was the right chap to do it.' Lady Home disagreed: 'As far as I am concerned he is able enough for any post in the Government,' she told reporters, adding prophetically, 'even Prime Minister.'

The burthen of the criticism was that it was wrong and almost unconstitutional to have a Foreign Secretary in the Lords. 'Unnecessary and unwise,' said Gaitskell, 'constitutionally objectionable and not good for the conduct of our affairs in the world.'[1] Some Tories agreed. A passage in Eden's memoirs, *Full Circle*, then recently published, was quoted. He had wanted in 1955 to make Lord Salisbury Foreign Secretary but had reluctantly decided not to because 'I was sure that there was a danger of misunderstanding if foreign policy statements, or an important part of them, were made in the Upper House, and if the main debates were held there.'

Eden did not believe that the Commons would take an important statement on foreign affairs from a junior Minister. So a Cabinet member would have to be spokesman in the Commons—and 'this could only be the Prime Minister'. Why it had to be the Prime Minister is not clear. Macmillan simply appointed Edward Heath as Lord Privy Seal in the Cabinet to handle foreign affairs in the Commons.

These arrangements and Home himself were stoutly defended by Macmillan in the Commons during a no-confidence debate on 28th July 1960. He had appointed Home because he was 'absolutely convinced that he was the best man for the job'—why otherwise would he have risked the complication of having a Foreign Secretary in the Lords? 'I did not think that the mere accident of birth,' said Macmillan, 'or the mere fact that my noble friend sits in another place, should

[1] Parliamentary Reports. Commons, 28th July 1960, cols. 1997–8.

debar me from the right to choose the man I wanted at my side or deprive him of the right to serve.'

By this time the newspapers began to change their tune. Rejecting the idea that Home was to be a stop-gap or simply an instrument of Macmillan, *The Times* now noted that he was 'unmistakably patrician . . . with the aristocrat's assurance about where he stands and about what really matters', and added: 'Lord Home's closest colleagues reckon him tough, persistent, and sometimes unmovable in argument and negotiation; and it could be argued that Mr Macmillan wants him where he has been placed because he does not give readily under pressure from anybody.'[1]

This was true. He had learned the ropes of government and begun to be much more his own man. He could be indecisive through doubt, as over the Central African Federation, or through loyalty, but never through lack of determination, much less fear of consequences. Macmillan, who in May when the 'summit' fizzled out 'seemed close to collapse,'[2] was purposefully shifting some of the foreign burden.

Hidden from the public eye were the attitudes to the appointment of some of Home's colleagues. Reginald Maudling, the ambitious young President of the Board of Trade, and one of Butler's former protégés at the Research Department, had aspired to the post and complained bitterly to at least one member of the Cabinet when he failed to get it.[3]

Edward Heath, who Macmillan intended to be Home's spokesman in the Commons as Lord Privy Seal 'with Foreign Office responsibilities', is said to have had many hesitations whether he could serve under Home. If so his doubts were removed when Home explained his concept of partnership in conducting foreign policy. There was no doubt in Home's mind who was head of the office but neither was there a thought of top and bottom dog.

Heath, who had been a highly successful Chief Whip and briefly Minister of Labour, came to respect Home's fairness and judgment and to appreciate his lack of lust for the limelight; and, in any case, was to get his own very special limelight leading the team negotiating Britain's entry into the Common Market.

More flattering criticism of Home's appointment came from Sir

[1] *The Times*, 28th July 1960.
[2] Sampson, p. 151. See note, p. 87 above.
[3] Private information.

Roy Welensky, angry with Macmillan for moving Home before the Monckton Commission reported. To him, it marked a definite change of direction in British policy, prejudicing the future of Rhodesia and the Federation. Home continued to exercise some influence on Central African affairs in Cabinet but, Welensky believed, 'from my experience of Macmillan as Prime Minister, he ran his Cabinet on the basis of he and the Minister concerned making the decisions on a particular issue and the Cabinet being brought in as a rubber stamp. I personally have no doubt that Home felt very strongly on some of the issues, and, if he had been made aware of them in time, would certainly have expressed his views with some vigour. But I have a feeling that many of the decisions were taken before he was aware of what was happening.' [1]

Alec Home's three years at the Foreign Office, though begun amid sneers and stupefaction, made his name, and at the end of his time there were those who hailed him as the greatest Foreign Secretary, certainly since Ernest Bevin and perhaps since the Marquess of Salisbury.

This was unrealistic. Home came at the fag-end of what has been called Britain's 'great retreat'. Since foreign policy is the exercise of influence based on power, his scope was more constricted than was his predecessors'. His point of view in, for example, the Congo issue, had little effect and he regarded the affair as one of his failures.

In other fields—Berlin, South East Asia—Britain was a partner, usually a junior partner; over Cuba in 1962, when nuclear war was at hand, she could do little more than stand on the touch-line, encouraging the protagonist and tut-tutting to the antagonist. It was the period when Dean Acheson, American Secretary of State from 1949 to 1953, bluntly observed that Britain had lost an empire and had not succeeded in finding a new role.

Neither the decline in influence nor that in power should be exaggerated. The fact was that *no* major power for a decade and more 'had any foreign "policy" worthy of the name, apart from the effort to keep everyone else as quiet as possible'; and Britain still had enormous commitments throughout the world and 'formidable' capacity to deal with them.[2] Diplomacy, in the full sense, was at a higher premium than ever

[1] To the author, Welensky adds: 'I know this won't be liked, but I have ample evidence of it.'

[2] W. N. Medlicott, *British Foreign Policy since Versailles, 1919-1963*, London, second edn. enlarged, 1968, pp. 330 and 332.

and Home used it with great effect to influence in particular United States policy. Initiatives, great and small, could be taken and he took them, sometimes successfully, sometimes not, over Laos, Spain and Portugal, disarmament, the United Nations.

But what endeared Foreign Secretary Home to the British in general was his firmness, straightforwardness and on occasion blunt language. He refused to have Britain pushed around by Americans, Russians, French or the neo-racialists of Africa and Asia. What oft was thought and tactfully suppressed he said out loud, for instance about the anti-Western bias of the United Nations. With him the 'endless negative', felt by the British as 'a weariness of the flesh',[1] ended.

He knew his own mind. Equally importantly he knew Macmillan's. The Prime Minister had learned the lessons of the past, not least from his own brief but chastening experience under Eden.

Apart from Cabinet discussions, Home remembered, 'we had an arrangement by which we met twice a week, for a quarter of an hour, twenty minutes. Privately, off-the-record so to speak, and without officials. We reviewed the scene every third day, and so we knew exactly how we were thinking on the issues of the time. If he took an initiative, say the Test Ban Treaty, we would have planned this at one of our meetings.

'I think this is a very good plan for the Foreign Secretary—to be able to walk in on the P.M. for an informal look at the whole field. It is economical in time and fruitful in result! Of course the P.M. most often takes the public initiative in the big issues of policy.'

Home never resented Macmillan's occupying the international lime-light though he did not always agree with some of his initiatives: 'I was much less keen about summits than Harold.' He thought that, with the Russians, 'nothing would come of them and nothing ever did. So my own strong advice was to work behind the scenes as on the Test Ban Treaty, and the Laos settlement.'

This, Home concluded, 'is the only way you can ever get anything done with the Russians—on a limited front on a particular issue at a particular time that happens to suit them.' It was little enough but at least it did not lead to disappointment and the feeling of desperation which follows public failure.

In public Home was far less conciliatory, tougher, towards the

[1] Lord Franks, *Sunday Times*, 26th April 1964, quoted in W. N. Medlicott; see note, p. 123 above.

Communist powers than was Macmillan and this, too, was an advantage: 'He thought on the whole that this was quite a useful division of functions—that I should pursue this line. Sometimes he may have thought that I went a little bit far. But still he didn't object to this. He could always say "Oh, that's only my damned awful Foreign Secretary. I'm much more peaceful-minded myself!"'

Early and late in his Foreign Office years, the Congo harassed him. At first he saw the Congo, so precipitately abandoned by the Belgians, as likely to be penetrated by the Russians, who would use it 'as a base for the extension of Communist power', posing as champions of independence for colonial peoples. Lumumba received their backing, Belgian residents fled or were massacred, and law and order collapsed. Only in Katanga Province under Prime Minister Moise Tshombe was there peace and work. Home had no hesitation in November 1960, in putting Britain strongly behind a United Nations Security Council vote for intervention with a peace-keeping force, which was heavily backed by the United States, already deeply interested in Africa and the Middle East. There was, however, in Home's mind a great difference between policing rival tribal forces and intervening as a combatant on one side or the other.

Indeed when he learned that the United Nations, with American support, intended to use force 'in the last resort' against the flourishing Katanga Home insisted that 'there can be no question of empowering the United Nations to use its forces to impose a political settlement'. He agreed only that forces could intervene to prevent clashes between Congolese troops. His careful proviso was, as we shall see, ignored.

Meanwhile, he attended his first meeting of the U.N. General Assembly, when Khrushchev took off his shoe and used it to bang the rostrum. 'It might,' Home lightheartedly told the Lords, 'be held to my credit that I sat opposite the Opposition Front Benches for four years and never once took off my shoe.'

He was in reality shocked by his first encounter face-to-face with the Russians, who were openly using the United Nations as a propaganda organization and as a means of subverting the newly independent nations: 'Unless a newly independent nation is hostile to the West,' he remarked, 'it is not really independent.'

He came back from New York, after conversations with Gromyko, confirmed in his view that peace could be maintained only by 'the balance of terror'. Of this reality the Socialists, he thought, had no inkling; either that, or some of them simply swallowed Communist propaganda. In their opinion, he said: 'Every Russian rocket is a contribution to security and peace and every British and American weapon is an offence against morality.'

'I did not hear a squeak of protest,' he noted in the Lords, 'when Mr Khrushchev said his rockets could sink this country like an aircraft carrier. Not a word. But when we come to strengthen our own defence deterrent, immediately there is criticism heaped upon us.'

Dangerous as it was, brinkmanship was the only way: 'I trust and believe our people will have the spirit to see this through.' Talking was right enough but he gave a warning about 'summitry': If there were to be another failure 'there could come despair and from despair war. What I am after is an honourable draw. Only peace itself is the victor.'

What he saw starkly he expressed without frills. So much so that in Paris in December 1960, a Soviet diplomat walked out during a luncheon address Home was giving to the French diplomatic association. 'A charter of hate' was his phrase for the communiqué that had followed the recent Russo-Chinese talks. Where in reality, he inquired, was the 'new imperialism' if not in Estonia, Latvia and Lithuania where Russia had colonialized 22 million people?

At this the flushed Russian scraped his chair back and abruptly left. Lord Home, a newspaper reported, seemed one of the few who did not realize what was happening. The Foreign Secretary, one newspaper advised, ought 'to take a refresher course in diplomacy before venturing abroad again'.

As it happened, a diplomatic initiative of the most intricate, yet vital, kind was preoccupying him. The Americans were proposing to back, with force if necessary, a Right-wing government in Laos, one of the Indo-China states, where a Russian-aided Communist insurrection seemed, at the end of 1960, as if it were about to succeed. If the Americans intervened to prevent it, so would the Sino-Soviet bloc. This could be the start of a third world war.

Home wanted to neutralize the situation by reviving the International Supervisory Commission of the 1954 agreement on Vietnam to encourage the formation of a broadly based government of 'national unity' in Laos. The United States—where John F. Kennedy had become President—disagreed.

They turned a deaf ear to Home's arguments, the more so because he was not in their good books at the time. He had recently, on 8th February 1961, restated the long-held British view that Communist China should have a seat at the United Nations: 'they weren't particularly angry with *me*. They just didn't like the British attitude and I repeated it. Britain thought that though the Chinese would be a cursed nuisance in the place—worse than the Russians—it was better to have them in since at least it was possible to see what they were doing. The Americans understood the point really, but they disagreed with it and they carried the day. On the last two votes whether China should come in or not they got a bigger majority each time against it. It was something on which our opinions differed.'

Nevertheless Home quietly persisted with his persuasion of the Americans while at the same time publicly making it clear to the Sino-Soviet bloc that Britain would not allow Laos to become Communist because next door was Thailand and Thailand was a member of SEATO: 'A member of our alliance is threatened with a permanent state of Communist rebellion,' he said at a SEATO Conference in Bangkok on 27th March 1961, 'in a country with which it shares a long and vulnerable frontier, vulnerable not only to direct aggression but to more than a threat of subversion.'

Home's persistence was rewarded. The Laos negotiation was an achievement for the British point of view and because the American policy was reversed. The Americans had been inclined to get involved in Laos, and wanted to back the Right-wing element but it was clear that if they did they would get involved in a sort of Vietnam in even worse country than Vietnam.

Home recalled some of the diplomacy: 'Harold Macmillan and I took the opportunity of talking about this at one of our conferences with Jack Kennedy and persuaded him that he ought to have a closer look at American policy. He agreed and said he would send Averell Harriman along. Averell came and talked and was convinced that we were right and the State Department and the Pentagon were wrong.

'So Kennedy reversed American policy on Laos and we did manage to fix up a settlement with the Chinese and the Russians. It was 50-50 satisfactory in the sense that, although the Communists cheated and did not get out of a third of Laos, nevertheless the Royal Kingdom of Laos still exists today. It was in fact about as satisfactory a settlement as could be got in that part of the world in these sort of circumstances, where bands of Vietminh and Pathet Lao and Vietcong were challenging the governments, royal or republican, in that part of Asia.'

Just how touch-and-go the situation had been Home revealed to the Lords in July, 1962 after an agreement had been signed: 'I could not say it at the time but I should like to say it now, that when I went to the SEATO conference it was not just a question of war between North Vietnam and Laos. War between the SEATO alliance, including America and the Communist powers, including Russia and China, was so near that it could have turned on the spin of a coin.

'Britain would have been once more engaged in a world war—not less because it happened to be on the continent of Asia.'

With justifiable satisfaction, he added: 'I hope the British people realize that this kind of situation is not solved by luck.'

There were plenty of problems and crises nearer home than South-East Asia. In March 1961 South Africa, driven out of the Commonwealth, despite all Macmillan's arts, became a Republic and so part of Home's domain at the Foreign Office. Britain itself was undergoing a 'counter-inflationary budget', a Bank Rate increase, more purchase tax, cuts in public expenditure and a 'pay pause' on wages and salaries. Productivity had fallen back to the 1960 level and domestic consumption ceased to rise.

With the Commonwealth shaky and the economy shakier still, Macmillan cautiously produced a new initiative: Britain would apply to join the European Economic Community which seemed to be flourishing while Britain flagged, an oasis of prosperity and peace in a desperately dangerous world. To join Europe, Macmillan believed, could be Britain's salvation, her new, invigorating role in the world. If not this, what else was there? He knew, however, that advantages and disadvantages were finely balanced. He introduced the idea gently, almost surreptitiously.

Not so Home. Influenced perhaps by the enthusiasm of his second-in-command, Edward Heath, he informed the world before Macmillan did that the Government was not merely weighing the idea but had decided to apply for entry to the Common Market.

Britain, he told the Lords, needed more money to fulfil her commitments in the world. She had tried everything—Crippsian austerity, exhortation by kindness and inducement (Amory's remedy), wage increases only for increased productivity. None had succeeded more than temporarily. Now we should 'expose ourselves to the astringent of competition', because it would open new opportunities for investment and expansion.

Moreover, he claimed, Britain would serve the Commonwealth better inside than outside Europe. As for the political connotations of the Treaty of Rome, once inside the E.E.C. we should have a hand in deciding them; in any case he saw no signs of any Common Market country sacrificing any significant amount of sovereignty:

'The question of sovereignty should be judged by whether there would be compensating gain. It really is a question of balance of advantage. We should not make sovereignty into a shibboleth.'

With a broad smile he added, 'It occurs to me that a bachelor surrenders some of his sovereignty on marriage, with material advantage to the human race.' Some sovereignty was surrendered when Britain joined NATO and GATT, the General Agreement on Tariffs and Trade. 'Let me admit that the Treaty of Rome would involve considerable derogation of sovereignty', but only in connection with economic matters.

Home had some special reasons, which he did not explain to the Lords, for wanting Britain to join the Common Market, though at first believing it was not possible:

'I'd written it off as almost impracticable after the original Maudling idea [1] of the Free Trade Area collapsed,' he remembered. 'Then I thought that it was very unlikely we would get back into serious negotiations on it. But the opportunity did occur again.'

It was to be Britain's economic salvation—'this was certainly my feeling. Britain needed that sort of market unity in order to mobilize the wealth and get the wealth in particular for research on anything like the scale the Americans could command.' He later cited the huge Concorde aircraft development as an example: 'It has been almost beyond the resources of Britain and France together.' Only by joining the European community could a country of 55 million people like Britain hope to steal a march on the Americans, who would 'nine times out of ten beat Britain purely because their research goes on at eight times the scale of this country.' Home, remembering Suez perhaps, and the Empire as it once was, believed the road back to power

---

[1] Maudling, President of the Board of Trade 1959-61, first tried to get a free trade area of virtually the whole of Europe instead of the E.E.C. This attempt failed, after which the E.F.T.A. agreement was concluded as a substitute alongside the E.E.C.

lay through Europe. Heath began haggling at the toll-gate in October, 1961.

Meantime, despite a mounting din from Moscow, Home coolly flew off to Portugal and Spain on projects of his own. Portugal, Britain's oldest ally, was an ally still in both NATO and EFTA. British troops exercised there and Portugal had bought two British frigates. Under the benevolent rule of President Salazar she had prospered. Unfortunately for her, so too had her African territories, Angola and Mozambique, which, therefore, the Communists coveted. The usual courses of action were set in motion. Bands of desperadoes were infiltrated, calling themselves 'freedom fighters'. At the United Nations, the Communist spider set its Afro-Asian flies to work and soon a General Assembly resolution demanded that independence should be given without conditions or reservations to all trust and non-selfgoverning territories no matter how inadequate the territories' preparedness might be. It was an open invitation to chaos from which the Communists hoped to benefit or at least to damage their enemies.

The resolution, directed at the British in Central Africa and the High Commission territories as at the Portuguese, was 'impracticable and very dangerous', Home told the Lords, and infringed articles of the Charter. 'I don't care who votes for it. The United Kingdom is not going to do so, as long as I am Foreign Secretary.'

Home's visit to Portugal was intended both to show solidarity— 'I couldn't stomach the U.N. attacks on Portugal for her colonial policy. The Portuguese have done rather well'—but also to advise a certain caution while the 'wind of change' was still blowing. To avoid visits from U.N.'s touring investigators, he proposed that a fact-finding mission should go to Angola led by the British Consul-General at Luanda. This was agreed between Britain and Portugal. Portugal in later years was to prove a true friend to her neighbour, Rhodesia.

Home's Spanish visit had different motives. He had long believed that Spain should be brought into closer relation with the West, and his opinion was backed by the United States on strategic grounds. A quarter of a century had passed since the civil war, General Franco had resisted German blandishments during the second world war and throughout had lived peaceably with his neighbours.

A trial balloon had been sent up by Butler, the Home Secretary, during a private visit to Spain in May when he spoke of wanting Spain 'fully incorporated in the Western world'. There was a small explosion from the elderly British Left but not elsewhere; Michael Foot, M.P., referred to Home's 'blind, clumsy posturing which passes for skilful diplomacy in the Tory mind.'[1]

Home, undaunted, pressed on with the visit, and his purpose. 'I thought Spain ought to be in NATO. I am quite certain we should not, for example, have had all this trouble with Spain about Gibraltar if our policy, which was beginning to mature—though the Scandinavians disliked it—of introducing Spain into NATO, had been achieved.'

By the time Home was back in London, it was evident that Khrushchev was banging the gong for another crisis. The Leftist and Communist organizations were in full cry in Britain. With one such group, the Campaign for Nuclear Disarmament, Home had 'great fun'. Speaking of the Campaign's attempt to turn young people into unilateral disarmers, he asserted that the C.N.D. executive, led by Canon J. Collins and others, contained Communist propagandists. Collins threatened to sue Home: 'I carried on a desultory correspondence for six months saying he really must be very innocent if he did not know what was happening.

'Then one day the *Daily Express* came out with a report of two members of his executive who had resigned and both said they were paid-up members of the Communist party. So I just cut out the report and sent it to him in an envelope without any covering letter, and never heard any more. Great fun.'

Far less fun, Home found, was the crisis unleashed during the summer by the other Communists in the Kremlin. In fact there were moments, he later admitted, when he suffered 'acute anxiety . . . a nasty prickling feeling'. Once more Khrushchev raised the question of Berlin, demanding in effect that it should be incorporated in the East German satellite republic—'What is mine is mine and what is yours is negotiable', as Home put it. But this time he had gone further: it must be done by the end of the year. It was an ultimatum.

Home stood firm. At the end of July he warned Khrushchev 'that one false step over Berlin could easily plunge the continent of Europe into war'. He spoke of living in 'international anarchy', and of his preference for 'the quiet, serious, patient techniques of diplomacy, free from the threat of force'[2] (20th July 1961). But he left no doubt in Khrushchev's mind: the British had always 'stood in the path of the

[1] Michael Foot, *Daily Herald*, 27th June 1961.
[2] House of Lords, 20th July 1961.

highway robber from Philip of Spain to Hitler'. They always would. As for rumours, probably Communist-inspired, that the United States was wobbly, Home said: 'I know of no disunity, only a common purpose to do what is right for the alliance and for free men.'

In early August, as the East Germans blocked movement from East Berlin to the Western sectors, plans were discussed in London for calling up reservists to bring the British Army of the Rhine up to full strength. The Western Foreign Ministers met in Paris where Home spoke of 'a very dangerous situation and possibly war'. The Russians announced that they would resume testing of nuclear weapons and talked of having developed nuclear bombs equivalent to 100 million tons of T.N.T. 'We,' said Home, 'have enough nuclear striking power of our own to put most of Russia's big cities out of existence.' On 13th August hordes of workmen hurriedly erected a high wall round the eastern sector of Berlin.

During these tense days, Home stood largely alone. Macmillan, in the north for the grouse, carried his unflappability to embarrassing lengths by observing that the crisis was 'all got up by the press'. Home persuaded him to issue a correction.

Before long, Khrushchev quietly dropped the year-end ultimatum. The deterrent had deterred. 'The balance of terror', as Home called it, had been on the side of the West. The war of nerves slackened but did not end.

The Russians started dropping metal 'chaff' in the western air corridors to Berlin to confuse Allied radar. Home, in Geneva with Dean Rusk and Gromyko for disarmament talks, grasped the nettle: ' The Russian bombers were dropping chaff in the path of our aircraft and, because it upset the radar, there was very great danger that an aircraft carrying 100 people might crash.

'So we really set about Gromyko. We knew where the Russian bombers were coming from and where they returned to and we let him know it. He of course said they weren't doing anything, that he couldn't understand what our accusations were about. But he did get the orders cancelled. From that moment we never had any real air trouble in Berlin again.'

In these days Home was on top form and still rising. Far from being 'faceless' he became a prominent public figure: 'The one star that has continued to climb to a meridian of respect and influence has been that of a peer—Lord Home,' observed *The Times* on 26th June 1961, comparing him favourably with some of his colleagues whose stars appeared to be in the descendant. 'Lord Home,' agreed the *Mail* on 23rd June, 'has emerged as an independent, lucid and powerful force, a hard worker who has made much of the running in the Western diplomatic camp and who has now capped everything by putting himself at the head of the Tory lurch towards the Common Market.'

Sometimes in public he half-jokingly complained that he was working *too* hard and spending too little time on British soil. He felt like a soldier who had answered the recruiting poster's invitation to 'join the Army and see the world', he told the Scottish Unionist conference at Ayr on 20th April. More seriously he added that, while it was a good thing to see one's opposite numbers in other countries, 'this perambulation is seriously overdone and interferes with the continuity which there should be in the direction of British foreign policy.'

Was he tiring? Had Macmillan been right in July 1960 when he had spoken of 'the cruel and gruelling position at the Foreign Office . . . the decay of one man after another under the frightful pressure'?[1] Elsewhere, he talked of it as a 'killing' job. Home hotly repudiated the idea: 'It *isn't* a killing job. I never felt it a killing job,' he insisted later on. 'Mind you it is a bit overdoing it if you have to fly the Atlantic or out to Singapore seven times in three months.' He found it exacting: 'But it *needn't* be a killing job.' Macmillan spent eight months as Foreign Secretary in 1955, and left it very reluctantly.[2]

The post was undeniably taxing in another sense; its occupant had the issue of peace or war in his hands. But, 'I was not overpressed by the responsibilities—no, definitely not,' Home recalled. 'Mind you, I was very lucky. I had very good people to work with. Dean Rusk was a supremely good operator. The Foreign Office is extremely good and a Foreign Secretary is very well advised. Harold Macmillan was a very good P.M. to work with.'

Undoubtedly it was an advantage to be in the Lords. There was more time to think. Thinking, however, Home cheerfully informed the Lords on 25th January 1961, was the part of his job he found the most exhausting.

---

[1] Parliamentary Reports. Commons, 28th July 1960, col. 627. The decayed men, incidentally, could refer only to Eden and himself.

[2] 'I love the Foreign Office—the work and the people,' he wrote to Eden (*Tides of Fortune, 1945–55*, p. 692).

13. U.N. Arraigned: 1961–2

Katanga under fire. 1,000-lb. bombs. Cabinet divided. U Thant 'leaning'.
Coloured racialists. U.N. 'beginning of the end?'

Home was the least suspicious of men but towards the end of 1961 he began to doubt the motives of the United Nations Secretariat.

He saw that in the Congo, the U.N. forces, composed largely of Indians, were attacking Katanga, the rich and only stable part of the territory, under the diaphanous pretext of restoring 'freedom of movement'. He sent off a Foreign Under-Secretary, Lord Lansdowne, to demand that Hammarskjöld, U.N. Secretary-General, should stop the assault. 'If the United Nations got deeply involved in a war extending over the years, or was tempted itself to become a Colonial power, that would be the end of the United Nations,' he said in the Lords on 7th December 1961. Though he did not spell the message out, he observed that, while Britain was giving £10 million a year to the U.N., eighty-seven other countries were not paying their dues.

Realizing that Home was a thorn in their side, the U.N. officials tried to entangle him irrevocably in their plan to destroy Katanga. They asked Britain to supply twenty-four 1,000-lb. bombs for use by Indian Canberra bombers against Katangese roads, bridges, fuel dumps. At first, Homer nodded and Home agreed. When the nature of the trap was pointed out to him by Welensky, his old Oxford friend Lord Clitheroe, and others, he swiftly rescinded the agreement; the U.N. Secretariat delicately explained that because of 'considerable anxiety' in Britain they had withdrawn their request.

The lack of British block-busters did not prevent the start of an all-out assault on Katanga under the significant code word MORTHOR, a Hindi word meaning 'smash'. Later the U.N.'s indiscriminate bombing of Elisabethville, combined with the killing of civilians and Red Cross personnel, turned smash into terror.

'I thought it was disgraceful,' Home recalled. 'They were deliberately setting about the only part of the Congo on which stability could have been based. I was very much against U.N. interference with Katanga. I took the view that Katanga could make the basis of a sound government for the Congo. Breaking up the only bit that was stable was a damn silly thing to do. We couldn't do anything except express a point of view; time and time again, the Foreign Office would propose a course of action but it was sat on at the U.N. We *were* caught up in the U.N. policy; it was out of our hands.'

The Americans were no help. They strove to shore up their candidate, Adoula, as the head of a central government, and believed that U.N. force would help them to this end. 'The Americans strongly backed the U.N. Force and they made no distinction between the rest of Congo and Katanga. In other words, they didn't see Katanga as an element of stability in the situation. On the contrary, having backed the U.N., they were inclined to back them right through.

'I always suggested to them that this was a bad policy, but they didn't take this advice, though I think for a long time we acted as a restraint on the Americans at U.N. in not going for Tshombe, President of Katanga, straight away. It did not amount to what I would call trouble with the Americans. But it *was* a difference of opinion.'

Home's efforts did not always meet with approval from his own colleagues. There was inside the Cabinet some division of opinion; a few colleagues held that he was being too strongly anti-United Nations and thought it might be best if the U.N. *did* take over the whole affair. It went without saying that Home's attitude did not make him very popular with the Labour Party.

Home had scant doubt where the responsibility lay for the bloody attack on Katanga: the U.N. officials,[1] acting partly anarchistically, partly on the side of the Afro-Asian bloc supported by the Communist countries. O'Brien, the U.N. representative in Katanga, accused him of being the obstacle to a perfectly smooth operation.[2]

Behind the U.N. officials in the Congo stood the Secretary-General

[1] 'I have always believed the bloodshed in the Congo can be fairly placed on the heads of the United Nations officials who forced the showdown in Katanga with Tshombe.' (Welensky to the author.)

[2] C. C. O'Brien was on secondment from the Foreign Service of Eire to the U.N. Secretariat and was for a time U.N. representative in Katanga. 'He was hostile to the idea of Katanga's secession,' Welensky wrote, 'because he hated the secession of Northern Ireland from Eire.'

in New York. After the death of Hammarskjöld in a plane crash, his place was taken by a Burmese, U Thant. He was impervious to Home's views: indeed 'he leaned strongly the other way'.

U Thant remained 'leaning' over the coming years, blasting the United States for resuming nuclear testing and keeping silence about the Russian resumption that preceded it. He condemned Britain's 'grave error' in not bringing down the elected Rhodesian Government by force, and in 1967 removed the U.N. peace-keeping force in Egypt. In consequence Nasser's attack on Israel was facilitated. Home was required to propose a vote of thanks to U Thant when he spoke to the House of Lords in the Royal Gallery, and did it reluctantly.

The Congo affair was a minor defeat for British policy. 'The conclusion is,' Home later thought, 'that we could not alter the course of events with America against our point of view.' The Americans here, as at Suez, were the stumbling-block, a fact, as we saw, that had bearing on Home's enthusiasm for a European entity. Nevertheless Welensky, whose own territory of Northern Rhodesia was also threatened by the U.N., believed that Home had handled the Congo situation 'with both courage and skill . . . the best that could have been achieved in the extremely difficult circumstances.'[1]

Yet it also damaged the U.N. organization itself. Who, Home asked the General Council of the United Nations Association in Britain on 13th July 1962, could agree to put an international force under the command of a U.N. inspired by bias and prejudice?

Home learned the lesson if the British Government did not. In April 1962 the U.N. formed an 'anti-colonial' committee of seventeen nations from the General Assembly to 'investigate' Rhodesia. The General Assembly, Home peremptorily remarked, could make recommendations but members were in no way bound to accept them. Though he was willing to give the committee information on 'our dependent territories, we shall not allow resolutions or recommendations to influence our colonial policy . . .

'What I will not do under any circumstances is to allow irresponsible actions by some members of the U.N. to divert us from a programme of orderly and peaceful transfer of power from the United Kingdom to elected governments of our colonial territories.'

The 'anti-colonial' committee arrived in London and 'warned' the British Government that there must be no independence for Rhodesia

[1] Welensky to the author.

before an election with 'one-man, one-vote'. This sort of racialism will wreck the United Nations, Home pointedly observed, and if that happens the racialist members 'will have killed their own protector'.

All southern Africa was heavily under attack during 1962 from the racialists, their allies and 'their protector'. Britain, allied to the Republic of South Africa through the Simonstown agreement, supplied her under licence with the muniments of war, including Buccaneer aircraft. This the British Socialist leadership condemned, hinting that they would cancel the contract if they came to power. 'I hope,' said Home on 18th May 1962, at Nostell Priory, 'that they will think again and again before they make speeches linking British exports with the ideology of other governments.'

While the attack on Africa and the Congo was at its height, Home got together some facts about the functioning of the United Nations in the world at large, and drew up a kind of balance sheet. This he presented in a speech to a handful, no more than twenty, members of the Berwick-on-Tweed United Nations Association on 28th December 1961. Though he came down 'decidedly' in favour of retaining the United Nations Organization, there was a howl of rage from the Socialists and their allies across the world, outraged at any hint of criticism. With his usual understatement, Home observed only that the speech 'caused quite a ruffling of feathers in the political dove-cotes'.

Why, he asked, was there 'a crisis of confidence' in the United Nations at a time when everybody realized that what Byron called 'that immortal fry of almost everybody born to die' could literally come true?

It was because for the first time since the U.N.'s foundation 'a number of countries have voted publicly and without shame in favour of the use of force to achieve national ends'. He mentioned the four Security Council members who had condoned India's use of force against Goa, despite the fact that India's aggression was 'a direct breach of the Charter and of international law'. When the U.N. approved that 'it could be, as Mr Adlai Stevenson a strong supporter of the U.N. had said, "the beginning of the end".'

Recently the General Assembly had passed resolutions, particularly on 'colonialism', which were 'reckless and careless of peace and security'. They demanded that trust and non-self-governing territories should immediately be handed over to the natives of those territories. Doing exactly that had resulted in the chaos of the Congo.

He noted that the countries who voted for such things were often in serious arrears with their payments; 87 out of 104 were defaulting. Russia and her satellites refused to pay for Congo or Israel-Egypt border operations; France did not pay towards the Congo expenses.

'We have reached a stage when a large part of the organization which is dedicated to peace openly condones aggression . . . when a refusal by many to carry their share of the cost brings a prospect of power without responsibility.' To say there was cause for anxiety was an understatement.

Home came to the nub of the matter. Russia, which had always employed the veto to 'further the international objectives of Communism', was now manipulating the U.N. 'to prosecute the cold war, using racialism, nationalism and the exuberant individualism of newly independent countries to further their ends.'

Yet United Nations members knew perfectly well that 'Russia's Empire is occupied by military force and ruled by fear. No one who has witnessed what has happened in Hungary and East Germany can have any doubt that Russia's colonialism is the most cruel and ruthless in history. In the United Nations her technique is undisguised—it is that of the bully.

'By contrast the British record is one which has freed 600 million people in fifteen years and transferred them from colonial dependence to complete independence within the Commonwealth, where they are equal partners and in no way subordinate. We are moving fast—perhaps faster than in prudence we ought—in the direction in which the new countries want to go.'

United Nations members knew all that. But 'they seldom condemn the Russians and constantly harass us.' They had a double-standard of behaviour.

'It seems as if pushing at an open door is not good enough for them. Apparently it is emotionally unsatisfying and politically unrewarding for them to co-operate with the metropolitan power in completing the process of independence in an orderly way, and to ensure that new nations get a good start in international life.

'Since we in Britain are agreed on independence anyway, the only way to pick a quarrel is over timing. "Self-government today", regardless of whether there is anyone capable of governing: "independence tomorrow" even though it would mean other Congos.'

The fact that there was 'one rule for the Communist countries and another for the democracies, one rule for the bully, who deals in fear, and another for the democracy because their stock in trade is reason and compromise'—this put Britain 'in an appalling dilemma'.

Britain, 'a most vulnerable island,' wanted peace, wanted the rule of law abroad 'where we have to earn our living,' wanted above all to co-operate with all nations without exception.

Naturally, therefore, since 'our safety lies in making and keeping friends, all our instincts and interests combine to urge support for the kind of United Nations for which the founders drew up the Charter'.

But could Britain continue to give such support in view of U.N. practices? 'Has the United Nations of the authors of the Charter had its day?' That question was being asked by 'many sober and responsible observers'.

Yet, on 'the other side of the balance sheet', the aims and aspirations of the U.N. were sound. Britain could not 'afford lightly to discard an instrument dedicated to peace' at a time when man was not so far removed from the jungle that he could afford to dispense with 'any discipline there may be to hand'.

Moreover Russia would not always win—her *troika* secretariat proposal had been defeated.[1] The 'colonialism' cry was transient (except in the Russian empire). There had been the success of collective action in Korea (made possible only by Russia's absence from the Security Council). The U.N. police had helped keep the peace on the Israel-Egypt frontier. In education, farming, medicine and labour relations, U.N. agencies had done quiet, valuable work.

'I come down decidedly on the side of hope,' he concluded. But the U.N.'s primary aims—peace and security—must be reinstated. We must, Home concluded, 'neither sail off into the blue of Utopia nor founder upon the reefs of cynicism.'

The speech was frank and fair. Home believed, and was later to write, that the nation must 'be really well educated in the basic facts of community and international living', otherwise the future of the democratic system was doubtful.

The explosion that followed the Berwick speech was essentially obscurantist in aim. There was little real criticism and less careful consideration of the facts. For example, Harold Wilson, later to become Leader of the Labour Party, avoided the gravamen of the speech and

[1] The *troika* proposal was for three Secretaries-General whose terms of duty would be in rotation.

used it for party political purposes. Lord Home 'condemns the U.N. and its members because the wind of change blows too freshly through Africa and Asia', he wrote: it was all part of a struggle between the colonialist and anti-colonialist powers. 'Lord Home seems to resent the aims and aspirations of the new world which is coming into being.'

Wilson reduced Home's anxieties to personalities. There were a large number of Ministers and M.P.s (Tories) who had 'past or present financial involvements' in Katanga,[1] he alleged. (In fact, British industrial and commercial interests in the Congo lay 45 per cent in Katanga and 55 per cent in the rest of the Congo.) The Labour Party, he added, wanted to strengthen U.N.—'as a first step towards our ideal of ultimate World Government'.

Three years later, however, Home had little to add to or retract from his statement. He still believed that irresponsible use of the veto would 'doom the organization to impotence, at worst death.'[2] By that time, his analysis was scarcely challenged.

[1] Article in *Reynolds News*, 4th February 1962.
[2] See also his speech on the U.N. in 1967, pp. 247-8 below.

14. Long Knives and Hot Lines: 1962 – 3

'Beastly politics'. Cuba: Khrushchev's 'aberration'. Kennedy's 'rare gift'.
De Gaulle infuriated. Defence dilemma. Nightmare at the theatre.

In less than twenty-four hours in mid-July 1962 'unflappable' Prime Minister Macmillan dismissed six Cabinet Ministers and a number of others of less senior status. Home was not among them. This 'night of the long knives', as some journalists dubbed it, has never been fully explained. Home knew that Macmillan was planning a reshuffle of ministers but the speed of the operation surprised him.

The Ministers so summarily removed—not shuffled—included Lord Kilmuir, the Lord Chancellor, Selwyn Lloyd, Chancellor of the Exchequer, Harold Watkinson, Defence, Sir David Eccles, Education, Charles Hill, Minister of Housing and Local Government, Lord Mills, Minister without Portfolio, John Maclay, Secretary of State for Scotland.

Home's first thought was for Selwyn Lloyd for whom he had the greatest admiration, and he at once wrote to him: 'Politics are really beastly at times and Friday was a bleak day for all of us with whom you have worked in the Cabinet so loyally and long.

'I would like to thank you for your example and all the countless kindnesses you have shown to me during your years at the Foreign Office when I was along the passage and later at the Treasury when I was constantly pestering and you never impatient.

'More than anyone I have benefited by the foundations which you laid at the F.O. and the careful judgments which you made on this and that problem which are still with us because they are insoluble in our time, but are still faithfully treated with your prescriptions.

'This letter could turn into an obituary! But happily it is nothing of the sort because all of us will hope that after a rest (and do make it real) you will return to the political scene like a lion.

'Please keep in touch and let me go on drawing on your wisdom as I fear I have done so shamelessly for many years.'

Lloyd's removal was not, however, altogether a surprise to Home: 'I knew,' he called to mind, 'that Macmillan was beginning to think that Selwyn had had too long at the Treasury and was getting stale. Possibly true, though nobody has done as well there since.' He did not know why Lloyd had not been transferred to the Home Office instead of being relegated to the Back Benches. Some of the others, such as Eccles and Watkinson, had probably done enough, he thought. He never understood what had panicked Macmillan, although the *Daily Mail* on 12th July had forecast sweeping changes; not all its forecast was accurate but it was correct in stating that Butler would leave the Home Office and become 'deputy premier', a non-constitutional position unused since Attlee deputized for Churchill during his wartime absences from the country.

Home, never concerned with the fight for place and seldom hearing 'in-gossip', saw no hidden significance in the substitution of one set of people for another. To him Macmillan was simply giving a new look to the Government, for whom affairs were not going well. The economy was slack, there had been a Liberal victory in Conservative Orpington; at the Leicester North West by-election the Conservative had come third to Labour and Liberal, and there were Back Bench rumblings against the Leadership.

What escaped Home was the fact that naming Butler as deputy premier suggested to the public that in due course he would succeed Macmillan, now 69, as Prime Minister. Some said that Butler and Macleod had panicked Macmillan into the changes by telling him that Cabinet resignations were in the offing which would destroy the Government. If that were true, then Jeremy Thorpe, Liberal M.P., was justified in his quip about the Prime Minister: 'Greater love hath no man than this, that he lay down his friends for his life.' There were, however, other explanations advanced for Macmillan's precipitate actions, which did not involve Butler and Macleod.

Was it not also clear that the main beneficiaries of the change were those close to Butler in the post-war years—Maudling who became Chancellor of the Exchequer, while Boyle (Education), Powell (Health), Joseph (Housing), entered the Cabinet?

The suggestion startled Home: 'Till you said it this minute,' he exclaimed in 1969, 'this interpretation had not occurred to me, nor do

I think it rings true.' Butler's young associates were in any case ripe for promotion. Moreover it was unlikely that Macmillan would appease Butler. It was generally known that the Prime Minister sometimes thought Butler too adept at making ambiguous remarks about him. It was doubtful whether he was intentionally equivocal but he could certainly rub the Prime Minister up the wrong way—a fact that was to have national significance in the coming months.

Whether Macmillan appeased Butler or not, what he gave him with one hand he removed with the other, saddling his new deputy, or more officially First Secretary of State, with the task of breaking up the Central African Federation in the teeth of Sir Roy Welensky's steadfast opposition. A Ministry, the Central African Office, was specially created so that Butler became overlord to the Commonwealth and Colonial Secretaries, thus avoiding some of the clashes between them which had continued when Sandys succeeded Home and Maudling succeeded Macleod. Butler did his job with subtle skill but at the expense of alienating Rhodesia, and thus increasing the distrust some Conservatives already felt for him. Macmillan, with one cunning stroke, created a deputy premier and reduced his chances of ever becoming premier.

Macmillan's lack of love for the heir-apparent was divined, if not by the public at large, certainly by sharp-eyed M.P.s and political correspondents. After the 'night of the long knives', which in essence was a revelation of Macmillan's weakness, there was some speculation— confined mainly to the pundits—as to who his successor would be. Some thought of Maudling, others of Macleod, as front-runners. A few wondered, rather idly, whether such members of the Cabinet as Lord Home and Lord Hailsham (Quintin Hogg),[1] might renounce their titles. A joint committee of both Houses, urged on by Lord Stansgate (Wedgwood Benn), was then considering whether peers should be allowed to give up their titles for their lifetime so enabling them, if elected, to sit as M.P.s in the Commons.

Home was asked whether he would do so if it became possible. With a broad grin he told a Foreign Press Association lunch on 31st July 1962: 'I had a constituency once. I know what it is like, and I am not terribly anxious to have another.' Nor, he said, was he in favour of weakening the House of Lords by some of its members deciding to go

[1] Leader of the House of Lords and Lord President of the Council since 1960; Minister for Science and Technology with special responsibility for sport.

to the Commons. He would wait till he had seen the joint committee's report before he answered the question.

The petty crisis of 'the night of the long knives' was within three months overshadowed by the major crisis of the days of the big bombs. In late September 1962 Home in New York told the U.N. General Assembly that, though he distrusted the Communist interpretation of 'peaceful co-existence', he detected nevertheless the beginning of a perceptible thaw in the cold war. A few weeks later he was referring to 'opportunist and two-faced Russia' who, as President Kennedy revealed on 22nd October 1962, had put medium-range and intermediate-range ballistic missiles into Cuba, thus threatening the United States, the Caribbean area and South America. 'A massive act of duplicity,' Home dubbed it in the Lords.

America and Russia faced each other like two dogs tensed to spring at the twitch of an ear and the world trembled. Home found the situation difficult to interpret. Khrushchev had up to then been, to his mind, the most convincing exponent of co-existence the Russian leadership had produced. Nevertheless he had always noted that 'Khrushchev was a gambler.' From his first meeting with Kennedy in Vienna he may well have taken away the impression that he would not stand up to a challenge. Probably he and the Kremlin 'hawks' had drawn the conclusion from the Kennedy administration's oft-declared liberalism, the fumbled 'Bay of Pigs', its support for the corrupt U.N. assault on Katanga, its attacks on anti-Communist South Africa, that it was soft.

If so, it was the same error into which Ribbentrop had led Hitler about Britain. Kennedy stood firm, and with him Home and Macmillan. All knew that if the balance of terror overbalanced there might be— as Home had told the United Nations a month before—300 million dead in the first few days of war. From the British side, the Prime Minister took the lead:

'Jack Kennedy used to telephone every night and Macmillan had a conversation with him. The objective of both was the same: how to avoid a showdown without losing the influence and authority of the West. Here Bobby [Robert Kennedy] played a considerable part, and helped his brother to handle this with a very considerable care and sensitivity. But Macmillan was always talking and counselling and discussing the sort of moves that might be made. It was a comfort to Kennedy to have his advice and experience ready on call.'

These conversations used to take place *every* night and Home sat in on them with Macmillan. Using the 'hot line' is not easy for the un-mechanical. It was necessary to lift the hand from the switch when listening and press it when speaking and often the two leaders did it the wrong way round. There were moments of hilarity which at least relieved tension. 'Still by and large they got through to each other on the same wavelength and there wasn't any difference of opinion what-ever on this with the Americans. But they did discuss all the various ways and means of diplomatic action,' he recalled.

Home considered that Britain's counsel had a considerable influence. More than anything else it was in strengthening Kennedy's feeling that he had a friend on his side with whom he could discuss things without reserve absolutely openly. There was no one else, outside America, with whom he could do this and he used to take full advan-tage of it. 'And the Ambassadors—Lord Harlech there and David Bruce here [1]—were both experienced and skilful. The contacts were very close. 'That', Home commented later, 'is how it should be between trusting allies.'

There was no question of Britain's acting the honest broker. Home told Russia in the most categorical terms that Britain would not mediate with the United States, as he revealed to the Oxford University Con-servative Society in November 1962. 'They had deliberately put missiles into Cuba and they must decide to take them out and quickly. If they did not neither I nor anyone else could answer for the consequences.'

While the exchanges were going on, Home dealt summarily with the British Leftists. Seeking to defend the Russians, they talked of the 'compatibility' of bases, that is, the Warsaw Pact countries and NATO being lined up against each other. That, he told Lady Summerskill in the Lords on 25th October 1962, was a recognized front. The point about the Russian planting of nuclear weapons on Cuba was 'that it is de-liberately opening up a new area of instability and putting nuclear weapons of great power into a new part of the world'.

The Russian aim was to test the American reaction to a threat of force: 'The reason the free world can breathe again,' Home frankly stated when the Russians withdrew, was 'that the President of the

---

[1] Lord Harlech, David Ormsby Gore at this time, was British Ambassador in Washington, 1961-5 and previously Minister of State for Foreign Affairs. David Bruce, wartime European Director of the Office of Strategic Services (now C.I.A.), was American Ambassador in London 1961-9.

United States did not fail and did not lose his nerve.' If he had accepted Russians missiles on Cuba, 'no ally of America would have had confidence in United States protection ever again,' he said on 31st October.

Privately Home thought that the Russians climbed down because they got 'cold feet. But they would not have had cold feet had there been no deterrent.' Yet how appalling it was—'unforgivable' he called it—that in the twentieth century we should have to face 'a demonstration of brinkmanship with nuclear weapons.'

On the other hand the uncomfortable thought occurred to him that had nuclear weapons existed earlier, 'my generation might have been spared two wars,' he wrote to the Scottish nuclear disarmers ('Committee of 100'): were Britain to disarm unilaterally it was 'only too likely that other powers would take advantage of it.' India, more or less disarmed, was not saved from an attack by Communist China.

The American attempt to save South Vietnam from the Communists had as yet scarcely begun, though the assault by the Viet Cong was already some years old. American military aid, under article 51 of the United Nations charter, was confined to advisers but was soon to include fighting men. The subject was sometimes introduced by Kennedy when Home and Macmillan talked with him: 'Every now and again he [Kennedy] used to say what did we think about it. We thought and said quite firmly that our role lay in Malaya and Singapore and not in Vietnam. Though we told Kennedy we were sympathetic to his dilemma and would support the American cause, nevertheless we could not support them to the extent of sending troops or military assistance.

'The Australians did. I think Kennedy understood our reasons but they were not well understood in America.'

Britain sent no forces because she had insufficient for use on the mainland of Asia. In any case, it was judged that the country would swallow up almost any army, as indeed it swallowed the French and then the American. Anything Britain could have added would have been only psychological assistance to U.S., and, Home thought, British public opinion would have been against it.

Home, who had many meetings with Kennedy during his brief Presidency, found him 'a man of great imagination. He was an individual who was not necessarily bound by the advice he got from his departmental officials. He had a gift very rare in a politician, in that he took his own time to make his own decisions. At several meetings

I've seen him get very strong advice from his own officials, but only after a few hours of contemplation would he say "yes" or "no". In the foreign field he was an extremely successful operator. He had imagination, endless drive, and energy. He would never let anything rest and stagnate.'

Home found Dean Rusk easy to work with at the State Department: 'Firm and strong and patient. Of course they [the American administration] were caught up in Vietnam which bedevilled Kennedy's Presidency to some extent and Johnson's entirely.'

With Khrushchev, whom he met in New York and in 1963 in Moscow, he got on well personally: 'An ebullient character, erratic, but human. When one was next to him at lunch he would be joking away and then he would suddenly turn and say "You're a representative of the Capitalist class." The tirade would end as suddenly and all would be sunny again. There was a strange duality in him.

'Like most of the Russian leaders, Khrushchev had purges and cruelties which could justly be laid at his door but he grew more flexible in his interpretation of co-existence and could be human when *not* on the job.

'I remember him once in the New York Waldorf where we had been meeting. When we left he got in one lift and I got in the other. At the bottom as he walked into the street an enormous crowd surrounded him and one of his companions told him that he ought to get into his car. He said "How can I leave without my Lord"!'

Home was involved in intricate matters of defence during 1962-3 though in most of them Macmillan took the lead. Conceptions of what NATO should be and do were changing, partly under de Gaulle's individualistic views, partly because of developments in nuclear weaponry. The British Government began to phase out the obsolescent V bombers for delivering the nuclear bomb and decided that the American Skybolt missile should replace them. After vast expenditure of money, however, Skybolt was deemed unsuccessful and the project ended, much to the dismay of the British Government. At this point de Gaulle proposed that the French and British should join to produce their own new deterrent, in effect to make Western Europe independent of the United States. Neither proposition seemed feasible or desirable to the British Government, who were thinking rather of asking the Americans for Polaris submarines, in some ways a militarily better proposition.

Confusion began when Macmillan visited de Gaulle in December 1962, while Home was also in Paris for a NATO ministerial council.

'The Skybolt weapon had failed us,' Home remembered, 'and we had to have something comparable or our strength would not be credible. The next best thing—and much the best thing—was the Polaris submarine; it was in fact the only weapon that made sense in the terms of a deterrent. The aeroplane was obviously going to lose its penetration and what was needed was a second strike weapon.'

At this time, however, Macmillan and Kennedy had not yet held their talks in Nassau, no one knew whether the Americans would part with the nuclear knowledge Polaris contained nor whether they would let Britain have it. Meanwhile, Macmillan had gone to talk over the possibilities with de Gaulle at Rambouillet, the President's official residence outside Paris.

At Rambouillet the impression de Gaulle seemed to get was that Macmillan was going to America not to fix up for any alternative to the Skybolt, but intended to co-operate with France in production of a nuclear weapon and would 'chuck' the American connection. 'De Gaulle must have got the wrong impression although nobody knows this because nobody can check up from a record. The vital conversations were held *à deux* without an interpreter there and were conducted in French.'

In January 1963 Macmillan went on to Nassau in the Bahamas for talks with President Kennedy and was promised the Polaris. To de Gaulle this sounded like another of perfidious Albion's tricks. To put this right, if it could be put right, Kennedy sent a message from Nassau to de Gaulle asking him to come and asking whether he would like exactly the same arrangements for Polaris submarine as Britain was going to get.

'This infuriated de Gaulle,' Home recalled. 'So far from pacifying him and letting him think that France could jump on the wagon of the United States deterrent and save a whole lot of work and a whole lot of money he declined to have anything to do with it. He decided to have a French deterrent which is French from start to finish. It was a decision which up to now has put the French at a considerable disadvantage for they have still a long way to go to perfect their delivery system.' Britain has her four Polaris submarines.

Home has always held that from the British point of view the Nassau decision was right. The question is whether Macmillan at Rambouillet ought to have tried to persuade de Gaulle to go to Kennedy and to ask for the Polaris submarine. Home is sure that de Gaulle would not have done that. His dislike of being beholden to the Anglo-Saxons was very strong in his mind.

Though Home was not present at the vital Macmillan meeting, he had opportunity to talk to de Gaulle during the NATO deliberations of December 1962: 'He was concentrating everything after the retreat from Algeria on teaching Frenchmen to think in terms of France and the defence of France by Frenchmen. The defence of Europe and the NATO alliance left him cold.' He disliked NATO and other such arrangements involving America and Britain largely because of their Anglo-Saxon origin. Contingency planning he rejected despite the fact that the Russians, under the cover of manœuvres, could attack France with great ease and speed. All he really wanted to have was occasional contact with the Allied Chiefs of Staff.

To Home the American military connection was essential. He felt it necessary to have the Americans tied to Europe, at any rate until there could be a credible Anglo-French deterrent. Even after that came about he was convinced that an American presence, conventional and nuclear, would be necessary to balance Russia's mobilized force.

During the early months of 1963 there was a real danger of NATO breaking up, one group of countries clinging to the U.S. deterrent, the other to a hypothetical French deterrent. A compromise was, however, agreed at the Atlantic Council ministerial meeting in Ottawa, when Home promised to assign the V-bomber force and three Polaris submarines to the Supreme Allied Commander, Europe. But he made it clear that Britain would retain her right individually to use the weapons she put under NATO command. One reason was that a situation could be visualized where Russia might blackmail Britain by saying 'If you move there, we will strike at you.'

It was, too, Home said, a very large assumption to make that the United States would in all conceivable circumstances cover Britain with her strategic deterrent and 'governments cannot take risks with national security.' He would, however, be no party, he told the conference, to excluding the U.S. from the European continent.

Home was attacked by the Labour Opposition for keeping the nuclear deterrent. Though as late as 1960 Labour leaders were opposed to Britain's giving up her nuclear weapons, by 1963 the pacifists, neutralists, unilateral-disarmers and crypto-Communists had the upper hand. Early in the year Gaitskell died suddenly and Harold Wilson took his place. Three years earlier P. Gordon Walker, afterwards shadow Foreign Secretary, had given warning that, were this to happen, Wilson would be the 'prisoner' of the unilateralists.

Wilson repeatedly cast doubt on the credibility of the British deterrent, asserted that Britain, even if she did not possess it, would still take a seat at the top table, and that in any case it was too expensive. His second shot was the suggestion that when Britain abolished her nuclear weapons she should increase her conventional forces.

Home agreed that they should at least not be reduced, but maintained that a total reliance on conventional forces 'could tempt an aggressor to think he could start a conventional war, keep it conventional and win it conventionally. Thus you would tend to invite what everyone is trying to avoid—war. I cannot stress too much that it is war we are trying to stop, not only nuclear war.' [1]

On the subject of conventional forces, Home was not at one with his colleagues. The Sandys 1957 plan for reductions was by 1962 seriously weakening the forces and causing awkward dilemmas. For example, Home strongly opposed the Government's intention to halve the Brigade of Gurkhas, and in the upshot only some 3,000 were cut. 'The difficulty is that as you go on progressively cutting you come to the most horrible choice. Do you, for example, disband the Gurkhas or do you disband the Argylls, a British Regiment? Cuts now have been taken too far.'

Home was very insistent on keeping at least a substantial number of Gurkhas, some 10,000, because they were such very good troops in the kind of warfare Britain might anticipate in various parts of the world. He argued that they could be used in the Gulf, in other places, even in Africa. They were as a matter of fact used in the Congo by the United Nations and were very successful. Home warned his colleagues of the danger of approaching rock bottom in cutting down on such forces.

Home, like the rest of his countrymen, had long been familiar with Left-wing protest marches but in July 1963 came personally face-to-face with the then relatively new 'rentacrowd' [2] disturbances organized

---

[1] 14th March 1962.

[2] This word, first used in the *Daily Telegraph*'s sardonic column 'The Way of the World,' suggested that the Leftists could draw upon a force of all-purpose demonstrators.

by Trotskyists, Communists, Anarchists and others to create disorder in all non-Communist countries. The experience gave him a considerable shock.

It happened during the State visit to London of King Paul and Queen Frederika in July 1963. The Greek monarch and more particularly his Queen had long been objects of detestation to the Left, who had never forgiven the Greeks for successfully resisting and indeed crushing the repeated Communist attempt to take over their country. Six weeks earlier, during a private visit to London, Queen Frederika had been assaulted by a crowd who, like the apprentices of Elizabethan London, were always ready to be called out to molest or 'demonstrate' by their puppet-masters. Home apologized officially for their behaviour: 'I thought if we failed to protect someone who after all was the Queen of her country, an apology was due. It was after all only good manners.' For this he was furiously abused by the Left and its satellite organs.

During the State visit of the Greek royals—who were closely connected by ancestry and more recently marriage with the British royal family—something similar occurred. This time Home was present. Queen Elizabeth, the Queen Mother, took her relations to see a play at the Aldwych Theatre. There was booing and jeering from an ugly crowd. Home realized that the booing was organized; 'it gave one quite a nasty feeling walking into the foyer of the theatre.' The play they saw was *Midsummer Night's Dream* where another Queen with Greek connections had a disturbing experience but had some comfort at least in being told afterwards:

> Think but this, and all is mended,
> That you have but slumber'd here,
> While these visions did appear.
> And this weak and idle theme,
> No more yielding but a dream . .

15. Surprising Decision: January – August 1963

The Six: 'no sulking'. Khrushchev's jollification. Christian politics. Colleagues accused: Vassall. Profumo. Home changes his mind.

While Britain lay in the grip of the worst winter for two hundred years, her Government was suddenly winded by a sledge-hammer blow from abroad. President de Gaulle's blunt 'Non!' ended the negotiations for Britain's entry into the Common Market, and Heath trailed disconsolately home from Brussels.

'There was,' Home told the Lords on 6th March 1963, 'a fundamental difference of principle about what the future of Europe should be.' The French Government saw it as 'an inward-looking, tightly-knit Continental group from which British and United States influence would be removed: a Europe pursuing the role of a third force balancing between the United States and Russia. We are totally opposed to such a conception of Europe and it has become clear that the other five in the Six are also opposed to it.'

However, he added, Britain would 'not sulk and retire from the game'; with her E.F.T.A. partners, he said in Brussels on 7th February 1963, she would continue to seek rapprochements with the Six.

In fact the game was nearly up as far as the Macmillan Government was concerned. The Labour Party, which opposed entry into Europe, knew it and Lord Attlee observed with satisfaction that only a corpse of a government remained.

Looking back Home agreed that the collapse of the negotiations let the wind out of Macmillan's sails: 'He had set so much store on this particular adventure and initiative.' 'It was,' a senior Party official is quoted as saying, 'Macmillan's ace, and de Gaulle trumped it. The Conservatives never fully recovered.' [1]

There was happier news from the wider foreign front. In August

[1] D. E. Butler and A. King, *The British General Election of 1964*, London, 1965.

Home went to Moscow to sign the Test-Ban Treaty, which had resulted from a joint approach to Khrushchev by Macmillan and Kennedy. Home recalled an extraordinary dinner at which Khrushchev presided. U Thant was there as well as large American and British delegations. Rusk brought with him a number of American leaders, both Democrats and Republicans.

Proposing the health of his guests, Khrushchev said: 'Forgive me Mr Rusk if I describe you because of the nature of your supporters, as part clean and part unclean.'

Then, turning to Home, he said: 'I don't know what to say about you, Lord Home? Are you clean or unclean?'

Home replied: 'I am a biased judge. I'll refer it to U Thant who is obviously the arbiter of all things.'

Then, Home recalled, Khrushchev had an 'outrageous piece of luck'. U Thant said: 'I don't know that I can judge either, but do you, Mr Khrushchev, know what my name means in Burmese? It means Mr Clean.'

From then on, the dinner became 'a great jollification'. As always these dinners lasted over three hours but the days when Khrushchev drank too much and had to stop his colleagues from emulating him were over by then. Home regretted Khrushchev's departure from the international scene.

When Home spoke at the opening of the U.N. General Assembly in New York on 1st October 1963 Russia had set up the 'hot line' direct teletype with Washington and expelled five Chinese citizens. A note of optimism crept into his references to the Russians. 'I believe that Russia has publicly and finally renounced force . . . I believe we are at the beginning of a period in which we can organize peace.'

Khrushchev had said repeatedly in recent months that it was folly to interpret the Communist doctrine as leading inevitably to war—and had unsuccessfully argued his point with China, thus splitting the Communist world in two.

China too, Home believed, would eventually have to drop force from her programme if she wished to survive: 'Nuclear dust knows no frontiers and all her millions will not save China from it.'

And if the Russians, having dropped force, subversion and exploitation of other people's problems to propagate Communism, still succeeded in converting the world, then they would have won by fair means.

Home was mistaken in thinking Russia had 'finally' renounced force; he was assuming that Khrushchev was a fixture in Moscow. Yet he was correct in observing 'a reduction in tension'; it was the beginning of the lull in Russian pressure which convinced many in the West that they could afford to lower their defences.

Alec Home was almost certainly the only politician of world stature in the 1960s who publicly inquired whether the wielding of political power could be reconciled with the teachings of Christ. He asked because, as a Christian, the question was often in his mind and he gave some tentative answers to the General Assembly of the Church of Scotland on 28th May 1963.

The Church, he thought, must primarily be concerned with the relationship of the individual man to his God—'with the salvation of his soul.'

On the other hand, 'the individual is not merely a soul: he is an operator in earthly human society, a society which from the day of creation has embraced good and evil.' Thus the Church was also concerned with man in society and 'could not escape from a duty to hold before the community the ideal of the good life.'

If the Church succeeded in making individuals into good Christians, then society would be organized and administered by people and politicians guided by the Christian ideal. Home would have agreed with T. S. Eliot that 'it is the general ethos of the people they have to govern, not their own piety, that determines the behaviour of politicians.'[1]

Home had found no precise guidance for a politician seeking to translate Christianity into political practice. In fact Christ came into the world to do one thing, to redeem, which no one else could or can do. He kept himself detached from all ordinary local or sectional obligations, as Archbishop William Temple had pointed out. So it was not a question of what Christ would do in any given situation of the complex modern life, national or international: 'Is there,' asked Home, 'any Christian *principle* involved in social insurance or free education or one-man, one-vote, or self-determination or the possession of nuclear arms?' Christ did not require the centurion he praised so highly to leave the army; if he had been teaching pacifism, why were there two swords in the possession of his apostles right at the end of his ministry?

[1] T. S. Eliot, *The Idea of a Christian Society*, London, 1939, p. 27.

To the question whether the acts of the British people and their politicians are inspired by a Christian ethic, the surface answer would seem to be no. Yet 'how for instance do you explain the voluntary national decision by a sharing of wealth to sustain free education so that each child may have equal opportunity? Or the British people's constant crusade for disarmament and universal peace? Or that politicians undoubtedly find it easier to pass a law if, as well as being practical, it is recognized to be morally right?'

He dismissed the idea that such acts were done because there was likely to be a material dividend: 'I believe that in such matters of profound human value a national conscience works even if it is almost subconscious.'

It was true that, while the teaching 'do unto others as you would they should do unto you' had sunk into 'our national bones', there had been an increase in crimes of cruelty to each other, for the veneer of civilization was very thin. Yet on balance 'I would give politicians and people the benefit of the doubt.'

The politician, however, must resist the temptation to 'claim that every political act is approved by the angels.' Nevertheless 'in the leadership of a Christian nation there should be an element of witness.'

Nor should the search for truth in religion be feared today when there seemed to be a passionate desire that religion should appeal to the mind. In the end 'we may yet claim to be a God-fearing Christian country'.

But the Church should pay less attention to forms of worship, to doctrine and dogma (against which the intelligence revolts), and more to educating people in the simple basic teachings of Christ. 'Do not allow the pure teaching of the good neighbour to be overlaid.' The more complicated life becomes on earth 'the greater the need for simple rules of human behaviour'.

In such fashion the British Foreign Secretary bore rather lonely witness to his simple Christian faith during a year when a Bishop proposed a 'religionless Christianity' and the 'progressives' pumped atheism and a decadent liberalism through the organs of instruction and entertainment.

Ironically, as Alec Home spoke of the Christian ethic, campaigns were being mounted against some of his ministerial colleagues alleged to have broken it. When Vassall, a junior civil servant, was sentenced for espionage, wild stories of total inaccuracy appeared in the newspapers hinting at his close relations with Thomas Galbraith, one of the Admiralty Ministers. Macmillan set up an inquiry; two journalists who refused to reveal the sources of their allegations were sent to prison. Although the imprisonment was at the hands of a judge, Macmillan was blamed for instituting the proceedings that led to it. 'I don't think Macmillan was ever forgiven by a section of the press,' Home reflected. Some newspapers certainly turned violently against Macmillan; and the B.B.C. made him and his Ministers the chief political butts of disparaging skits.

More visibly damaging to the Government was the long-drawn-out affair involving John Profumo, Minister of War (i.e. of the Army). He had become sexually involved with a woman of easy virtue through a plausible physiotherapist, Stephen Ward, who had professional clients in high places. One of the woman's other sexual partners was a Russian Embassy intelligence officer, Capt. Evyeni Ivanov.

Rumours of the affair had been rife amongst parliamentarians and journalists since February 1963. So strong—and embellished —did they become that Profumo made a personal statement in the Commons to the effect that, although he had once or twice met the woman, he had no intimate relationship with her.

In June, however, Profumo wrote to the Prime Minister admitting that he had lied in his statement to the Commons and wished to resign. The Press accused Macmillan of closing his eyes to scandal to shield Profumo and of being careless of security in view of the Ivanov involvement.

Home heard of the rumours from a Conservative M.P. Certain that no question of security was involved, he conveyed his information to Macmillan who already had it, and gave his attention to other matters. Home was not officially involved in the matter nor in the subsequent inquiries. As War Minister, Profumo came under the Minister of Defence, then Peter Thorneycroft.

Home was said by some newspapers to have contemplated resignation. It was quite untrue. He had never been a censorious man, knowing that the flesh is weak. Profumo's lie to the Commons was indefensible and meant that he had to resign. But there were many who felt sympathy for him, believing that he had lied because he could not bear his wife [1] to know, fearing that it might break up the marriage.

[1] Profumo's wife, Valerie Hobson, was a popular film and stage actress; she was sister-in-law of Lord Balfour of Inchrye, a former M.P.

If Profumo had resigned before his lie to the Commons, the damage to the Government might have been small. As it was, Jo Grimond, the Liberal leader, put the prosecution case succinctly: 'Either he [Macmillan] knew the dangers of the company which his Secretary of State was keeping and did nothing about it, or he did not know and should have made effective inquiries, for there were plenty of warning rumours.' It is clear that Macmillan was slow to act: his reasons can only be the subject of speculation but were almost certainly psychological and perhaps connected with the prostate trouble, later to become acute, which notoriously casts its shadow before in the shape of lassitude.

Wilson, the Opposition leader, insisted on treating the affair exclusively as a neglect of security rather than, in *The Times*'s words, 'a moral issue'. The security aspect, in reality, was negligible. Home in an interview with the American Associated Press said: 'I am absolutely satisfied that there was no breach of security.' What angered him was the suggestion on the basis of one Minister's folly, that there had been a general degeneration in the standards of British public life. (Rumours had been spread that other Ministers had been as indiscreet as Profumo; the Denning report showed them to have been baseless.)

The Profumo affair was a gift to unscrupulous political opponents who suggested that this was the sort of thing Tories naturally did. In any case, the public was getting tired of the Conservatives, doubting their competence and ready to be persuaded that they behaved immorally as well.

While recognizing this, Home had no sympathy at this time with those Conservatives, long restless under Macmillan, who took the opportunity of the Profumo debate on 17th June 1963, to tell the Prime Minister, then 69, that he 'ought to make way for a much younger colleague'. One of them, Nigel Birch, quoted Browning—

> 'let him never come back to us!
> There would be doubt, hesitation and pain:
> Forced praise on our part—the glimmer of twilight . . .'

Some of the anti-Macmillan M.P.s gave newspaper correspondents to understand that Home was their ally; Home repudiated the suggestion with indignation.

After the first shock of the Profumo affair, the dispirited Macmillan had in fact considered resigning. Lord Hailsham, he thought, might be his successor. The Peerage Act, passed in June 1963, allowed hereditary peers to renounce their titles for life; and, against the Government's wishes, the Lords voted for the Act to take effect as soon as the Royal Assent was given rather than after the Dissolution.

Home would have supported Hailsham but most of the Cabinet M.P.s would not. Many more would, during July, have accepted Reginald Maudling, the Chancellor of the Exchequer.[1] But there was far from general agreement.

A few colleagues and some Party members, looked towards Home himself; two or three journalists suggested that he alone was the man behind whom the dismayed and divided Party could unite. Home took none of it seriously; and, seriously, none believed that he would ever renounce his ancient titles.

During the summer recess, however, Macmillan, recovered from his deep depression of June and July, let it be known that he intended to remain Prime Minister and, health permitting, lead the party at the general election due at the latest by the end of the next year, 1964.

A far more surprising—and hitherto unrevealed—change of heart came to Home himself. During August and early September a number of leading Conservatives spoke to him of their conviction that Macmillan ought to resign, and Home came to share their opinion. He decided that it was his duty to inform Macmillan of this opinion and of his own change of mind.

---

[1] Lord Redmayne (then Chief Whip) to the author.

158

16. Blackpool to No. 10: September – October 1963

Chequers dinner. Butler's 'Cross'. Strange Cabinet: Powell listens. Macmillan's surprise. Conference manœuvres. Doctors' verdict. Palace call. Dissenters.

A Prime Minister, inured to Opposition demands for his departure, takes fright when his chief colleagues echo the cry, for they alone have power to enforce his resignation if sufficient of them hand in their own. But for one lone colleague to suggest that he should retire is daring, not to say risky, and likely to evoke a lofty counter-proposition.

Home, however, was in a strong position. His loyalty to Macmillan was unassailable. He was, as the Prime Minister easily divined, the only colleague who had never even secretly dreamed of occupying No. 10, and advice from a transparently unselfseeking 14th Earl was more acceptable, galling as it might be, than from an ambitious Mister.

One September evening Home, invited to dine at Chequers, broached the subject—'reluctantly' because he greatly enjoyed working with Macmillan. Nevertheless, he was quite firm. The party had had 'terrible luck' with the Profumo affair, and he had come to the conclusion, he said, that Macmillan 'had lost too much ground to recover his winning form.' This opinion was shared by other colleagues, was gaining currency in the Party, and Macmillan should know about it.

'There was most emphatically no plot to oust him', he emphasized. Nor was he bringing 'pressure' to bear. To stay or to go was entirely a matter for Macmillan to decide: 'I didn't seek to influence him at all, and I said that whatever his decision it would be supported.'

But the bowed, dispirited Macmillan of June and July had vanished completely. He was perky, full of vitality, and brushed aside Home's suggestion: 'He talked about himself and his determination to stay, not desire to go! He just told me that he wanted to stay, and that was that,' Home remembered: 'After that evening at Chequers, I knew he had decided to go on, providing his health allowed. '

Since Macmillan would not even consider resigning, there was naturally nothing said about a successor. It was, however, widely known that even if his health broke down, Macmillan would never countenance Butler as his heir, even though he had made him deputy Prime Minister. The reason for this immoveable attitude was the subject of much speculation, some suggesting that it was because Macmillan thought that Butler lacked capacity for decision-making, others that his desire to be all things to all men led him into indiscretions. Yet few who knew him would deny his great intellectual qualities and his capacity for hard work. It was appropriate that the postal address of Chequers was Butler's Cross.

Macmillan, in reality, was not as confident in his ability to carry on as his words to Home suggested. Unknown to anyone, he had for some time suffered from mild prostate trouble, and this might become acute. During the early days of September he discussed with Martin Redmayne, the Chief Whip, what should be done if he were to be suddenly incapacitated and had to resign. How should his successor be chosen? He himself had been chosen to follow the stricken Eden by the Cabinet alone, but the procedure left him dissatisfied. He determined therefore that if it became necessary for his own successor to be found, the Party as a whole should have its say. There would be, he instructed Redmayne, a fourfold inquiry. The Cabinet would be sounded by the Lord Chancellor, Dilhorne; the Chief Whip would take the opinions of all Tory M.P.s; the Chief Whip in the Lords would hear the views of active Tory peers; and the leaders of the National Union would, through agents, chairmen, candidates and Young Conservative leaders, discover the wishes of the Party in the country. These arrangements were prepared before the month was out.

At the end of September Home was away from England at the United Nations in New York. During his absence a group of Tory M.P.s, mainly on the Left of the Party, though supported by one or two from the Radical Right, had continued to agitate for Macmillan's retirement. They suggested he should announce it at the end of the Party Conference due to begin in Blackpool on Wednesday, 9th October. They were still not agreed on who should take his place.

On Sunday, 6th October Home was again invited to Chequers, mainly because the Prime Minister wanted to hear his personal impression of the United Nations meetings and of his talks with Dean Rusk.

Maurice Macmillan, the Prime Minister's son, and his son-in-law Julian Amery, Minister of Aviation, were also at dinner. Talk turned to the prospects of an election which if it were to take place at that time the Central Office believed the Tories would lose by about 100 seats. Though Macmillan showed no sign of wanting to resign, his son and son-in-law urged that there was all the more reason to stay if defeat was likely since it would be a splendid last service for him to carry the responsibility and then allow someone else to take up the leadership in Opposition.

Home having spoken his mind the month before, did not demur. Macmillan intended to address the last session of the Party Conference on Saturday afternoon, as was then customary, and to announce that he would lead the Party into the next election. The newspapers got the message; on the Monday morning after the Chequers dinner they unanimously announced 'Macmillan to stay'.

At ten o'clock next day, Tuesday morning, 8th October Home went to a routine Cabinet meeting at 10 Downing Street over which Macmillan, looking pale and drawn, presided. Home thought he seemed to be in 'a baddish way' but neither he nor any other Minister knew that doctors had been called in the early hours to relieve him of bladder pains. Macmillan did not refer to the matter, nor did he mention his future intentions except to say that he expected to arrive in Blackpool on Friday evening. As Home recalled, 'I had absolutely no impression that Macmillan was resigning. Quite the contrary. He meant to go on; but my impression was that he might *have* to go because he looked so dreadfully ill.'

Towards the end of the Cabinet meeting Macmillan excused himself and left the room. A buzz of conversation followed, centring on the Prime Minister's ill appearance. Would he have to resign? And if he did resign . . .

Then, it is said, an authoritative voice intervened. Viscount Dilhorne, the Lord Chancellor, told his colleagues that if Macmillan were suddenly to be compelled to resign, it would be his duty under the arrangements made in September to seek Ministers' opinions on a successor. As he was not a candidate for the leadership he would be available to help any discussion or to give any advice his colleagues might desire. Home broke in to say that as he was in the same position as Dilhorne, not a candidate for the leadership, he also was ready to help in any way required.

It was a remark he was afterwards to regret. He made it quite casually: 'If Macmillan *did* have to resign,' he recalled six years later, 'I had no more idea of competing than Reggie Dilhorne.'

Home's observation was in fact lost in the hubbub of conversation and most of those present, including Redmayne, the Chief Whip, could not remember his making it. One Minister, however, did hear it, did remember it, and took it to be not casual but committing. The consequences were to be unhelpful to Home.

The meeting broke up before lunch and some Ministers took the train for Blackpool. Butler, the deputy premier, and Dilhorne remained in London. So did Home. He was to exchange the instruments ratifying the Test-Ban Treaty with the Russians and Americans on Thursday morning and would go to Blackpool later that day to be ready to deliver his foreign affairs survey on Friday.

At 6.30 p.m. on Tuesday evening, however, the Chief Whip was called to 10 Downing Street. Macmillan told him that he was entering hospital that evening for an early operation and that he should make ready the four-pronged inquiry to elicit opinions about a successor. Home saw him for a few moments only at 7 p.m. and was given the same opinion.

The world at large, however, was told only that Macmillan was to have an operation for prostatic obstruction and would be absent from official duties for some weeks. He would therefore not be going to Blackpool. The deputy Prime Minister, Butler, would be in charge of the Government during his absence.

Next day, Wednesday, 9th October Home was summoned in the afternoon to the King Edward VII Hospital for Officers in London where Macmillan was being prepared for his operation. The Prime Minister, speaking under considerable strain, confirmed that he intended to resign. He talked of possible successors and to Home's astonishment indicated that he regarded Home as a real possibility.

This, Home recalled, was 'the first time I heard any suggestion that I might succeed Harold. I told Macmillan that it was impossible. I was a peer and it was useless even to think about it. I simply dismissed the idea and left it like that so it played no part in my thinking.'

That being so, Macmillan had to decide in effect between Butler and Hailsham. Home left the hospital with the firm impression that Hailsham was Macmillan's choice; and he knew that Macmillan's backing of Hailsham, once it became known, would carry great weight with

Party opinion. He also took with him Macmillan's message of his intention to resign from the Premiership and the leadership of the Party which Home, as that year's President of the National Union of Conservative and Unionist Associations, was to read out to the Conference in the Winter Gardens at Blackpool the next afternoon.

Home was content with Macmillan's preference for Hailsham. He had known him a very long time, and had the highest opinion of his intellect and capabilities. He had been a good chairman of the party and was a cheerful, robust colleague. Some doubted Hailsham's judgment. If Home did so, he did not think that it amounted to a disqualification for leadership. But within a week Home had perforce to change his opinion.

Hailsham had other known supporters in the Cabinet, among them Soames (Agriculture), Marples (Transport) and Hare (Labour). But because he was Macmillan's choice did not mean he would automatically win the day. The quadripartite soundings, which unofficially Redmayne now set in motion, might yield a surprising result. There was no certainty; nor, as yet, was there, as far as the country at large was concerned, uncertainty either since Macmillan's decision to resign had not been announced.

Home arrived in Blackpool by air on Thursday afternoon, 10th October, and delivered the Prime Minister's announcement from the platform. The Conference generally was astounded by the news, though a number of the Party leaders and M.P.s had received an inkling of his decision. Maurice Macmillan, the Prime Minister's son, and Julian Amery were aware of it; they also knew that Hailsham was the Prime Minister's choice, and they now set about getting the Conference as a whole on their side. Their lobbying was intense and they did not despise a certain ballyhoo, including the distribution of lapel-badges bearing the letter 'Q', the initial of Hailsham's first name Quintin.

They had some success but there were many doubters, believing that Hailsham's good qualities were gravely outweighed by what they regarded as his irresponsibility and lack of judgment. Their doubts were now to be greatly reinforced.

Uninhibitedly garrulous, festooned with gimmicks, Hailsham rushed excitedly hither and thither, and late on Thursday evening dramatically announced at the end of a lecture to the Conservative Political Centre that he would disclaim his peerage and hoped to stand for Parliament. His bid for the leadership was now public. There was tumultuous, even hysterical, applause from his supporters, singing and shouting, and mass fervour of a kind distasteful to less ardent Hailsham-ites. Whisked away from his lecture by fast car, Hailsham made a triumphal entry to the Young Conservatives ball, where he was received with the sort of rapture more often accorded by teenage girls to pop singers than to potential Prime Ministers. But his evident eagerness for the Premiership nauseated many who would at least have tolerated him before.

In retrospect, these antics, which persisted till the end of the conference, convinced Home reluctantly that Hailsham had messed up his chances with Conservative members—and irrevocably. In the opinion of many his judgment had been publicly shown as extremely faulty and his succession impossible.

For the time being, however, this was by no means clear to Home. No whiff of the feverish atmosphere surrounding Hailsham's bid had reached him. He was aware, of course, that there was, and had always been, opposition to the choice of Hailsham and that Butler had a strong following, particularly in the Cabinet. But on Friday and even on Saturday, 12th October, he still believed that Hailsham was the best prospect: 'Harold Macmillan had really designated him. I was perfectly prepared to support Quintin.'

Others, more sensitive to Conference atmosphere, disagreed, and some leading lights in the Party were against both Hailsham and Butler. One of these was Duncan Sandys, the Commonwealth Secretary. Unknown to Home, he had seen the Prime Minister in hospital and urged that he should press the Foreign Secretary to become a candidate. This, as we saw, Macmillan had tried to do and failed.

On Friday it was bruited through the Conference halls that Home might be, as it was quaintly put, 'drafted', and the day's newspapers carried references to it. But, opening his foreign affairs survey that morning, Home said: 'I am offering a prize to any newspaper man who can find a clue in my speech that this is Lord Home's bid for the leadership.' The speech was the success of the Conference, the applause loud and long.

During the day Home received a stream of visitors in his hotel room. They had a single theme: 'They wouldn't have Rab and they wouldn't have Quintin. Then Selwyn Lloyd [sacked by Macmillan in July 1962] and a number of others, Dilhorne and Duncan Sandys among them, came along and begged me to run for the leadership.' The 'others' included John Hare, Anstruther-Gray, Mott-Radcliffe, and, as a representative of Back Bench M.P.s, Col. C. G. Lancaster, M.P. for the Fylde. To all, Home's reply was, 'No.'

But his visitors persisted, arguing that if he would not consent at least to be 'drafted' as a candidate, there would be a leadership feud, a split displayed to the world, from which only the Socialists could benefit.

It was shrewdly phrased. Home saw it as an appeal to put Party before self, to follow duty rather than desire. It was perhaps the only call he could not resist. Even so he would not agree to enter a contest.

He promised only that 'if you get into a terrible jam what I will consent to do—and nothing else—is to go and see my doctor and see if I'd be fit.' He was not playing the reluctant débutante. 'I really didn't think I was fit enough, as a matter of fact, because I'd had rather a long strenuous time and my eyes had been bad. So I simply said I would do that—no more.' He informed Macmillan, whose operation had been successful, of what he had said.

Home's undertaking was so conditional that he did not mention it to Hailsham, with whom he strolled from the Conference to lunch on Saturday: 'Walking down the street, Quintin asked what chances I thought he had and I said I think you've got a pretty good chance. I think you are the fellow really—and I did think so.'

Nevertheless, however little the Conference delegates knew of Home's conditions, a ground swell was rising in his favour. On Saturday afternoon when, as President of the National Union he introduced Butler's keynote speech, he was received with an enthusiasm far surpassing that accorded to the deputy Prime Minister. His references to the leadership question were non-committal although they included one curious comment: 'We choose a leader not for what he does or does not do at the Party Conference but because the leader we choose is in every respect a whole man who in all circumstances is fit to lead the nation.' Who was the un-whole man? Perhaps himself since he doubted his health; perhaps the erratic Hailsham. But it was Hailsham whom he sought to defend when he said to the delegates: 'I hope you will discount what people do at Blackpool whether on the land or in the water.' (Hailsham always made a point of sea-bathing at party conferences.)

When the Conference broke up, Home returned to London. During the weekend it became clear to him that Hailsham's antics had lost him the leadership, and that the heart was rapidly going out of his supporters. This left Butler. While there was some backing for him in the Cabinet, though it was far from unanimous, elsewhere it appeared half-hearted. Macmillan was inflexibly against him. Even if support for Butler became more visible, he might when he came to hand his official resignation to the Queen refuse to give her the customary advice on a successor if that successor might be Butler.

Clearly an impasse was at hand. The party *was* 'in a jam'. Home, therefore, fulfilled his promise and submitted himself for medical examination. 'The doctor unfortunately said I was fit'—and he conveyed the news to Macmillan. He then took the Czech Foreign Minister, David, to Covent Garden to see *The Sleeping Beauty*.

Meanwhile Macmillan had ordered his four-pronged soundings into intensive action. This move was unanimously approved by the Cabinet, presided over by Butler, on Tuesday morning. Macmillan received the results on Thursday morning, 17th October.

Reports from the constituencies were indecisive, mainly because it was still not definitely known that Home might be in the running. In the Cabinet, Dilhorne reported an overwhelming consensus for Home, as did Lord St Aldwyn speaking for the Tory peers. In the Commons the Whips had asked Tory M.P.s, including junior Ministers, for their first, second and third preferences. They had also noted objections to any of the known candidates, and the shades of opinion expressed were considered by Redmayne, the Chief Whip, who gave weight to 'people on whose opinion one would more strongly rely than on others'. On first choice Home was 'marginally' the leader and became 'outstandingly' so 'as you took it further through the field.'[1] No figures were ever published.

Later in the day Macmillan called the four groups of reporters together and required each to inform the others of the advice they had separately given him in the morning. Some weeks later Macleod was to suggest that the results of the soundings had been manipulated because there was insufficient support for Macmillan's first choice, Hailsham, and he refused to accept Butler. There is no evidence for this; equally, since those concerned refused—and still refuse—to give details or figures where applicable, none against. The accusation deeply wounded Home, who would later insist on an entirely new mechanism for choosing the Party leader.

Home never saw the results. He was informed by Redmayne early

[1] Interview in *The Listener*, 19th December 1963, pp. 1011–12.

on Thursday evening, 17th October that he was in the lead and it never occurred to him to question the word of Macmillan and all the other prominent and honourable men concerned. Redmayne also gave the news over the telephone to Butler, as acting Prime Minister. Twice Butler assured him that he accepted the position.[1]

Macmillan intended to give his resignation and recommendation to the Queen next morning. But on Thursday evening as rumours of the result of the soundings spread, Home's telephone at Carlton Gardens, the Foreign Secretary's official residence, rang continuously and almost always with bad news. Sometimes Lady Home took the calls, sometimes Selwyn Lloyd who, with Dilhorne, was spending the evening with the Homes.

Hailsham telephoned to say that he would not join a Home administration but would serve under Butler; Lloyd replied that such an attitude would look very like sour grapes. Macleod and Powell saw Redmayne and told him they could not accept the result of the soundings (though they had agreed to their being taken two days before) and would not accept Home as Prime Minister; neither, they implied, would Maudling, and Errol (President of the Board of Trade).

Home knew that if it was true that Butler, Hailsham and Maudling would all refuse to join him, it would be impossible for him to form anything more than a rump administration able to do little but limp towards an election where defeat would be foreordained. 'I made up my mind then that I would see them all individually', he recalled, to find out the truth of the matter.

Macmillan, however, would brook no delay. Next morning, Friday, 18th October, he telephoned Carlton Gardens, to say that his resignation had gone to the Palace and that he was advising the Queen to ask Home to form a government. He had heard all about the previous evening's events and brushed them aside: 'Go ahead, get on with it' was his peremptory instruction, adding that Home would have to consult his colleagues later.

At 12.15 Her Majesty's Secretary of State for Foreign Affairs, the Earl of Home, was called to the Palace and invited by the Queen to form a government. Rushed into so awkward a position, he felt bound to inform her that, since the situation had come as a complete surprise, he could not forecast the attitude of his Cabinet colleagues and asked for time to see if he could form a government.

[1] Lord Redmayne to the author.

Thus at 12.56 it was announced simply that 'The Queen has received the Earl of Home in audience and invited him to form an administration'. There was—and could be—no reference to his acceptance of the invitation. For this situation no exact modern parallel exists, though in the earlier nineteenth century both the Duke of Wellington and Lord Aberdeen accepted invitations to form governments with no promise that they would or could. The question of what would happen were Home to return to the Queen empty-handed led to speculation, some of it worried, some merely wild.

Home began his vital interviews after lunch and, armed with the Queen's Commission, he conducted them in the Cabinet room at 10, Downing Street. Embarrassing though it was to ask old colleagues 'are you for me or against me?', he was his usual amiable self, business-like and brisk. At first Hailsham, Butler and Maudling were reluctant, arguing that Home lacked experience on the 'home front'. But they could not agree among themselves who should be Prime Minister; their individual *amours propres* outweighed their common unity, which alone could have defeated Home. In the end they all consented to serve under him, though not until next morning did Butler and Maudling finally give their words.

So at the last only two Ministers, Macleod and Powell, stood out against Home, despite Maudling's pleas to them not to throw their careers away. Their reason was simply that they did not believe that the Conservatives could win a general election led by someone with his aristocratic background.

'It was in vain that I said to them, "Well, I don't think you are right," but if they held this view they must do what they thought fit.' It was Home's view that the defection of these two Conservatives, who attracted the 'intellectual vote', probably cost the Conservatives the 1964 election. He was conscious of an 'unnecessary and serious' handicap in trying later to collect the floating vote, the unaligned. Also it was a weakness in the Party to have two prominent people who said they would not serve with the leader.

Powell had an extra reason for refusing to join Home. He was the Minister at the Cabinet meeting on 8th October who had made a mental note of Home's casual disclaimer of being a candidate for the leadership. He took this as a pledge by Home to the Cabinet that he would never consider the leadership. It was a rather purist view.

'I regret that the totally changed circumstances,' Home later reflected, 'had driven the incident out of my mind. None of my colleagues, except Powell, had recalled it—I had seen them all. Nothing would have been easier than to get release from the supposed pledge.'

To the outside observer the 'blame' may seem exaggerated but Home, a man of honour, hated the thought that even accidentally he might have misled even one of his colleagues.

The refusal by Macleod and Powell did not hinder his ability to form a government and in fact, as we shall see, gave him a tactical advantage in doing so. Thus it was that shortly before lunch on Saturday, 19th October 1963, Home drove to the Palace and kissed hands with the Queen on his appointment as Prime Minister and First Lord of the Treasury. After the most frenzied fortnight in British political history within living memory, the leadership crisis was over, and the inhabitants of the British Isles, returning from football and preparing for an evening out, discovered to their astonishment that their new Prime Minister was a sixty-year-old hereditary peer without a seat in the House of Commons, the first since Lord Salisbury resigned sixty-one years before.

It is no small thing to be Prime Minister of the United Kingdom but the business in hand precludes much pleasurable contemplation of either the glamour or the glory. Home, probably alone among the Prime Ministers in this century, had, as we noted above, genuinely never daydreamed of entering No. 10 as its master. He did not think it other than the greatest of all honours, but he would have understood the rich Bostonian who firmly told the evangelist: 'A man who has been born in Boston feels no need to be born again.' The man born to be 14th Earl of Home, Baron Douglas and the rest felt no need to be born again as Prime Minister. Far from it. Clasping the hand of his friend Lord Ogmore, at a Downing Street reception a few weeks later, Home whispered with unwonted feeling: 'Never, never let them persuade you to leave the House of Lords.'[1]

What satisfaction he felt was in any case blunted by his nagging awareness that many believed there was something contrived about what he later called 'the sort of *sub rosa* election'. The point was skilfully exploited the very evening of his accession by Wilson, who claimed to descry 'the machinery of aristocratic cabal producing a result based on family and hereditary connections.'

No matter that Home knew his own motives to be unassailable, nor

[1] Lord Ogmore to the author.

that, as Lord Blakenham put it later, unless all those conducting the soundings were crooks, the method by which Home was chosen was far more democratic than had ever happened before—or could happen again—since it gave due weight to the opinion not merely of the Cabinet but of Tory M.P.s, the Lords and the constituency parties.[1]

Still Home felt tarnished. Nor was this just a result of the Socialist outcry at the time. Six years later doubt still nagged him, even to the point where he wondered whether after all Butler ought to have become Prime Minister: True, 'his stock was extremely low at that time, but whether a party ought to take any notice of that I don't know'.

He was inclined to think, looking back at his own experience, that only 'on the rarest occasion' was a party wise to by-pass a tried heir-apparent and never unless there was an overwhelming reason. With Butler as leader, the election might have been lost by a heavy majority but recovery afterwards might have been quicker; or the election might have been won.

On the other hand future political historians may judge that what George Canning called 'the stupid old Tory party' had once more bumbled its instinctive way into choosing the right man for the unhappy situation that prevailed at the fag end of the Macmillan regime.

[1] Lord Blakenham to the author.

17. Sir Alec and the 14th Mr Wilson: October – November 1963

'Straight talking'. Cabinet-making. Matchsticks. P.M. without a seat. By-election at Kinross and W. Perthshire. Shaky start in Commons. Relations with Opposition.

Home, at sixty entering the busiest year of his life, hustled on to the air on Saturday evening, 19th October with a brief, crisp message to the nation: 'First,' he said in his cool, clear voice, 'my task is to serve the whole nation. Second, no one need expect any stunts from me—merely plain, straight talking.'

It did not take him long to discover that straight talk was 'easier to say than to do.'

By Sunday evening 20th October, he had completed his Cabinet and the list was announced at 6 p.m. His room for manoeuvre had been small. He could not on Friday ask members of the previous Cabinet whether they would serve under him and on Sunday tell them he did not want them. 'One had to rely on the support of the colleagues with whom one had served all that time. Even if one had wanted to change, one could not just before an election. It would have been too disruptive.'

So, as Wilson observed, it was largely the 'same old gang'. Butler moved into Home's place at the Foreign Office and his former posts as First Secretary of State and Minister in charge of the Central African Office lapsed. Maudling remained at the Exchequer, Dilhorne as Lord Chancellor, Henry Brooke at the Home Office, Sandys at the Commonwealth and Colonies, Thorneycroft at Defence.

Home's only real chance to make changes was, ironically enough, provided by the dissent of Macleod, replaced as Leader of the House by Selwyn Lloyd, and of Powell, into whose shoes as Minister of Health stepped Anthony Barber. Hogg (formerly Hailsham) having renounced his peerage, ceased to be Leader in the Lords and was succeeded by Lord Carrington, though Hogg remained Lord President and Minister for Science.

171

For Edward Heath, who had carried out the Common Market negotiations of 1961–3, a new post was created and he became Secretary of State for Industry, Trade and Regional Development as well as President of the Board of Trade. This was an encouraging step forward for it gave industry and commerce an able, energetic spokesman in the Cabinet—former Presidents of the Board of Trade had sat very much below the salt—and at the same time boosted the Macmillan plan for regionalization. (Whether this sort of Government 'regionalizing' was *dirigisme* rather than Toryism was a matter of opinion.)

John Hare—Macmillan's Minister of Labour, and a former Party vice-chairman under Lord Woolton—was given a viscountcy as Lord Blakenham and made chairman of the Party and Deputy Leader of the Lords with a seat in the Cabinet. He was to prove an invaluable chief of the Party. Lord Poole, who had successfully master-minded the 1959 election, became an additional vice-chairman. The team could scarcely have been bettered: Poole, Blakenham said later, was an inventive, creative genius, 75 per cent of whose ideas were brilliant, the rest less so.[1]

The old gang perhaps; nevertheless, as Home observed six years later: 'It's worth remembering that what Wilson called "the old gang" then are still the gang now in the Shadow Cabinet. They have lasted until 1969—with a new leader, a young member of the old gang.'[2]

One further change Home effected early in the New Year, making Hogg overlord for education and science, thus putting Edward Boyle, the Minister of Education, in second place. Ghosts of the past were not soon laid and it was at once suggested that this was part of a bargain Home made for Hogg's support when he was forming his Government. 'I don't make bargains of that kind,' he tartly told a television interviewer. Privately he commented: 'I thought there ought to be a super-viser over all education, particularly as the Robbins report was coming along, which had far wider boundaries than the Ministry of Education. It was demotion for Boyle in the sense that someone was put over his head but there was no sort of acrimony or trouble: Edward was perfectly co-operative.'

Scarcely had Home announced his Cabinet than he faced the In-

[1] To the author.

[2] In fact only nine of those in the Douglas-Home Cabinet were in the Shadow Cabinet—Douglas-Home, Heath, Maudling, Hogg, Joseph, Barber, Rippon, Godber and Carrington. Macleod had been in the Macmillan Cabinet.

quisitor, presenting himself on Monday evening, 21st October, before television's quizzical stare. He dealt with the questions vigorously. Did he know how the other half lived? *Inverted snobbery! There weren't two halves to the nation. In any case, he had represented miners in Parliament and knew all about farming.*

Did he become leader by a democratic process? *If anyone else had been chosen by the same process he would not have complained.* Was it a fact that by rejecting Butler the party did not deserve progressive support? *Plain, flat nonsense—he would pursue progressive policies and he had appointed Heath to carry forward a modernization-of-Britain programme.*

Was his attitude to Communism inflexible? *Yes, as long as it includes force in its programme; otherwise full co-operation.* Did he want to apply again for admission to the European Economic Community? *We can't do it.* Was he going to be cut to pieces by Wilson in the Commons? *'I should be surprised!'*

One question was more tricky. The interviewers resurrected a remark he had made in the February before: 'When I have to read economic documents I have to have a box of matches and start moving them into position to illustrate and simplify the points to myself.'

He extricated himself quite well, but privately admitted later: 'It was a frightful bit of bad luck. I was having lunch with Kenneth Harris. He said do you think you could ever be P.M. and I said I thought not because I do my economics from a match-box! While I was eating my mutton chop! I never gave another thought to it. I saw it in the draft and I ought to have taken it out. But then I never thought about being Prime Minister.

'Harold Wilson made full use of it: "Look at this fellow, in a year when economics matters *supremely*—this fellow's put in charge who knows nothing about it, simply match-box stuff." There's no one cleverer at making use of that sort of thing than Wilson.'

Home had his revenge for the 'match-box' taunt the same evening on another programme. Wilson, who would have much preferred the visibly shaken Macmillan to have remained his opponent,[1] had sneered at Home, the 'scion of an effete establishment', incautiously adding: 'After half a century of democratic advance . . . the whole process has ground to a halt with a 14th Earl.'

Innocently, Home observed: 'As far as the 14th Earl is concerned,

[1] A. Howard and R. West, *The Making of the Prime Minister*, London, 1965, pp. 60–1, 104.

I suppose Mr Wilson, when you come to think of it, is the 14th Mr Wilson.' The nation round their television sets roared with laughter.

'I don't,' Home continued, 'really see why criticism should centre on this. If all men are equal—well, that's a very good doctrine. But are we to say that all men are equal except peers? And nobody can be a Prime Minister because he happens to be an earl?' Wilson showed his irritation in private.[1]

Two days later Home disclaimed his peerage, putting in cold storage for his son, David, the ancient titles, Earldom of Home, Lordship of Dunglass, Lordship of Home, Lordship of Home of Berwick—all in the Scottish peerage—and the Barony of Douglas in Lanarkshire and the Barony of Home of Berwick, both in the United Kingdom peerage. As he was a Knight of the Thistle, he became Sir Alec Douglas-Home. The wrench was real. But over a decision once taken he seldom repined.

So from 23rd October 1963, the Prime Minister of the United Kingdom possessed a seat neither in the Lords nor the Commons, a situation unparalleled in modern British history. To give him time to get one, the opening of Parliament was postponed. A by-election was due at Kinross and West Perthshire and the Unionist candidate, George Younger—Viscount Younger's heir, and later M.P. for Ayr—stood down in Home's favour.

On 25th October the Prime Minister's office was moved to Comrie eight miles west of Crieff and the Prime Minister began his campaign. During the next fortnight he delivered forty-eight speeches: 'That was rather fun,' he remembered. 'I enjoyed that. It was strenuous but it was all in lovely country among very agreeable people. Of course there was a mammoth press following—whom we managed to leave behind! About 15 per cent of them usually managed to arrive at the meetings, up the country roads.'

But to his old tutor, John Masterman, who had sent a letter of encouragement 'at the moment of trial and opportunity', he wrote: 'Oh, for the cricket field!' and even in public he referred to himself as 'the long-stop'.

He played a sound innings against Liberal, Labour, Scottish Nationalists and three Independent candidates. Though there was a drop in the Conservative vote of nearly 3,000, his majority of 9,328 was a resounding personal achievement, sufficient to offset the loss of Luton in a by-election on the same day.

[1] Op. cit., p. 95.

Five days later a scene was enacted in Church House, Westminster, inconceivable in politics almost anywhere else than in England. R. A. Butler, whose hopes of the premiership had so recently been dashed, made a graceful, almost touching, speech supporting Home's adoption as Party leader: 'Sir Alec stands on the side of progress. I knew this before I consented to serve with him. I look forward to lending the weight of my influence and support for the forward-looking programme which is going to lead us to victory in the next election.

'Sir Alec has the great advantage of looking and being ageless. I am quite certain he will make a direct appeal to the young, and that we shall in fact be a Government young in heart under his leadership.'

Thus fortified, Sir Alec responded with fighting words that infuriated the Socialists. 'From this moment on,' he told the assembled Party delegates, 'the fact that there is a General Election ahead of us must never be out of our minds. Every act that we take, every attitude that we strike, every speech that we make in Parliament or elsewhere, must have that in mind, because the one thing that matters is that this country should be saved from Socialism and that a Conservative Government should be returned.'

The implication that the Prime Minister would never make a speech without a party political flavour was eagerly seized upon: 'Callaghan [1] made a good deal of this, suggesting it meant that national policies were to go by the board. I expect what I said led to this interpretation, though I was talking of course in a Party organizational sense.' But the Socialists did not let it go. They brought it up constantly in the Commons in an economic context. Flowing from it arose the insinuation that somehow the Prime Minister was covering up the difficulties of the economy and their effect on the £ sterling.

While the adoption meeting was proceeding at Church House, strange scenes were taking place outside the front door of No. 10, Downing Street. Young people were arriving carrying clothes over their arms, coat-hangers, guitars, Beatle records and piles of books. They knocked on the door and sought to enter. The doorman barred the way, and asked their names. 'Dunglass,' the boy said; 'Douglas-Home,' the girls claimed. Only after the doorman had inquired 'above', were the Prime Minister's children admitted. So the young Douglas-Homes, unpretentious and casual as their parents, entered No. 10;

[1] James Callaghan, M.P., then in the Opposition Shadow Cabinet.

there during the following months were held a christening party for the first grandchild and an engagement party for the youngest daughter.

Next day Sir Alec Douglas-Home, M.P., walked into the Commons for the first time for twelve years; in 1950 he was a back-Bencher, now . . . 'The difference between the atmosphere of the two Houses! My knees literally shook the first time I got up. I was glad to sit down. The sheer impact of noise!'

He spoke stumblingly, and many sitting behind him thought he would be made into mincemeat as the Socialists had threatened. Would it not after all have been better to have had the skilled, suave parliamentarian, Butler?

When the Opposition were not jeering, they ignored him. Towards the end of his speech, however, Sir Alec gained confidence, taunting the Opposition with its vagueness on defence; when by a slip of the tongue he seemed to suggest that Wilson might become Prime Minister he quickly recovered by saying: 'I have always faced facts—however horrible they are—even if they have not.'

Within a few weeks, however, Sir Alec was providing some nasty surprises for the Opposition: 'A funny thing has happened to Sir Alec Douglas-Home since he came to the Commons,' one newspaper noted. 'He has become genially dangerous. Every time you think you are hitting him on his aristocratic head, he pops up like a jack-in-the-box and clobbers you.' [1]

During question time a Labour M.P. claimed that it was not Sir Alec but his speech-writer who had described Wilson as 'a slick salesman of synthetic science'. With every appearance of seriousness, the Prime Minister quietly replied: 'I am very interested that you should have noticed that phrase. Have you anything better to suggest?'

When someone claimed that Hogg, Minister of Education and Science, also had to employ a speech-writer, he peered astonished over his half-moon spectacles, known as 'Homes': 'It has never occurred to me that anyone could possibly write Mr Hogg's speeches.'

Courteous ridicule delighted the House. Wilson became more wary of the opponent he professed to despise but he lifted his guard too often. To his derisory comment about the alleged drift of scientists to America, Sir Alec sweetly returned: 'I think the Right Honourable Gentleman is himself going to America soon—I hope it is not because he does not find room for his talents here.'

[1] *Daily Mail*, 19th February 1964.

176

Once William Hamilton, a Labour M.P., found the ground neatly cut from under his feet; Wilson, hurrying to his support, fell flat on his face. On 16th July Hamilton asked why Sir Alec gave oral answers to 55 questions last month, but transferred 48 to other Ministers.

Sir Alec retorted that since he entered the Commons last November he had answered more questions than Earl Attlee did in three whole sessions as Labour Prime Minister.

Mr Hamilton: 'Lord Attlee had a much less effective Opposition.'

Sir Alec: 'Whatever we were like in Opposition, we did not ask silly questions like this.'

Mr Harold Wilson, Leader of the Opposition: 'In the days of Lord Attlee's administration, not only the country but the House was three times as satisfied with the Prime Minister as it is today.'

Sir Alec: 'I seem to remember Lord Attlee was defeated.'

Sometimes honours between the ex-14th Earl and the 14th Mr Wilson were more equally divided. During Wilson's visit to the United States in early March 1964, agency reports claimed that he had said that he wanted to put the Royal Navy under U.N. control, and on 3rd March the *Evening Standard* had the headline 'Royal U.N. Navy' starts a row.

Sir Alec commented: 'Mr Wilson goes to the United States and makes a great speech on behalf of the Socialist Party suggesting they are going to take some new initiative by putting the British Navy at the disposal of the United Nations. He calculated he will get the headlines and make a great impression and no one will question it. And someone has questioned it.'

Wilson furiously—and correctly—denied in the Commons making any such speech. Courteously as ever Sir Alec made what reads like an apology but with its nuanced pauses and calculated hesitations sounded quite the opposite. It went: 'If the—er—um—Right Honourable Gentleman *says* he did not say these—things—in a speech and I have *insinuated* that he did, of course I withdraw it—naturally. That's the thing to *do*. But we still have to have explained these extraordinary headlines that came to us.'

The truth was a quibble. Wilson had not made the remarks in a *speech*, but off the record to journalists had, it appears, suggested that R.N. ships should be allocated to the U.N. Sir Alec's 'mud-slinging antics in the last few days have been disgraceful' [1] one Wilson supporter wrote.

[1] Richard Marsh, M.P., reported in the *Sunday Times*, 8th March 1964.

It is hard, probably impossible, for Sir Alec Douglas-Home to hate. Tearing a passion into tatters is not his line. He prefers to steer a ball through the slips and does not object when an opponent does the same to his bowling. Wilson 'was genuinely trying to do me down. This was legitimate party stuff, the hard knocking and all that.' Probably, however, Wilson's personal relations across the floor were worse with Heath; they seemed to annoy each other more. 'Life's much too short to dislike one's political opponents and I don't,' Sir Alec concluded.

There was, for instance, the debate on the Denning report into the Profumo-Keeler affair of 16th December 1963, used by the Opposition to make party capital. Sir Alec threw Wilson off his stride by calmly observing: 'I can only think that the right honourable gentleman composed his speech before I made mine.'

Nevertheless in private talks the two agreed that in any such situation in the future a commission should, at the Prime Minister's request, investigate any allegedly serious breach of security in the public service; and that the Prime Minister and the Leader of the Opposition should 'try to agree how to handle it'.

'After Profumo,' Sir Alec recalled, 'even the Socialist Opposition, who had made so much capital out of it, were shocked into feeling that really this was something that oughtn't to happen again, and that if there was a security case involving Ministers—which Profumo's wasn't—it's much better to handle it by a machinery agreed by the two leaders in Parliament.'

Sir Alec had always believed that Government and Opposition should do their best to create a bi-partisan approach to foreign affairs. He thought that knowledge should be conveyed by Ministers to their opposite numbers on a Privy Council basis, always on the condition that it was clearly understood that this did not inhibit free debate in the House of Commons. Sir Alec knew no less clearly than Walter Bagehot that the success of the British governmental system stemmed from the fact that Her Majesty's Opposition was as integral a part 'of the polity as the administration itself.' [1]

[1] *The English Constitution*, London, 1867, Chapter 1.

18. Errors and Irritations: October 1963 – April 1964

No case for squeeze. Television 'mistake'. Modernization without bossing. R.P.M. and expediency. Saddled with policy statements. Speeches and writers.

Sir Alec Douglas-Home's first act as Prime Minister was to inquire of Maudling, the Chancellor of the Exchequer, to see whether there was a case for a 'squeeze', that is, for economic restraint. A criticism of the Macmillan Government was that it had been too inflationary and that the economic situation was running away, that there would be a big deficit and that, therefore, the 'regulator' should be applied.

The advice given to Sir Alec boiled down to 'no change'. The Treasury forecast was for a recovery in the winter and spring of the next year, 1964. So Sir Alec proceeded with the financial policies as they were.

Yet three months later the January figures—issued in February 1964—showed a large trade deficit. Just before they were published Sir Alec, who was to broadcast on television, again sought advice. Again he was told that there was no need for restrictions, that all was going according to a considered plan and that the deficit would be absorbed later in the year and in the spring of 1965, even though there might be a deficit in the autumn of 1964.

Thus armed, on the eve of the publication of the figures Sir Alec appeared on television.[1] Half way through his interview with Robin Day, the following exchange occurred:

Day: Is it correct that you have been warned by the Treasury that there is a danger of a serious Balance of Payments crisis in the autumn?

Douglas-Home: Well, I can answer that in one word—and that word is no.

Day: On January 1st of this year you said the economic outlook was very good; do you still think so?

[1] 17th February 1964.

179

Douglas-Home: Yes, I think it's seldom been stronger. Of course, there's always a danger of the pressure on the economy of these great programmes of capital investment, on education, housing, roads and the rest of it on which we're engaged. But the economy is very strong; exports are going up. Almost everything depends on whether we can really maintain the 4 per cent overall increase in the national production, year in and year out.

Day: But the head of NEDDY [1] warned, I think on Friday, that the economy is coming to a difficult period. Are you saying that no precautionary measures are necessary—between now and October?

Douglas-Home: If the Chancellor judges that the economy is running into what you call a difficult period, which might be quite different from a critical period, he would take the necessary action—election or no election. This is a matter of the national interest and the national economy, not, I hope of party politics.

With such unexceptionable sentiments Sir Alec drove back to No. 10.

Next day, 18th February 1964, the balance of payments figures were the worst ever published, though far worse were to come in the years of Socialist government.

The outcry was deafening. How could the Prime Minister have claimed that the economy had seldom been stronger? From the Socialist side it was alleged that Sir Alec had been electioneering regardless of the perilous state of the nation; there were rumours that he had ignored a Treasury memorandum giving warning of the serious economic situation. The Tories were dismayed and some complained that the Prime Minister had not been properly briefed.

Little enough of this criticism was true. But the wording of Sir Alec's answer was a mistake. In a sense the economy never *had* been stronger, but there was the deficit, and his reply should therefore have been qualified. It gave the hostage for which Wilson and the Opposition were looking, and they began those exaggerated forecasts of financial doom which came home to roost in the crisis of confidence under the next Government. It was of little avail for Sir Alec to plead 'Do not let us talk ourselves into a crisis or write ourselves into one on the basis of one set of monthly figures.'

Gloom was uncalled for. Production was rising, unemployment

[1] The National Economic Development Council.

had fallen to 2 per cent, export order books were full, as he correctly pointed out at Glasgow on 24th February. It was true that on 27th February the Chancellor had to give 'a touch on the tiller' by raising Bank Rate half per cent to 5 per cent: the smallness of the rise was 'an indication that in financial and Treasury circles there was no great feeling of crisis around'.

A month later, in March, he could claim that his boast that the economy had never been stronger was justified: the imbalance had been halved. Exports were at a record peak of £369m. and the trend was still upwards. The visible trade gap had narrowed from £120m. in January to £68m. in March. By April indeed there was something of a boom, which Maudling in his Budget corrected by mild increases in taxes to the order of £100m. in higher drink and tobacco duties.

Castigating the Socialists for 'scrounging round the economic dustbins', Sir Alec remarked that everyone could understand that things were, as he forecast, going well: 'I do not even need my box of matches and economic son-in-law.'[1]

The economy was Sir Alec's first priority. The next thing was the Regional Policy. He had deliberately put Heath in charge of the growth areas and regional development as a major act of policy. Macmillan had started it by sending Hogg to the North East of England.

'This conception of growth areas in Scotland and the North East and North West and various places was, I thought, a very good and exciting one and Ted, I knew, would put a great deal into making the policy a success, and he did.'

The 'major act of policy' was part of the 'modernization' fervour which gripped the Tories and became the subject of many of their speeches in the early months of Sir Alec's premiership. Though genuine enough, it was also intended to take the shine off the new Labour Party gospel, enunciated by Wilson at the 1963 party conference in Scarborough: 'We must harness Socialism to science and science to Socialism'.

Sir Alec himself spoke on 20th November 1963, on television of 'our plans for the modernization of Britain ... Every department of our national life must be kept up-to-date ... industry must be equipped with the latest machines . . . And that indeed is why Mr Heath has been appointed to his new post—to bring all the resources of the country simultaneously to the task of modernizing Britain.' As part of this,

[1] His daughter Meriel married an Oxford economist, Adrian Darby.

there was to be a vast programme for starting new colleges and universities, roughly according to the Robbins report.

Almost alone among Tories, Enoch Powell, now a saturnine Back-
Bencher, complained that much of this foreshadowed *dirigiste* Socialism.
He doubted whether the 'inducing or cajoling particular firms and
industries to establish themselves in places which they would not otherwise have chosen,' could be effective 'unless, as the Socialists envisage,
the entire economy is so controlled as to make it so'.

Sir Alec sensed the dangers: 'We are not going to get things done,
I can promise you this, by directing you or bossing you in any way.
It is not orders but opportunity.'

The educational plan was more open to criticism: why, for example,
start new universities when it would be infinitely cheaper to expand
old ones? Where were first-class dons to be found in sufficient numbers? Why the excessive emphasis on higher education when it was
primary education, for long the Cinderella of education, which self-
evidently needed expansion to cope with the swelling birth-rate?

Later on Sir Alec recognized the folly of a Tory Government legis-
lating for Socialist measures: 'I think if there is a criticism of the twelve
years of Tory Government—from the party point of view or perhaps
from the *democracy* point of view—it was that we weren't able to make
our policies sufficiently distinctive for the ordinary worker to understand the difference between the Left-wing Conservative and the Right-
wing Socialist. There wasn't a clean enough cut. I think this is valid
criticism.'

The indistinctive policy might be summed up in the neologism
"Butskellism".[1] It arose out of the Welfare State, which Sir Alec had
always approved, insisting that a nation must have a public conscience
and be willing to devote a proportion of its national wealth to the
unfortunate. 'But the net was spread so wide—so many were included
in this.' It was welfare run riot, damaging to character and morals. Yet
in 1963 neither party dare officially suggest a more selective system.

Another piece of 'modernization', laudable in itself but politically
mistimed, was the Bill to abolish price-fixing by manufacturers, the
abolition of Resale Price Maintenance. This upset the Party from January to April 1964, and in the opinion of many was electorally damag-

[1] 'Butskellism' was a journalist's invention to describe the alleged similarity between
many of the political attitudes of R. A. Butler and Hugh Gaitskell, the former
Labour leader.

ing. It was all part of the Government's itch to be seen doing something, no matter what.

The Bill had the praiseworthy object of increasing competition between retailers and so bringing prices down. Clearly, however, the small shopkeeper would be hit, since chain-stores with their large turnover could more easily reduce prices. The small man might find himself in liquidation.

The Bill was 'one of the things that some people think cost us the Election, because with only four seats redistributed we would have won it,' Sir Alec recalled. Heath was very keen on the Bill, but most of the Cabinet were not.

Sir Alec came down on Heath's side and decisively. He was sure the Act was right, even though it brought severe damage to many small traders: 'It probably did sacrifice quite a lot of Conservative votes', and it was troublesome in the House and the constituencies.

Selwyn Lloyd, then Leader of the House, firmly believed that such a Bill should have been enacted only at the beginning of a five-year term, not at the end. Conservative M.P.s under constituency pressure, particularly from the small chemists, vacillated, and the Government's majority on a section of the Bill was reduced to one. Tories of the 1960s had, like 'Christopher North', to say 'I cannot sit still and hear you abuse the shopocracy.' [1]

'We are, as you may have heard,' Sir Alec admitted to a Plymouth rally at Devonport on 13th March 1964, 'having our own little local difficulties over the Resale Prices Bill.' His next sentence has now a hollow ring: 'But I can tell you in the spirit of Drake at Plymouth nearly 400 years ago that we have plenty of time to settle our own differences and thrash the Socialists too.'

The Bill passed into law in April, an example of Sir Alec's preference for right (as he saw it) over expediency. It has to be admitted that it did not generally reduce prices, although such price reductions as have since been enjoyed by hard-pressed consumers have in the main resulted from its provisions.

Sir Alec conducted Cabinet business methodically, almost impersonally, rather in the Attlee style. His colleagues suffered no Churchillian monologues, no sotto voce, donnish asides such as occasionally escaped from Macmillan. Unlike Eden he never chased his colleagues;

---

[1] *Noctes Ambrosianae*, No. 39, February 1835.

unlike Macmillan he had never himself to be chased. He was easily available for consultation and seldom hedged a decision.

His Civil Service staff became devoted to him. His speed in extracting the essentials from long memoranda was by this time legendary. Though he could be advised, he knew his own mind, a mind as clear as running water and notably free from passion and prejudice. He had no side. Sauntering through No. 10, one hand in trouser pocket, he was as casually at home as at the Hirsel, and indeed through Lady Douglas-Home, who knew everybody from the Principal Private Secretary to the switchboard operators, the hub of the Kingdom took on a quiet, family atmosphere.

Apart from the Prime Ministerial and Cabinet Office officials, Sir Alec had a Party political staff, minute by comparison with that of his successor. The only politician with an office at No. 10 was his P.P.S., Sir Frank Pearson, and two women secretaries, one to deal with his own constituency, the other for general Party work. The Prime Minister was modest in his requirements; he needed neither court jesters nor ego-boosting *aides*.

With the Conservative Central Office in neighbouring Smith Square, Sir Alec had less happy relations. He had promised the nation 'plain, straight talking' but, he remembered, 'I found it easier to say than to do, because I was always being saddled with policy statements that they said one had to make. Over a five-year period that would have been all very well. But the effect of the kind of speeches one had to make was damned dull.'

The difficulty was that not only had Sir Alec unexpectedly become Prime Minister but a Prime Minister who must fight a General Election within at the latest twelve months. The Central Office tactic was to get him out and about in the country: 'One had to get oneself known and begin to hot up the pace.'

This meant constant speech-making, over and above that normally required of Prime Ministers—whose speeches, he thought, 'ought to have a scarcity value'—and the assistance of speech-drafters: 'A contrast has been pointed out between the speeches I made as P.M. and as Foreign Secretary—perfectly justifiably. As Foreign Secretary one had time. The officials used to produce good stuff on foreign affairs and I could put my own stamp and flavour on it,' he recalled. 'As P.M. the time was too full and too short'. This did not mean that he simply read out all that was put before him. He rewrote the material, added to it and subtracted from it, writing it in his own hand with a 3s. 9d. Biro pen on thin white sheets of Basildon Bond. The process became known to his staff as 'basildonizing'. It was always more natural to him to write than to dictate to a secretary.

Nevertheless when time pressed as it almost always did, wordy passages were delivered unaltered: 'I ought not to have allowed so much stereotyped stuff to get into the speeches.' In a private memorandum on 30th December 1963, to Sir Michael Fraser at the Conservative Research Department, he wrote: 'I think that part of the reason people are bored with us is that we have been boring. We fill our speeches with statistics which anaesthetize rather than animate. People need visual aid but they fight shy of figures and percentages (their instinct is right—there is too often a trap in them). We should, I am sure, talk in terms of things which people see and know.' [1]

But when on one occasion he said that the Conservatives 'had got off the wavelength of "the people", somebody came down on me like a ton of bricks. I was sharply pulled up.'

He was helped with his political speeches by George Christ of the Central Office and two journalists, Eldon Griffiths [2] and Nigel Lawson, who had been engaged originally to help Macmillan but who had resigned before they did anything.

On their side, the Central Office officials did not always find Sir Alec an easy man to help. They were accustomed to the style of Macmillan who, when speeches were being drafted, would toss the ball of ideas back and forth with his *aides*, plucking what he regarded as the best thoughts from the discussion and using them in his speech.

Sir Alec, under far greater time pressure, tended to accept drafts without comment, much less contradiction. He would alter them but would not usually discuss his alterations with his *aides*. His own views he largely kept to himself and he was not inquisitive about the views of others. He was, in this respect at least, a private man keeping his own counsel.

The fact was that Sir Alec had a natural gift for 'simple, straightforward' speaking, delivered off the cuff. As Prime Minister it was a

[1] Prime Minister's Personal Minute No. M.48 H/63, 30th December 1963, to Sir Michael Fraser, Director of the Conservative Research Department, and from 1964 Deputy Chairman of the Party and Secretary to the Shadow Cabinet.
[2] Griffiths became a Tory M.P. in May 1964.

gift he had to curb since a chance word or hint could give rise to dangerous misunderstandings.

Not that his speeches were as dreary or as crammed with heavily hedged policy statements as in retrospect he supposed. Often they had a startling humour. Asked on an American television programme what he would do about Castro if he were Dean Rusk, he at once replied: 'I think I would shoot myself'.

His jokes went down well, particularly the one about the two statisticians who already had four children and refused to have another because they knew that every fifth baby born is Chinese. Most of his sallies had a homely, even agricultural flavour. Speaking about uneven export performances, he reminded his audience of the rooster which pushed an ostrich egg into the hen-run, saying 'I don't want to cast aspersions but *this* is what is being done in other places'. Nor could one of his favourite sports be omitted: the salmon on the fishmonger's slab would, he pointed out, have done better if it had kept its mouth shut—and so would certain Socialists.

His beau ideal as a speaker was, however, a man who never cracked jokes: de Gaulle. 'Nobody had any doubt what he meant. It was simple stuff and his French was beautiful, classical—even when he was talking about Quebec!'

Kennedy's speeches he admired and he thought his speech-writing arrangements were worthy of emulation. The speeches were made for him not so much by experts on this or that subject but by 'masters of style'. Then he added his own sentences.

Sir Alec could scarcely hope to equal either de Gaulle or Kennedy since in the first five months of his premiership—before the election campaign proper began—he had to make sixty-four full-dress speeches and about 150 whistle-stop chats, amounting to some 330,000 words.

From the first, however, the experts of Central Office divined correctly that it was not Sir Alec's oratory but the man himself who could turn the 'don't knows' into Tory votes. Though he spoke clearly and well, he was no crowd-swayer. He could marshal an argument, direct a good-humoured laugh against his opponents, even deliver a crushing rejoinder. Yet he somehow lacked bite and had no gift for raising an audience's temperature, let alone blood pressure.

He knew his weaknesses and became sensitive and rather finicky about his speech-making. Everywhere he went an *aide* carried a special metal lectern, adjustable for height. Then the experts thought he ought not to use his famous 'Homes', the half-moon spectacles he favoured, because they had been seized upon by cartoonists. So a larger lectern was constructed, equipped with a specially bright light by which, it was hoped, he would be able to read without his 'Homes'. One disability he never overcame. He could not easily separate a pile of paper, so that he frequently turned over two sheets instead of one with sometimes embarrassing results.

He was at his best when he was most himself, chatting with people on whistle-stop tours, at fêtes, in factories or fields, 'getting himself known', as the Central Office thought of it. Yet this was very curious. He could scarcely be considered by the public as 'one of us', and was not. He had never nipped in for a quick one or a cup of tea at Lyons. He had nursed babies, his own and those of his children, but he had never pushed them in a pram in the park. Sir Alec filling the boiler or standing in a queue in the pouring rain waiting for a bus was inconceivable. He did not borrow books from the public library; the books flooded in, mint new, from the authors and publishers. He did not try to make ends meet: they met.

For all that, people of the most diverse kinds took him to their hearts. He was so obviously nice and they knew instinctively that he was sincere and not 'on the make'. He truly tried to put the interests of the nation first; he was a man who inspired trust. Some, too, felt a desire to protect him. His spareness gave him an appearance of frailty. Though he was in fact 6 ft 1 in. tall, he seemed smaller partly because of his large head which required a hat, when he wore one, of size 7⅜. The broad forehead and tufted eyebrows above deep-set eyes gave the rest of his face a tight bony appearance in certain lights. But when the ascetic look melted, as it often did, into a wide, boyish grin, the contrast between the death's head depicted by cartoonists and the real man simply delighted his audiences. Perhaps, after all, he *was* 'one of us'; certainly he could not be the aristocratic, high falutin relic of the cruder Socialist propaganda.

So the magic began to work and in April Lord Blakenham reported that Central Office estimates showed that while in November 1963, the Party would have lost an election by 100 seats, the loss in April would have been halved.

19. A Candid Minute: 30th December 1963

Affluence no answer. Tories 'let things slide'. Hustle to wind up Colonies. Britain must be in First XI. Slipping into neutralism. Democracy touch-and-go.

While the Christmas lights of 1963 still twinkled and the Scots made ready for first footing, Sir Alec, who had been called to London from the Hirsel because of violence in Cyprus, sat down in No. 10 and dictated a brief political testament.

It was not intended as such: 'I don't naturally sit down and write a thing like that', he observed afterwards. He did so because those helping him with speeches and other political work sought guidance, after a long period of Macmillan, on his basic attitudes to help them 'change gear'. This was of necessity something of a 'forced exercise'!

Forced or not, the four-page minute (now for the first time made public) is self-revealing and full of his natural candour.[1] It is also unorthodox in its attitudes. Running through it is the certainty that material prosperity is not enough, a far cry from Macmillan's 'you've never had it so good'.

'If drab equality,' he wrote, 'is no answer to Britain's future, nor is "affluence" if that means the purely materialist grab for wealth. I have, therefore, never really believed that the well-off society is the answer to Socialism or even to Communism.

'If people gain riches and lose their feelings for religion, service and sacrifice, they will be discontented within their own society and they will be bad neighbours.

'The Christian religion is still the basic if subconscious[2] influence in the life of the British people and they will respond best if they are asked for service and an element of sacrifice.'

Later he used to say that unless a nation has a conscience and there-

---

[1] Prime Minister's Personal Minute No. M.48 H/63, see note, p. 185 above.
[2] 'If subconscious' is added in his own handwriting.

fore has some sort of welfare state—'though ours has been grossly abused'—running parallel to the accumulation of wealth, then society was safe neither from Communism nor dictatorship. He might have taken France as example, an undoubtedly rich country with a high percentage of Communist votes.

'Profit-making and the welfare state are compatible, necessary to each other,' he believed. 'The welfare state is a deliberate sacrifice on the part of the tax-payers for a moral, public purpose.'

Sir Alec was sure that, as he wrote, 'In the truth about anything—from economics to sport—there is an element of self-discipline and un-selfishness and therefore sacrifice. It runs from wage-restraint to help-ing the underdeveloped.'

But where in this was the 'service' and the 'idealism'? 'I agree with you,' he commented in 1969, 'that it's a difficult thing to put the service side . . .' In the past, the sense of serving had come largely from working abroad in the overseas possessions of Britain. As he wrote in the document: 'We have lost an Empire where one member of most families had a direct interest and was working for something visibly worth while.'

Elaborating on this, Sir Alec said: 'The letters would come pouring back giving great stories of what each was doing for the Empire. The whole of British society was permeated by the feeling that they were doing something worth while.'

Such idealism of service to the poor and backward peoples had gone and gone precipitately. He wrote: 'I have felt that in this respect Conservatives have let things slide. Possibly because with a loss of power we have had to yield to expediency. Our colonial policy is in some ways an example of that, but partly because a moral content in politics had become unfashionable.'

Pondering this, he said: 'If we'd had our own way we wouldn't have wound up our colonies in the manner we did. We'd have taken another forty years or so and then done it. The two wars undoubtedly hustled the pace along. The wind was anyhow blowing. Macmillan gave it a puff.'

He was, however, convinced in 1963 that the opportunities for service, though different, still existed: 'Quite a lot of opportunities will open up for us if we have the sense to equip ourselves to seize them. They can mean greatly increased wealth and by that means we can recover a deal of our lost power and influence.' He was here thinking of British participation in the Europe of the Common Market. But, it might be asked, would the European Economic Community, with its Brussels bureaucrats, attract the idealism of young Britons?

It seemed nevertheless that to bring out the best in the island British they had to serve abroad: 'Certainly the Scots know that!' he smilingly commented. 'Once we are parochial and concentrate solely on taking in our own washing we are lost.'

Service undoubtedly moulded the character of the young, the feeling of working for something visibly worth while. Some Conservatives pondered the possibility of some form of conscription for public service—nursing, reading to the blind, and so on. Such good works, however, would not provide the discipline of the armed forces and moreover the employers and industrialists disliked the idea of two years being taken from the lives of future employees, who should be equipping themselves for their jobs.

The Christian religion, Sir Alec had written, was still the basic if subconscious influence in the life of the British. He had spoken on the subject in public over the years. But 'it's terribly difficult for a politician because he is too easily thought to be using religion as part of his propaganda machine, and calling in God on his side.' It has to be done with 'discretion and sensitive antennae'.

He attached great value to the 'good neighbour' doctrine which, he believed, lay at the heart of Christian teaching, particularly at a time when values were 'falling like ninepins'. No religion, he thought, presented any better rules for social conduct than Christianity. Without the practice of good neighbourliness 'life was intolerable'. Perhaps it was a matter of age group. There were some ten to fifteen years between Sir Alec and Quintin Hogg, a declared Christian, on the one hand, and the rest of their Shadow Cabinet colleagues.

Closely connected with religion is the question of patriotism. Sir Alec was probably the only leading politician in the later 1960s openly to mention patriotism in his speeches. Speaking as Prime Minister at Grantham on 29th November 1963, he said:

'It seems to have gone out of fashion to be proud of our national flag, but patriotism in the twentieth century is still a noble thing if we think of our flag not as a symbol of conquest but as a banner proclaiming the image of the kind of life and the values in which the British people believe . . . If we are true to our history and to our beliefs, our flag proclaims an evolutionary not a revolutionary society.'

Again, it is worth noting that some other Conservative leaders seemed to shrink from incurring Left-wing taunts at the word patriotism, though it is possible that some of their more junior colleagues might belong to a generation with other views. A reaction among the young was likely.

When he wrote his 1963 'testament', Sir Alec was firmly optimistic about Britain's future: 'I believe that Britain has a fine part to play on the world stage. Not as a "trimmer" in international politics but as a country standing for true values.

'But to carry weight we must be in the First XI and not only that but one of the four opening batsmen.

'It is fashionable to think that power can be discarded but those who think that way are moving unconsciously towards neutralism and there should be no such word in the English vocabulary.

'It is not in the British character. We cannot lead from behind or from the middle ranks—we must be in front.'

With the emergence of the super-powers—the United States, Russia and China—Britain would presumably be fourth of the 'opening batsmen'; it was a matter, largely, of population. Britain would have an atomic and a world military presence though not possibly on the scale of the new 'Big Three'.

Sir Alec's horizons were wide, extending far beyond the concept of Britain as leader of Western Europe: 'I think,' he reflected in 1969, 'that the evolution we ought to go for is to be a partner in Europe, but with the knowledge from the start that the European community ought to merge later with an Atlantic community. This would really make sense. This is the sort of pattern that ought to emerge. No tariffs on such a scale would create a vast area of activity and service for our people. The scale of it would inspire.'

Sir Alec's vision would line up the non-predatory States as equals with the predatory, i.e. Russia and China, and would therefore rationalize an irrational situation, a point made by such distinguished writers as Brian Crozier, Herman Kahn and Anthony J. Wiener.[1] It would, in their view, though not in Sir Alec's, involve 'the dissolution of the U.N. and its replacement by a new international body excluding the predatory states,' as Crozier writes.[2]

[1] Crozier. See note, p. 104 above. H. Kahn and A. J. Wiener: *The Year 2000*, London, 1968.

[2] Crozier, p. 388. See note, p. 104 above.

Such outward-looking, expansive conceptions may seem like dreams but 'perhaps someone will label them foresight later on'. They were certainly the antithesis of the neutralist aims of Socialism; for them Europe was the limit, the confine into which they sought to put Britain, though for the time being they could not wriggle out of the NATO machine.

One of Sir Alec's most startling remarks in the 1963 document is: 'I have always thought it to be touch-and-go whether democracy (one-man, one-vote) will last. Certainly it will relapse into some more authoritarian form of government unless the great majority are really well educated in the basic facts of community and international living. At present the British people decide by instinct rather than reason and while that period lasts leadership and government by explanation is all-important.' As he was convinced in his earlier political days that the Conservatives had the answer to Britain's political problems, so now he was certain that the Party was an essential buttress of democracy.

The one-man one-vote electorate—preserved in Britain, the United States, Australia, New Zealand and Scandinavia—was not always equipped to understand difficult issues, particularly those involving economic matters, and to take intelligent decisions. Therefore to Sir Alec the essence of the matter was a society in which 'if democracy is really going to work, it's got to be educated and pretty highly. Individuals and corporate bodies must reconcile their own interest with the wider interest of the nation. We've got a long way to go before we can say democracy is secure and stands on its feet. It is under great pressures and strain.'

The Conservative leadership was pledged to tackle the question of making freely negotiated trade union contracts with employers enforceable at law, not by government intervention; the courts would be empowered to exact civil damages up to a statutory limit against unions—or companies—which broke contracts.[1] That such legislation, even though it had worked satisfactorily in other countries, might lead to widespread defiance was evident from the statements of certain union leaders. Supposing that unions refused to pay civil damages, were their leaders or members to be sent to prison en masse? What would happen if the unions called a general strike in protest—despite

---

[1] The Conservative proposals covered many other aspects of industrial relations, as Heath made clear in a speech to the Conservative Trade Unionists' annual conference on 4th April 1970.

the fact that a newly elected Conservative Government had received an electoral mandate for the proposed legislation? Undoubtedly the British democratic system could be severely strained.

Sir Alec, rightly, had paid much attention to meeting and speaking to young people, believing that the Conservative policy emphasizing the individual and the need to give scope to personality would appeal to them. But the Party had often forfeited the support of the young because they had talked loftily—and often confusingly—in terms of money and millions, and had scarcely touched young people's real problems or sparked their idealism. What British electors, old and young, needed 'in the complexities of modern politics' was a 'simple clear lead', wrote Sir Alec, more especially the town-dwellers and the industrial masses for, in the opinion of many Conservatives, people who lived close to nature were natural Conservatives who might think slowly but often got closer to the true values of life.

Sir Alec in his 'testament' reflected on his own position: 'I took on the job of Prime Minister,' he wrote, 'because throughout my political career I have done what I have been asked to do when I thought it my duty.' He became Prime Minister 'with many misgivings' but with one certainty: 'That if the Conservative Party allowed itself to be split and weakened, the Socialist would be "in" for long enough to do the country serious damage here and abroad.' His foreboding was to be amply justified.

But, Prime Minister or not, Sir Alec found the role of weighty prophet too much to bear for long. Like Boswell's friend Oliver Edwards, he might say 'I have tried too in my time to be a philosopher; but, I don't know how, cheerfulness was always breaking in.'

So to Sir Michael Fraser he ended his Prime Minister's 'minute': 'Is this enough and is there enough of "me" in it? Anyway, I am bored with myself for the time being!'

When he could, he took his own advice about 'simple, straightforward talking'. Few Prime Ministers have put the essence of modern, radical Toryism more lucidly and briefly than did Sir Alec, addressing the 'industrial masses' of Leeds on 19th June 1964:

'I have always placed the following ingredients in the forefront of Conservative philosophy and practice:

Work, because man is a creator and discontented if he is idle and because I believe that work at good steady wages is the secret of a happy home.

The home, if possible owned by the individual because that gives him a stake and a pride in his locality and country, but anyhow a home which is modern and well-equipped.

Education, because it is that which guarantees equal opportunity and is the passport to the fuller life.

Value for money, because that matters supremely when you are bringing up a family or when you are old or sick.

Thrift, because that means security.

Service, because that turns affluence into unselfishness and spreads prosperity throughout the whole community.

Such a credo was a clear statement of Conservative 'practice'; it could scarcely be maintained that it expressed Conservative 'philosophy'. Sir Alec was neither a Burke nor a Coleridge. His cast of mind was religious not philosophical, intuitive, practical, a man of principle rather than principles.

20. The Strong Suit: 1963 – 4

Canada's vacillation. President Johnson leaves it to Rusk. Home truths for Robert Kennedy. In Lagos. Ian Smith and the principles. The nuclear future.

Sir Alec generally left his Ministers to get on with their jobs but foreign affairs were traditionally overseen by the Prime Minister. Besides, no one inside or outside Parliament knew more about the field as a whole than he did, and Butler, the Foreign Secretary, was willing, even anxious, to be given a lead.

The Near East was always a bother, with Turks and Greeks at daggers drawn over, and in, Cyprus, which had become an independent Commonwealth country in 1960. Here, in fact, Britain could not lead. It was true that British troops could be drafted in to preserve law and order and pressure brought to bear on a vacillating U Thant to send a U.N. peace-keeping force.

But when the position deteriorated to the point where Turkey threatened to invade Cyprus to protect the Turkish minority, and there was a chance of a Near-Eastern war, Britain took second place:

'The danger was that the Turks, outraged by the treatment of the Turkish Cypriots, would invade,' Sir Alec recalled. 'We used our influence with them.' But he recognized the hard, cold fact: 'We had some influence; but the Americans had much more.' It was American pressure that caused the Turks to hold their hand, just as it was in a similar situation in the autumn of 1967.

Sir Alec at least knew the position and ran rings around the Opposition leader, Wilson, who distinguished himself by demanding that Britain should send to Cyprus her 'heaviest tanks', vehicles totally unsuitable for the terrain or for internal security operations in general.

Far more scope for exercising the cool, rational influence that Douglas-Home had made his *métier* was offered by the United States. In November Sir Alec attended the funeral of the assassinated Kennedy whom, as we saw, he had held in high regard, and in February 1964 set out again for North America. En route to Washington he had brief talks in Canada with Lester Pearson, then Prime Minister, and a personal friend. Sir Alec had sometimes thought that Canadian foreign policy was vacillating, and perhaps sympathetic to neutralism. So long, however, as the Canadians remained in NATO, Britain asked for no more.

Successfully persuasive in private with Pearson, Sir Alec hammered home the point in a striking speech in Toronto on 11th February. Describing how Communism imposed '"paradise" at the gun-point,' and how during the Cuban crisis, 'in a moment of arresting, blinding clarity, men saw that force had no meaning but death,' he emphasized the 'absolute interdependence of all nations'. Then he gave anyone who might be hesitating about the value of the military alliance a strong warning:

'Great prizes can be won if we act together. If we do not, we may not even be alive to collect the prizes. It will be small comfort to them for a few poverty-stricken survivors to apportion blame.' This indeed was 'simple, straight talking'.

His task in the United States was quite different. Two small clouds had appeared on the Anglo-American horizon. But first he had to weigh up the calibre of Kennedy's successor, President Lyndon Johnson, whom he had previously met only briefly. He was in for a surprise.

The President, at this Washington meeting in February 1964, left the discussion of foreign affairs almost entirely to Dean Rusk, the Secretary of State. Johnson was 'very reticent' on the subject. Though Sir Alec found him courteous and hospitable, he judged that his success in the United States (before he was harassed by Vietnam) was due to his 'extraordinary ascendancy' over Congress. His skill, as the Americans testified, was exercised in the field of domestic politics.

Sir Alec, however, raised the question of Cuba, one of the two small clouds. The United States had embargoed trade with the Castro dictatorship; Britain continued to trade and in particular sold 400 Leyland buses to Cuba in January. There were reports of American Government anger. Sir Alec was very polite and totally firm when the Americans sought to dissuade him from the trade. 'If this trade had had any strategic significance,' Sir Alec reflected later, 'we would have thought again, but double-decker buses were neither here nor there. It *was* awkward for the American administration because of their public opinion but they didn't press the objection too hard.'

British policy had generally been against the use of trade sanctions because they were an instrument of war, though they had been half-heartedly applied against Italy in the 1930s.

On television on his return to London Sir Alec insisted that 'nobody of the nature of Castro is brought down by economic sanctions and boycotts . . . At the beginning the impact is not on Castro, the leader, but on the people and, on the whole, people are willing to tighten their belts and back their national leader if they're really made hungry.'[1]

Sir Alec's convictions on sanctions were to be tested in quite another context twenty months later over Rhodesia.

The other cloud was more dragonish. America was giving money and other aid to Soekarno's Indonesia, which had continued to harass the Federation of Malaysia, a sovereign member of the Commonwealth and the United Nations since September 1963. Guerrilla activity was so widespread that in 1964 British and Malaysian forces were involved to the tune of £11 million a week.

At the root of the trouble lay that American anti-colonialism which Sir Alec had encountered from Suez onwards. It was as unaffected by the fact that Britain had given independence to Malaya, as by the fact that American anti-colonialism coincided with Leftist ideology end-lessly plugged by the Communist countries.

Sir Alec, however, had done some straight talking on the subject before arriving in Washington. A month before, in January 1964, one of the most violent anti-colonialists in the U.S. Government, Robert Kennedy, visited Britain.[2] Sir Alec invited him to Chequers.

'He started out,' Sir Alec recalled, 'with some ideas about Indonesia which I thought it well to correct. He shared with many Americans a strong anti-colonial feeling.' Kennedy was one of the Americans who had been vociferous against the colonialism of Britain and France. 'America had been very impatient with the Dutch in Indonesia and there was a good deal of sympathy with Soekarno.' It was right that Robert Kennedy should understand the reasons why Britain was fighting to defend Malaya, reasons he had not understood. He left London on his way to Indonesia with the knowledge that 'Britain's sole purpose was to safeguard the right to self-determination and inde-

[1] B.B.C. television, 17th February 1964.

[2] Robert Kennedy was assassinated on 6th June 1968.

pendence. Robert Kennedy's point of view was, I believe, influenced by his visit to London.'

His brother, President Kennedy, had been much more understanding on this issue. When it suited American interests, as in British Guiana, they pressed Britain to *stay* in possession. But it was different when the colonial problem was further away. Then the United States pressed Britain to get out, almost at any cost. One of the reasons was not far to seek. As long as the Americans went on condemning Britain for colonialism they had some chance of keeping the coloured population of the United States on their side.

Sir Alec's 'influence' on the American administration was unmistakable. At the end of his talks with Johnson on 12th–13th February, a joint communiqué was issued. On the whole it was banal and sidestepping. There was no pat on the back from the President such as Macmillan received from Eisenhower before the 1959 election; 'he was right not to do it because we were approaching a General Election,' Sir Alec reflected.

There was, however, one innocuous-seeming sentence in the communiqué which gave Sir Alec particular pleasure: 'The President reaffirmed the support of the United States for the peaceful national independence of Malaysia.' The point had been publicly made.

Africa remained an ever-present source of trouble. Without hesitation, Sir Alec as Prime Minister sent British troops to put down insurrections against the newly independent Commonwealth governments of Tanganyika and Uganda. There was constant fighting in the Yemen, where Egyptian troops and tribesmen were 'now equipped with mortars and radio and automatic weapons from a foreign source', Sir Alec told Socialist questioners in the Commons on 4th May. Sorties of various kinds were carried out successfully and with the minimum of force.

It did not take Sir Alec long to see into the heart of a situation and then to take speedy action. With his habitual modesty he later commented: 'Duncan Sandys at the C.R.O. was a great help. He is a man of decision and it made it much easier having him there to execute these operations.'

He did not doubt, he told a television interviewer on 20th February, that in East Africa 'there are a lot of people who are trained in Communist techniques in Moscow and China, and there are plenty of them around in the continent of Africa generally. Mr Chou En Lai said when he left Africa the other day that "the prospects for revolution in Africa are excellent"—he said it apparently with some satisfaction. There are Communist-trained agents right through Africa . . .'

Nigeria seemed an exception. For Sir Abubakar Tafawa Balewa, Federal Prime Minister of the Nigerian republic, Sir Alec had great respect: 'He was a very fine man, much the greatest of the African statesmen. He was one of the very few people who could in the early days have held that Federation together. A fine personality.'

Fulfilling a promise to visit Lagos, Sir Alec spoke in the Nigerian Parliament on 18th March. Nigeria, he told the Federal M.P.s, had achieved freedom and order with 'impressive speed: others have not been so fortunate—or so wise.' In Britain, he said, 'we believe that the Commonwealth has scope for growth—and I have come here to say so.' Twenty-two months later Sir Abubakar was assassinated, and Nigeria collapsed into a four-year civil war.

But for the British Prime Minister in 1964, not Nigeria but Rhodesia was the shoe that pinched. The Central African Federation had been broken up at the Victoria Falls Conference, conducted by Butler, in June 1963, when it was arranged that independence should be given to Nyasaland and Northern Rhodesia [1] but not to Southern Rhodesia.

It was a fatal mistake and foreshadowed things to come. There is little doubt that independence could have been given in June 1963, with the minimum of fuss; there would have been some Leftist shouting but it would soon have died away.[2] The trouble was, as Sir Roy Welensky put it, that 'Harold Macmillan was then in the process of completing the task Lord North had started with the American colonies—the liquidation of the British Empire.'[3]

Sir Roy Welensky, in London in December 1964, to take his leave of the Queen, lunched with Sir Alec at No. 10: 'I made it very clear to both him and Duncan Sandys that I had no doubt Rhodesia would move on to take U.D.I.'[1]

In January 1964 the late Winston Field, Southern Rhodesian Prime Minister, visited Sir Alec to begin negotiations for independence on the basis of the 1961-2 Constitution. Sir Alec saw the issue as a question of the 'pace' at which the franchise could be extended to larger num-

[1] They became independent as, respectively, Malawi on 6th July 1964, and Zambia on 24th October.
[2] See Kenneth Young, *Rhodesia and Independence*, London, 2nd edition, 1969.
[3] Sir Roy Welensky to the author.

199

bers of Rhodesian Africans, a point made in his paper on the colonies.[1]
There was no virtue in throwing the franchise open to great masses
of illiterate Africans, still living on the reservations under the tribal
system and occupied with subsistence-growing of food.

One of the answers, it seemed to him, was to increase African education. He offered Field some suggestions on possible British financial
aid for a big new educational programme and for African economic
advancement. About detailed franchise changes which Field discussed
with Sandys, Secretary of State for Commonwealth and Colonies, there
was deadlock.

Sir Alec's talks were 'basically inconclusive except that Field agreed
on education—to explore it, and we were going to put our civil servants
to work to get out a plan, particularly for secondary education. I've
never had doubt at all that we should have got agreement with Field.'

In April, however, Field was pushed out of the Premiership and his
place taken by his deputy, Ian Douglas Smith. For a time it seemed that
the new leadership might unilaterally announce the country's independence. This did not happen but African extremists began a reign
of terror in the townships.

In May Smith took up the negotiations with Sir Alec where Field
had left them. In July Rhodesia monopolized the Commonwealth
Prime Ministers' conference in London, although its Prime Minister
was not invited and it was contrary to precedent that the internal
affairs of a member country should be discussed in its absence. The
position was preserved with the strong assistance of Sir Robert Menzies
—that this was a British affair and therefore not something the 'Commonwealth P.M.s could order the British Government to do,' Sir Alec
remembered.

'We established this principle but it was very hard going.' There
were some sessions with rough talking from Ghana and from most of
the African countries, particularly Sierra Leone, led by Sir Albert
Margai, now exiled in Britain.

It was Menzies long afterwards who gave credit where credit was
due: Sir Alec, he wrote, 'presided with admirable firmness, great tact
and almost unbelievable patience . . . a wise and great man.'[2]

Although Sir Alec had not invited Smith to the Commonwealth
Conference, he suggested he should come for private talks: 'It is so

[1] See p. 108 above.
[2] *Afternoon Light,* pp. 220 and 227.

much easier to express oneself freely in conversation than in official communications', he wrote on 31st July, 'which, without the personal contact, can so easily lead to unfortunate misunderstandings.' If, however, the Rhodesian Prime Minister preferred to wait until after the British General Election in October, he would understand.[1] After some hesitation, Smith arrived at No. 10 early in September.[2]

Though Smith had been in London the previous year, Sir Alec had never met him except possibly, he thought, at a reception in Salisbury during his visits as Commonwealth Secretary. He seems to have liked him as a man, but Smith was a tough negotiator, refusing to be hurried or to sign more than a few sentences of a detailed paper at a time.

Smith, as others realized, was a countryman, his father a very small smallholder, and he lived close to the land. He had the countryman's suspicions of the civil servant and the big city, though he matured and acquired a shrewd knowledge of how to deal with people.

The September talks were, Sir Alec reflected, 'a holding operation with Smith. They couldn't be anything else because of our election in October. At that time nothing could be settled.'

Nevertheless the meeting was historic because the celebrated 'five principles' were enunciated. Contrary, however, to accepted belief these principles, later to prove to be giant stumbling-blocks, were *not* insisted upon by the British Government, who were in fact reluctant to commit them to paper, regarding them merely as a working agenda. Smith, however, had 'no sort of objection to them'.

Sir Alec himself disliked making an independence dependent upon its acceptance by a majority of the people.[3] He sensed that agreement would be hard-going. Nevertheless he has always believed he could have come to terms with Smith and, as we shall see, condemned the straits to which the Socialists were to reduce British relations with Rhodesia.

The last Premier-to-Premier rencontre of Ian Douglas Smith and

[1] Southern Rhodesia: Documents relating to the negotiations between the United Kingdom and Southern Rhodesian Governments, November 1963–November 1965 (H.M.S.O. Cmnd. 2807).

[2] A full account is given in *Rhodesia and Independence*, pp. 146–162. See note, p. 199 above.

[3] The Principles were not publicly stated until announced by the Labour Government on 21st September 1965. The fifth principle read: 'The British Government would need to be satisfied that any basis proposed for independence was acceptable to the people of Rhodesia as a whole.'

Alec Douglas-Home—two dissimilar Scots as could be found—had a smack of farce. On the very eve of the British General Election Smith telegraphed a message to Sir Alec about the testing of Rhodesian African opinion by means of an *indaba* (decision-taking meeting) of Chiefs and headmen. It was abruptly and immediately turned down. Smith afterwards said he had not intended the message to arrive until next day when the identity of the new Prime Minister would be known. Even so, it was the wrong time to try to carry on a technical negotiation: 'It was an idiotic thing to do,' Sir Alec reflected. Rhodesia, of course, was inexperienced in conducting foreign affairs; she would learn in the hard school of experience over the next five years.

Foreign affairs and defence matters, Sir Alec's strong suit, were the Labour Party's Achilles heel, mainly because a minority of the Party, wittingly or unwittingly, followed dogmatically the Russian Communist Party line. During June 1964 the Socialists learned that the Spanish Government were about to conclude contracts with British firms for the supply of frigates for the Spanish Navy. Even though the Spanish civil war had ended a quarter of a century before, 'Fascist' Spain was enshrined in Socialist dogma as a target for insult, and Wilson chose to attack Franco and his Government and indeed Spaniards at large.

The contract negotiations were broken off as an act of 'political prudence' by the Spanish, fearing no doubt that even if the contracts were signed a Labour Government would dishonour them. The order, worth £11 million—and possible future orders—was lost. Sir Alec who, as we saw, wished to bring Spain into NATO, condemned the Socialist intervention:

'Their attitude to the order from Spain is totally irresponsible. Here is a country which for the first time for years is anxious to buy British. A most valuable contract, worth a great deal in foreign exchange and in jobs, is about to be finalized. . . .Then in comes the British Socialist Party and deliberately wrecks the deal. They will do it again and again, for there are many countries in the world whose governments they do not approve.

'Can three-quarters of a million British citizens go to Spain for holidays by their own choice and yet Britain be denied the possibility of accepting an order for the Spanish Navy? I have always known that the Socialists were too dangerous to allow them to form a government. Now, even as an Opposition they are proving a disaster to the nation.

The only possible decision is to vote these men out of public life where they can do no harm.'

Wilson alleged that Sir Alec wanted General Franco as his running-mate in the Election, and that the affair was 'a put-up job for election-eering purposes.' In any case, he added, the Government had vetoed deals for supplying merchant ships to the Soviet Union.

To these accusations Sir Alec observed: 'Members opposite may have their own standards. We do not act on those standards.' There had been no veto on Russian deals: 'Soviet ships must be a question of an order coming from the Soviet Union. No order has come.' Wilson 'has made a deplorable mistake and he knows it. Opposition members must be feeling extraordinarily guilty.' [1]

On defence matters the Opposition was even wider open to criticism, partly because it was deeply divided and more because of sheer ignor-ance. Their reactions during a defence debate at the end of February were described by Sir Alec with some relish:

'Last week in the House of Commons, asked the simplest questions about their attitude to our nuclear arm, they passed the buck from Mr Brown to Mr Gordon Walker to Mr Healey so fast that they reached Olympic standards.

'They revealed themselves incredibly out of touch with events. Apparently they did not know that the nuclear freeze proposal would not affect existing plans for British or American nuclear weapons—they did not know that if there was a mixed-manned nuclear force it would not involve multilateral control—they did not answer for twenty-four hours when asked whether they would keep American bases for submarines in Scotland—they sat paralysed in hopeless confusion.

'Of course the Headmaster was away but he really ought to have told the prefects and left them their saying lesson.' [2]

Sir Alec's public attitudes on defence were clearly defined. He would *not* give up the nuclear deterrent and rely entirely on the Americans for the defence of the British Isles. He would give Britain's nuclear arm to NATO—on condition that it could be withdrawn. 'Govern-ments cannot gamble with the safety of the country.'

When the Socialists instead of nuclear weapons pressed for an increase in conventional arms and manpower they were caught again: 'If they want that they must say openly that they favour conscription,'

[1] House of Commons, 30th June 1964.
[2] Speech at Newcastle, 2nd March 1964.

Sir Alec told a rally at Bristol on 16th March. Meantime our 'compact trained army, voluntarily recruited' had proved themselves more than adequate for the 'fire-brigade police work' which had been done so efficiently in Africa, Cyprus and the Far East. The price for all forces, nuclear and conventional, was about $7\frac{1}{4}$ per cent of our total national expenditure; and of the defence budget less than 10 per cent was for nuclear armaments.

'The bomb is a deterrent and it has in fact deterred.' And if we abandoned the nuclear arm we should no longer be able to sit at the top table when matters of nuclear policy are discussed between East and West: 'I want to make it quite clear that I am not going to get out of that chair and I will not see it empty,' he said at Bury on 4th February. France and China would certainly get a nuclear deterrent; but they would not 'if I have anything to do with it supplant Britain'.

With the Socialists in office, the nuclear weapons are still there and doubtless for the same reasons that Sir Alec advanced and Wilson rejected with scorn.

But whether Sir Alec's argument—and Wilson's practice—with regard to Britain's nuclear strength would continue to be appropriate throughout the 1970s was doubtful. The time was clearly approaching when, unless reason prevailed, Russia and the United States would proceed to the next stages, the anti-ballistic-missile missile systems, the multiple heads. It would then be impossible, technically and financially, for Britain to maintain a credible deterrent and Sir Alec's argument would fall away. If, however, Britain joined the European community, European finance could make the next stages of nuclear weapons possible, even though only Britain and France possess the technical information, and as far as is known the French lack the knowledge of the delivery system.

Other developments might drive a coach-and-horses through Conservative policies. The Americans showed signs of wishing to withdraw from Europe and it was possible that they and the Russians, drawn together by mutual fear of China, would make an agreement above the heads of Britain and Europe. Britain then might have to take up the leadership of European defence and NATO would be dead. In any case there was always a flaw in Sir Alec's NATO defence argument: would the Americans let themselves be destroyed by the Russians for the sake of Britain or any other country? As in the 1930s, the outcome of a Russian assault on Europe would depend on whether, and at what stage, the Americans joined in.

This question remained unresolved. What, however, was blindingly clear to Sir Alec in 1970 was that NATO'S conventional forces alone could not hold a Russian attack on Europe. With conventional forces only, the Russians could occupy Europe up to the Channel ports. Then the tactical nuclear weapons would have to be used. These weapons could devastate and sterilize a whole belt of country about 400 miles deep so that nothing could live in it—and through which Russian reinforcements could not come except by air. This *cordon insanitaire* would isolate the Russians who had entered Europe during the first wave from their bases. If the Russians calculated that their lines of communication would thus be saturated, Sir Alec was sure that the knowledge would deter.

'It is not to man's credit that the peace is held by a balance of nuclear power but it is the fact of life and paradoxically the hope of life too,' he said at Grantham on 29th November 1963.

Then he bluntly added: 'But when that has been said, we know that if the nuclear deterrent fails to deter, the civilized world is lost.'

21. General Election, 1964

June or October? 'Drown out'. Television nightmare. The Chinese bomb.
Night of doubt. Call from a brother. Farewell to No. 10.

When was the General Election to be? The question was uppermost throughout the first six months of Sir Alec's Premiership and the final say in the matter was his. It turned mainly on another question: when were the Conservatives most likely to win? This was a teaser as much for Sir Alec as for his opponents.

There was little elbow-room. By statute the election must take place at latest on Thursday, 5th November 1964, but British governments traditionally shrank from appearing to cling to the felicities of office to the very last moment. If they did cling, much of their authority at home and abroad vanished.

At the fag-end of 1963 the omens, as we saw, were not propitious and in any case gave no time for Sir Alec to assert himself as leader, and to make his mark with the public. What then of the early spring or at any rate May? Sir Alec's key adviser was Lord Blakenham, chairman of the Party, who relied on detailed reports from the constituencies based on canvassers' census cards. By April he reported that the likely loss had been cut from 100 seats to 50 and his advice overrode Maudling and some others who pressed for a May election.[1]

Halving the loss in six months encouraged Sir Alec and he was sure that the favourable trend would continue. The Government was seen to be governing, the economic position was steady, and constituency Conservatives were rallying to him enthusiastically. Certainly more time was needed but—this was crucial—dare he wait for the autumn?

'I was rather in favour of June because I thought we should win. Things were going well about then. I didn't like the idea of being right

[1] This is Lord Blakenham's approximate figure; Sir Alec—see p. 207 below—recalled him as saying between 30 and 60.

up against the end of the allotted span.' The question of the balance of payments had not come up in June and was not going to do so until later. Sir Alec was very much torn between June and October, though inclined to the former, as was Soames, the Minister of Agriculture. The rest were doubtful. What was decisive was the advice of Lord Blakenham, the Party chairman: he told his leader that at a June election Central Office research showed the Tories would lose by between 30 and 60 seats, while they might just win in October or at any rate the result would be close. 'Still, I had the feeling we might win in June. We wouldn't have been up against what Wilson was able to say later on. If he'd said in June, "we think this balance of payments is going all wrong," I don't think people would have listened. He was able to say more in October and with more conviction.

'But Blakenham was absolutely decisive and he had the evidence of the polls; Central Office research was certain we would have lost by 30–60.'

Blakenham did not guarantee success even in October. In his opinion, the matter was 'marginal': the Tories *might* win and if they did by something between ten and twenty seats.[1]

If it was not to be early summer, then the holiday months made it impossible before the autumn and Sir Alec said so publicly on 9th April: 'In order to remove the present uncertainty about the date of the General Election the Prime Minister thinks it right to inform the country of his decision not to ask the Queen to dissolve Parliament before the autumn.' The actual date was not given nor even decided.

Most Tory M.P.s were unfeignedly relieved, and when heavy Labour gains were made at the G.L.C., county council and borough elections, the postponement seemed thoroughly justified. Correspondingly, the frustrated Socialists waxed furious, just as in turn did Conservatives in 1970.

On one aspect of the franchise, Sir Alec was adamant. Four by-elections were pending in the spring and Central Office advised postponement; others thought it pointless and expensive to elect four M.P.s for a few weeks only. Some younger Cabinet Ministers, however, wanted the by-elections to be held so as to rally confidence among Party workers; and also they resented advice from Lord Blakenham and Central Office.

'I thought we must do it, independently of what young Ministers

[1] Viscount Blakenham to the author.

may have said,' Sir Alec remembered. 'You can't keep people disfranchised for six months—at least you oughtn't to. I was told there was a considerable risk at Devizes and I said we can't help that: we must hold this election.'

Perhaps, too, Sir Alec wanted to test his hunch about June being a favourable month. From the results he could take some satisfaction, but more confusion. Rutherglen was lost; Bury St Edmunds and Winchester were held, though with much reduced Conservative majorities. Devizes, however, despite Labour hopes, remained Tory. On the other hand, the two June by-elections, at Liverpool Scotland and Faversham, were less favourable to Tory hopes. All the same the by-elections taken as a whole clearly demonstrated that the country was far from being decisively Socialist-inclined, despite twelve years of 'the old gang'. The battle could still be won. Blakenham's advice to wait had been vindicated.

Not all went well. Sir Alec had to move in as pacifier when there was trouble with the National Farmers' Union over the support price review. His tact won the farmers over. There was, however, little he could do when the Public Accounts Committee stated that excess profits of some £4m. had been paid to Ferranti Ltd, for its work on the Bloodhound missile. Although the firm agreed to repay part of the sum, Julian Amery, the Aviation Minister, had rough treatment in the Commons: 'One of those extras,' Sir Alec later commented, 'which one didn't want at that time.'

There was uproar, too, when it became known that the new military aircraft, the British TSR2, was suffering technical difficulties and its costs were soaring. Wilson denied that the Socialists would cancel the Government order (he did so later). 'It was a fine aircraft,' Sir Alec reflected, 'tremendously good. We would give a lot to have it now.'

Strikes harassed industry, particularly a big one at the Steel Company of Wales in Port Talbot, and there were go-slows in the power industry, the Post Office, Independent Television. With them came renewed Conservative calls for trade union reform, and the Government promised an inquiry—after the Election: 'I didn't think it was a thing we could tackle in those short nine months,' Sir Alec remembered. In fact all Ministers of Labour—Conservatives as much as the rest—had always been strongly against tackling the trade unions on this subject, though it was later adopted as prime policy by the Conservatives in Opposition.

The Government gave way to wage demands. After the Post Office had been granted a 6½ per cent increase in wages, the flood-gates were open. Electricity workers and busmen got rises above the 3½ per cent of the 'guiding light', and 'by the summer of 1964 top officials no longer bothered to pretend that an incomes policy existed.'[1] History repeated itself with placid monotony six years later.

The depredations of an unscrupulous landlord, Peter Rachman, highlighted the question of the prices of land for building. In the Cabinet, some Ministers pressed for the Government to declare that it would impose a betterment tax on development land. Nothing was done, the Conservative Manifesto rather feebly remarking that 'in considering any further measure to tax land transactions, the test must be that it should not adversely affect the price or supply of land'.

The problem was not easily susceptible of solution; but there were many who complained of the lack of firm proposals. 'There may have been a trick missed there,' Sir Alec reflected later. 'We said clearly that we would try to deal with the speculator. But, on the other hand, to have clamped down on everything would have had a very adverse effect on development.'

Despite all this, the Conservative Party steadily overhauled the Labour lead, and by September some opinion polls were showing the Tories actually in front by 2·9 per cent. It was Sir Alec, the anti-Government *Sunday Times* admitted, who had 'transformed morale and unity, and revitalized the fighting élan of the Conservatives' by his own simple honesty, sincerity and integrity. He had come near to 'Baldwin's "you can trust me" posture of thirty or forty years ago, without gimmicks, flamboyance or theatrical props.'[2]

The polls, however, also showed Wilson some 20 per cent in advance of Sir Alec in popularity. There would be no easy victory.

Sir Alec gave a clear thirty days' warning of the date of the election, announcing on 15th September that Parliament would be dissolved ten days later and that polling would take place on Thursday, 15th October. On Central Office advice—which he later questioned—he was to continue his round-the-country addresses and add to them whistle-stop tours, where he would speak for five or ten minutes on village greens, at street corners and shopping centres.

[1] Samuel Brittan, *The Treasury under the Tories, 1951–64*, London, 1965.

[2] *Sunday Times* editorial, 13th September 1964. Baldwin's posture was not 'thirty or forty years ago'; it was thirty.

At these scampering visits, as Central Office knew, Sir Alec excelled; his personality delighted his hearers, and even in the remoter villages he had good audiences. His success was undeniable for, as one reporter wrote: 'His speeches, lacking wit and short on verbs and full stops, convey the impression of honesty, sincerity and patriotism . . . He is fit and full of beans and is bounding round the country with not a visible care in the world.'[1]

He made some palpable hits about the Socialist Manifesto being a 'menu without prices'; and when Wilson talked of needing a 'hundred days' to get the nation right, he cracked back that a 'pep pill a hundred years old' (i.e. Marxist-Socialism) was more likely to kill than cure.

But his schedule was immensely tiring, which sometimes resulted in unfortunate slips of the tongue; once he talked of 'donations' when he meant pensions and spoke enthusiastically of the installation of 'imputers' rather than computers. Once he 'knighted' a Cabinet colleague, Geoffrey Rippon; and occasionally when commending a Tory candidate clapped the wrong man on the shoulder.

At a noisy meeting in Leeds he shouted at youthful hecklers, seeking to drown his speech, that 'the Labour Party must be very hard up if they have to hire this kind of people . . .' This caused, he well remembered, a 'bloody awful row. I did say they were hired—it was a slip of the tongue.' Perhaps he was not really far wrong: 'rentacrowd', even though not hired by Labour Party officials, were out in force during the Election and had perfected the 'drowning out' method of silencing speakers, common on the Continent between the wars.

The rowdyism reached its height at a meeting in the huge Rag Market hall in Birmingham on 8th October. It had serious results for the Tory party: 'Blakenham said the campaign went wrong after that,' Sir Alec recalled. 'Up till then he thought we were winning. After that the advantage began to slide away.'

The affair began quite humorously. When Sir Alec approached the hall, he saw a twenty-yard 'monster', manned by fifty people covered with a cloth painted to represent a dinosaur. Its face was Sir Alec's own, and it wore his half-moon spectacles. The label read: 'Too much armour, too little brain, now extinct.'

What happened in the hall was less amusing. Here the hand of rentacrowd was visible for all to see. As soon as the Prime Minister started his speech, bellowing, screaming, stamping broke out and the

[1] George Gale, *Daily Express*, 1st October 1964.

concerted shouting of slogans: 'Tories out! Home go Home.' Neither chairman nor stewards could quieten them. Sir Alec never once stopped speaking but few heard more than a stray sentence here and there.

'With 10,000 [1] yelling their heads off in an open space, I was left in front of the microphone, in front of the nation since it was televised, absolutely and totally unable to make oneself heard, looking strained and so on. The Labour party took the cue: they reproduced this wherever I spoke in the open air. Produced the din right under the microphone so loud you couldn't hear what you were saying.

'I never knew before that you had to be able to hear what you were saying to make sense.' The result was that Sir Alec was seen to be straining to hear while Wilson by contrast was always seen before a nice tame audience when deploying a case. He always seemed in control while Sir Alec was shown on the defensive, with his audience in turmoil.

When at the end he left the platform, he had to fight his way up the aisle. Blakenham thought the Birmingham affair was the turn of the tide, convincing electors that Sir Alec was losing, though in the upshot the tide did not turn very far.

It was a question whether Sir Alec should have spent so much time at large public meetings instead of being presented 'cosily'. Lord Blakenham, though admitting that the meeting got out of hand and affected his own confidence, believes that the tours were essentially right. It was important to let as many people as possible see 'the faceless Earl; and in fact the way Sir Alec got himself across to people was staggering'.[2]

It was not only Sir Alec and Lord Blakenham who recognized that what they faced in Birmingham and elsewhere was an organized attempt to prevent their being heard at all. The Tory M.P. Chataway was reminded of the chants of 'Jews out' in Nazi Germany. He spoke of the 'frightening element of mob rule in the unilateralists and fellow-travelling Left,' and added that it was with their support that Wilson had opposed Gaitskell and later won the leadership of the Labour party.[3] Quintin Hogg spoke of it as 'a deliberate conspiracy'.

By the time of the Birmingham 'conspiracy', however, other things

[1] The police estimated the crowd at 5,500 of whom 1,500 were anti-Tory. The Conservatives had reserved only 1,000 seats for their supporters.

[2] Viscount Blakenham to the author.

[3] Reported in the *Daily Express*, 10th October 1964.

had gone wrong. Despite the Treasury forecast, in August Sir Alec found it necessary to caution the nation that prosperity and full employment would disappear if prices were not kept down and export sales not kept up.[1] In short, the boom was slowing down; the growth of the economy was reduced to 4 per cent or less.

The situation was not altogether unexpected and would have occasioned little comment had it not been for the imminence of a General Election. There was a deficit of £73 million in the April–June figures, partly caused by a large, non-recurrent factor, ICI's purchase of the Montecatini works in Italy; and in any case the overseas account was rising.

Sir Alec and Maudling agreed that the way to deal with the deficit was by borrowing from the International Monetary Fund, and Sir Alec insisted that the matter should be announced publicly. He also insisted that the Treasury and foreign bank borrowing figures (suppressed after June 1966) should be published throughout the run-up to the election.

Though in reality there was no crisis, half the deficit being accounted for by foreign assets, the temptation was too great for some of the Socialist leaders to resist, particularly as on 29th September the *Daily Mail* 'National Opinion Poll' claimed that the Conservatives would win by 80 seats, their lead having risen to 2·9 per cent. Wilson accused Sir Alec of 'fatuous deception . . . twisted talk . . . crawling to the Americans'. He had 'been deliberately misleading the British public for electioneering reasons', and he compared the Prime Minister with John Bloom, the washing-machine magnate, who had run into financial difficulties earlier in the year.

Some of Wilson's followers, including Callaghan, the Shadow Chancellor of the Exchequer, were not happy about the exaggerations of their leader. They feared that such alarmist talk would threaten sterling; and the biographers of Wilson's election clearly state: 'The drain of British gold reserves really began from the time of the speech in which Wilson exposed the desperate plight of the economy.'[2] At Glasgow on 5th October Sir Alec said: 'They have staked everything on a desperate bid to talk the nation into financial crisis.'

But the damage was done and by 7th October the 2·9 per cent Tory lead of a week before had dropped to 0·9 per cent—and the stock-market had its worst day for two years.

[1] Speech at Aberfeldy, Perthshire, 22nd August 1964.
[2] Howard and West, p. 176, see note, p. 173 above.

The last ten days of the election campaign were not a happy time for Sir Alec. Out and about during the day, he generally found himself towards 6 p.m. in some hotel suite making ready for the evening's major speech. Though weary, he preserved his habitual calm, usually eating a little fish in his room before the speech, with whisky and sandwiches afterwards. Lady Douglas-Home and his small secretariat strove, generally successfully, to preserve a small oasis of peace around him and he never lost his ability to go to bed, to forget politics and to sleep.

Public speaking did not worry him much but television appearances did. He knew he was not a born television performer: 'If I had that time over again,' he thought later, 'I should have practised television assiduously or insisted on question and answer, which came naturally to me.'

Partly because of bone structure and taut facial skin, Central Office knew that he was difficult to present, and suspected that some television producers did not try very hard. So Norman Collins, a distinguished expert and director of A.T.V., was brought in to advise on the Party's television affairs and particularly on the presentation of the Prime Minister.

Collins's main problem was Sir Alec himself. Solo talks into the camera were Sir Alec's *bête noire*: 'I hated it. It was a burden all the time.' Sir Alec was not good at memorizing a speech, and the teleprompter was thought a too complicated aid to be mastered at short notice.

The television nightmare became most lurid on 11th October, the Sunday before polling day. He was to pre-record a fifteen-minute talk to be transmitted two days later as the final Conservative appeal to the nation.

It became obvious that, fatigued by the campaign, he could not memorize his lines. So small sections were recorded separately—again and again until the professionals were satisfied. The process continued on the day of the broadcast itself. Finally the separate pieces were stitched together. The result, though cogent, lacked spirit.

The Tories and television in general were not natural allies. It was not only that much of the B.B.C.'s news and current affairs output caused complaint on grounds of bias but that the B.B.C. had begun a series of programmes whose effect was to make a laughing stock both of the Government (with an occasional jibe at a Right-wing Socialist to 'keep the balance') and of those values for which the Conservatives had always stood: God, Queen and country and the civilized decencies. In addition, there were such B.B.C. serials as 'Swizzlewick' which showed Conservative local councillors as pompous, arrogant and corrupt.

Sir Alec recalled that there was a 'terrible lot of that sort of stuff to contend with. It became fashionable, and was called "satire"; it was a cult for two or three years which happened to overlap this period. I saw one or two of the programmes. I don't think they worried me very much. The only worry was the effect they might have on the public outside. I think they probably *did* have an effect, and it was nasty.'

'Considerable damage' was done to the Tories, he thought, by the Hardy Spicer affair, which began with a Wilson gaffe but was turned against the Government when the firm, then on strike, issued a writ against Wilson, thus making the case *sub judice*.

During the last few days of the campaigning, some of Sir Alec's colleagues said things he would have preferred them to avoid. Quintin Hogg, in a moment of exasperation after repeated heckling on the subject of Profumo, shouted back: 'If you can tell me there are no adulterers on the Front Bench of the Labour Party you can talk to me about Profumo. If you cannot tell me that, you had better not dabble your fingers in filth.'

This caused a sensation—though not all newspapers reported it—because rumours about the private lives of leading politicians of both parties had continued to circulate even after the Denning report. But Sir Alec did not believe that when the electors actually came to put their cross on the paper they were influenced by this.

But Sir Alec remembered vividly, 'it was nothing to the effect that Rab's interview with George Gale had!' Butler, though not prominent in the electioneering, had observed to Gale, the *Daily Express* reporter, that the election was neck-and-neck and 'things might start slipping in the last few days . . . They won't slip towards us.' Sir Alec, he conceded, had done very well but possibly had spent too much time out of London. Butler added that he thought Sir Alec was a 'bit bored' by Heath—'not as a Minister of course.'[1] These were vintage Butlerisms, typical, as Gale noted, of that 'most marvellous and most devious man'. But the suggestion coming from the Tory Foreign Secretary that things would not 'slip' in favour of the Tories was hardly bracing.

[1] *Daily Express*, 9th October 1964.

Sir Alec continued his whistle-stop tours up to the very end of the campaign; one trip to Chelmsford and East Anglia, decided on at the last moment, probably turned the scales at Maldon, Lord Blakenham thought. At Chelmsford Sir Alec said prophetically: 'Every time there has been a Labour Government in Britain, it has ended in financial and economic disaster. And it would happen again, if they got the chance . . . The Conservatives would eventually get back and clear up the mess. It would take a long time, but we would eventually do it.'

The Prime Minister's last bout of electioneering was in his own constituency in Scotland. Weary but far from downcast, he returned to London by plane in the early evening of polling day, Thursday 15th October.

A message awaited him at the airport. News had just come in that the Chinese had exploded their first atomic bomb. Though he regretted the fact, he also regretted that it had not been announced the day before since it would have driven home what he had so often said about the necessity of Britain's keeping her nuclear deterrent.

Back in Downing Street, Sir Alec, jaunty and smiling, was cheered by a small crowd of sightseers. Inside No. 10, family, friends and a few Ministers with London constituencies came and went as drinks were served and the television began to tick out the results.

It was soon clear that victory—if victory it was to be—would be by a narrow margin. At midnight, with the result still inconclusive, Sir Alec retired but returned in a dressing-gown. No one yet believed a defeat was inevitable.

Next morning, Friday 16th October, he woke early and as usual worked on his boxes from 7 to 8—'it's amazing how much paper you can get through at that time in the morning'—and breakfasted at 8.30. The morning newspapers were still uncertain, though most forecast a small Socialist majority.

Wilson, however, returning on the train from Liverpool, was gloomily foreseeing a narrow defeat. But during the morning Brighton Kemptown went to Labour—the first-ever Socialist win in Sussex—and South East Derbyshire was lost by 873. Even so the Socialists still lacked a majority over Tories plus Liberals.

It was, however, obvious that a precipitate departure from No. 10 might be necessary in the early afternoon and Sir Alec's staff, under his wife's direction, began to make the arrangements. Where, for example, if Wilson won, were Sir Alec and his wife to sleep that night? Although the ex-14th Earl had two houses and 50,000 acres in Scotland, he had no corner of London to call his own. An hotel would lack the privacy required for the appropriate licking of wounds. Might it be possible for him to spend the night at Chequers? The custodian of the Prime Minister's official country house, Mrs Hill, was telephoned and recalled a precedent: Winston Churchill had spent a few days there after his defeat in 1945. But the incoming Prime Minister's agreement must be obtained. In the afternoon, Wilson was tracked down to Transport House. He agreed.

During the morning, though defeat was not yet absolutely certain, offers of temporary accommodation flowed in from many friends and sympathizers, among them Hugh Wontner, chairman of a hotel group, who invited Sir Alec to occupy a penthouse at Claridges; the offer was provisionally accepted for the following Monday.

Before lunch too one of the private secretaries was instructed to arrange an audience with the Queen, on the same provisional basis. The time was fixed for 3.30 p.m.

A car hire firm was telephoned. Another irony of the situation was that although a retiring Prime Minister goes to take his leave of the Queen in an official car, he has to provide his own transport back from the Palace.

At 12.30 p.m. Sir Alec, still Prime Minister and spruce as ever, held a brief, final meeting of Ministers in the Cabinet room. When it was over, some of the Ministers walked upstairs for drinks in the drawing-room where staff and family—including Sir Alec's daughter, Diana Wolfe-Murray with her baby—still gazed gloomily at the television screen.

The atmosphere of a bedside vigil was strong: as the minutes ticked on, Sir Alec's year of supreme power was visibly ebbing away and would soon breathe its last. Some of those present were near to tears. Suddenly the tension broke. Sir Alec, watching the television screen where the inimitable George Brown was engaged in an altercation with an interviewer, burst out laughing.

A hurried lunch was eaten and the family returned to the drawing-room. The telephone rang and rang again. The calls were headed off by Lady Douglas-Home and the secretaries. But one was put through to Sir Alec. His brother William was on the line with a hot tip for the 3.30. Knowledgeable racing talk followed; Sir Alec, cool to the last, had already studied the form for the day.

The *coup de grâce* came shortly after lunch. At 2.45, television reported that Labour had won the crucial marginal seat of Meriden after a re-count. The Socialists were now only one seat away from an absolute majority; and at 2.48 they held Brecon and Radnor. It was all over. Sir Alec had lost.

In the drawing-room of No. 10 there was an awkward pause. The audience with the Queen had been arranged for 3.30: could it be advanced? It could not: a call to the Palace revealed that the Queen was somewhere in the grounds, walking with her dogs. Sir Alec went upstairs and changed into morning suit with tails and top-hat.

Outside in Downing Street cameramen and a small crowd waited. As the minutes passed, there was speculation whether in view of the closeness of the result, Sir Alec would challenge it, perhaps insist on putting the matter to the test of the Commons and, when defeated there, call another Election.

At 3.20, however, Sir Alec emerged unsmiling from the front door of No. 10 and, with his private detective, was swept off to see the Queen. Leave-taking over, the hired car bore him to Central Office, where he made an off-the-cuff television recording of farewell and a speech of thanks to the staff.

Shortly after 4 p.m. he was back at No. 10. Family, friends and a few Ministers had now retreated to the flat at the top of the building where tea and sympathy were being dispensed. The family hastily packed week-end bags—the rest of their belongings would be removed on Monday and Tuesday. The small office inhabited by Sir Alec's two Party secretaries was cleared, except for the 'Vote Conservative' posters to which a few more were added to welcome the Labour victors.

Suddenly a tremendous roar arose from the crowd in the street below: the Wilsons had arrived to invest the citadel they had won. It was 4.30. The party upstairs were trapped in what had so swiftly become someone else's home. Hastily they bundled into the lift, shot down to the basement and left through the garden.

There was no handover. Wilson and Sir Alec did not meet. The ex-Prime Minister simply scribbled a note and left it with the Principal Private Secretary. The envelope was addressed to 'The Prime Minister'. With it was the key to his despatch box.

The tumult and the shouting die. At 5.15 p.m., as darkness fell, the ex-Prime Minister and his wife, both wearing tweed suits, emerged alone from the garden gate at the back of No. 10. A few photographers' bulbs flashed. The hired car, waiting on Horse Guards Parade, drew up, the couple entered, and disappeared into the night.

So ended the great adventure, begun one night in a Blackpool hotel room little over a year before with the words, 'If you get into a terrible jam what I will do, and nothing else, is to go and see my doctor and see if I'd be fit.'

'The results were damned close,' Sir Alec reflected five years later. 'A few hundred votes redistributed and we would have been in. It was touch-and-go.' It was estimated that if 900 people in eight constituencies had voted Tory instead of Labour, or had simply abstained, Sir Alec would still have been in No. 10. The final results were: Labour 317, Conservative 304 (including the Speaker), and Liberals nine. The overall Labour majority was four.

Many Tories had expected a far bigger defeat, and after the catastrophic rout by almost 100 seats eighteen months later in March 1966, concluded that decisive defeat had only been postponed in 1964. Many believed that the man who had postponed it was Sir Alec Douglas-Home. His essential sincerity and decency had got through to the public at a moment when no other qualities would have done—neither the calculation of Macmillan nor the obvious professionalism of most of Sir Alec's colleagues.

So close was the result that it was impossible to isolate any single factor that might have turned the scale: if Macleod and Powell had not defected; if Sir Alec had not espoused the abolition of resale price maintenance; if there had been no economic downturn; if some Cabinet colleagues had exerted themselves more whole-heartedly—such were *post propter hoc* rationalizations. And too it might be said that the Tory Party lacked a slogan to fit the public mood: 'Keep Prosperity with the Conservatives' was not in the same class as Labour's '13 wasted years'.

A few Tories thought that Sir Alec himself had been a liability: his speeches lacked magic, he was not an economist (which by some sleight of hand Wilson had convinced them a Prime Minister must be), and perhaps he was not ambitious enough.

From Chequers on the Saturday after the Tory defeat, Sir Alec wrote to his friend Masterman: 'I think that the thirteen years was just too much and the public were a bit bored with both the parties who had claimed the centre of the stage for so long and, being the Government, we got the worst of it.'[1]

Or, as he succinctly put it five years later: 'People get stale, Ministers get stale and people get bored.'

Even supposing, however, that the Tories had won: 'it would have been by about ten I would guess,' Sir Alec reflected. 'We would have probably lasted a year or eighteen months, and then probably been shot out again, depending how the luck had run.

'An awful lot would have depended on the economy. If the Treasury forecast had come off and there'd been a real recovery, the deficit well cut by April 1965, this would have made a great difference to the future. But it is an "if".'

In his political 'testament' ten months earlier he had written: 'In life I have always thought it best to cut a loss quickly and look for the next chance.' To recriminate was pointless. Tomorrow was another day. To Sir Michael Fraser, head of the Conservative Research Department and soon to be appointed by Sir Alec as deputy Chairman of the Party and Secretary to his newly formed Shadow Cabinet, he wrote on that Saturday at Chequers:

'I marvel at the skill and resourcefulness with which you handled the months of preparation and the election campaign itself and I send you my warmest gratitude for all of it.

'I fear that it put a fearful strain on you but you were never at a loss and always seemed serenely and confidently in command. I do wish that success had crowned your efforts but I think that thirteen years were just too much of a drag.

'Anyhow we live to fight again and whatever may happen about that I would like you to know how much your unfailing help has meant to me.'

But when the thanks were given, the farewells said, the *dies irae* was already on the horizon.

[1] Letter to J. C. Masterman, 17th October 1964.

22. Does a Leader Matter? : October 1964 – July 1965

Opposition disliked. Hitting the Socialists. Du Cann chairman. Party discontent. Depression and decision. Heath acquitted. Not suicide but murder.

Defeat did not depress Sir Alec. In some ways it was a relief after the almost intolerable pressures of electioneering and ordeal by television. Only gradually was depression to steal up on him over the next six months, though when it came it was the worst of his life.

In the days immediately following the Election, there were some simple questions he must ask himself. Since he had been brought in to lead the Party as a stopgap, ought he to remain leader after defeat? Then again, if he withdrew, should he remain in the Commons or go to the Lords, presumably as a life peer?

There would be no dishonour in making a clean break at once. Yet it would be somehow ignominious to turn tail. He had acquired a taste for battle, a battle so nearly won. Moreover with a government so precariously in power, there could be a new election within a very short time. Again, he was determined that before he retired a new, unimpugnable method of choosing the leader should be ready.

He decided to stay and so told an informal meeting of what was to become the 'Consultative Committee', or Shadow Cabinet, which assembled a few days later in the penthouse flat at Claridges, his temporary home. Several of the ex-Ministers were late in arriving: they had not driven cars in London for years and forgot that meantime Brook Street had become one-way only.

Some changes were made. The two dissenters, Macleod and Powell, were forgiven and returned to the fold to deal, respectively, with the threatened steel nationalization and with transport. Sir Alec's two likeliest successors as leader were given nicely balanced advantages: Maudling, as Shadow Chancellor, was made No. 2 in the Shadow Cabinet; and Heath was given a remit to review and reconstitute all

Conservative policies and to set up panels of politicians, businessmen and academics to help him. William Whitelaw replaced Redmayne as Opposition Chief Whip in November 1964. Boyle took on Home Office affairs, Hogg education and science, Boyd-Carpenter housing and land, Keith Joseph social services. It was, observed one experienced political journalist, 'a more formidable and impressive alternative Government than Sir Alec had when he was Prime Minister.'[1]

When the Commons met on 3rd November the ex-Prime Minister was in sprightly form, telling the new Prime Minister that he would do his best to change places with him very soon. As for his thoughts about the new Government, he would not cover the 'whole range because I would be called to order for a filibuster'. However, there were some things he must deplore. The Cabinet, far from being 'streamlined' as promised, numbered twenty-three—no doubt because the Prime Minister had to make so many deals with so many people ('not my words but Mr Wilson's to me'). Then again the new Ministers looked so old—'much, much older than myself and my colleagues in the old Cabinet'. No doubt as in the Army, age and length of service had been the criteria for appointment; no doubt they would also find, as in the Army, that it would be 'first in, first out'.

He was distrustful of the number of unilateral disarmers in the Cabinet. Referring to Gordon Walker's oft-quoted remark that if Wilson became Prime Minister he would be prisoner of the unilateralists, Sir Alec commented that 'he does not seem to have disappointed his gaolers'. Another thing: the Government with its tiny majority had no real mandate to destroy the steel industry as they proposed; on that the Opposition would oppose them tooth and nail. He deplored too the violent language the Government had already begun to use about Rhodesian affairs. They should remember that 'the people of Southern Rhodesia are our own kith and kin and are faced with one of the most desperately difficult problems'.

But then Sir Alec, cast-iron as a statesman, staggered as a politician: 'I want to make it clear that it is not our intention so to exploit the Parliamentary situation that good government is made difficult,' he said.

'That is not the function of an Opposition. We shall judge each proposal as it comes, very strictly on its own merits, and the test we shall apply in every case is whether or not the matter proposed is in the

[1] James Margach, *Sunday Times*, 4th November 1964.

best interests of the nation. Our function will be to see that the programmes we left are, in fact, fulfilled.'

His followers cheered but before long some of them began to ask whether it was not the job of the Opposition at all times to oppose. Soon there were querulous complaints that the leadership was missing chances of harassing so unstable an administration.

'None of us were accustomed to Opposition—we didn't know quite how to handle it,' Sir Alec reflected later. 'It took a bit of settling down.' For Sir Alec it was particularly hard. He had always preferred 'doing things to criticizing others for not doing them'. He never disguised from himself that he did not like Opposition.

In those early weeks, however, it was not Sir Alec who lagged. He sparkled and hit hard. Practically single-handed he forced the Government to retain control over British nuclear forces consigned to NATO. Drily, he congratulated Wilson, who had castigated the British independent nuclear deterrent as neither British, independent nor a deterrent, on keeping the 'non-existing' deterrent, and pointed out that thirty-one unilateralist M.P.s, about to sponsor a C.N.D. march, had also voted for retention: 'Their seats won over their conscience.'

Wilson, reneging on yet another election promise, was referred to as 'the naughtiest neophyte since the '90s,' and when it was reported that at a Chequers meeting scores of mounted police were on guard Sir Alec inquired whether they were 'to prevent the outsiders from getting in, or the insiders from getting out'.

That was fun but Sir Alec struck to hurt—and succeeded—when he referred to the extremists among the Labour M.P.s as 'this craven core at the heart of the political party in power'. Their attempts to strip Britain of her defences were dangerous and their influence 'permeates the Socialist party. Inevitably it will affect their councils and weaken the resolve of leaders who wish to stand firm against the Communist challenge.'

For revenge, the Socialists resorted to the 'drowning out' technique they had used at election meetings. When in February Sir Alec pressed a censure motion on 'the hasty and ill-considered actions of the Government during their first hundred days,' the Commons, one journalist wrote, 'looked less like a debating chamber than a Rugby clubhouse at the climax of a victory celebration by the extra B XV.' [1] Thrice Sir

[1] *The Times*, 2nd February 1965.

Alec demanded the Government's resignation; each time the Socialists, according to one observer, 'wailed like dervishes'.

Tall, almost fragile, the leader whose knees had trembled at the noise when he returned to the Commons eighteen months before, stood his ground, and rushed again and again upon the foe as his Douglas ancestors centuries before hurled themselves at the English. As taxes rose, rates increased and the 'heaviest credit squeeze in history' was imposed, Sir Alec demanded an immediate General Election. The Government had authority neither at home nor abroad:

'This is a discreditable chapter in British politics. It has been one of double-talk and incompetence. The electors were led up the garden path. The chapter must now be closed.'

Whoever lacked aggression on the Opposition Front Bench it was not the leader. Yet it was his chapter, not the Government's, which would shortly be closed.

Sir Alec made some not entirely popular changes in the top Tory team in the early months of 1965. Lord Blakenham resigned as chairman—against Sir Alec's will and under doctors' orders—and both Heath and Selwyn Lloyd were thought likely to replace him. To the surprise of many, Sir Alec chose Edward du Cann, who had been Minister of State, Board of Trade, in the former Government. A barrister, he had made a fortune from unit trusts, a movement which he had largely fathered. At forty he was one of the youngest men ever to become Chairman; only J. C. C. Davidson (now Viscount Davidson) at thirty-eight was younger during recent times.

Sir Alec afterwards explained: 'I'd seen him operating at the Board of Trade. When he came into Cabinet, he was extremely good and efficient. His presentation of a case was masterly. I thought he was the right sort of age, a good speaker—and filled the bill.'

Not all the Tory leaders, however, were smitten by du Cann. He never in fact got on with Heath and Sir Alec sensed a clash of personalities for which no one was to blame.

In the Shadow Cabinet Maudling, still No. 2, became foreign spokesman in place of Butler, who retired to the Lords and Trinity College, Cambridge. Heath succeeded Maudling as Shadow Chancellor of the Exchequer, a swop that had considerable importance in the events of the coming July. Boyle went back to Education and Thorneycroft shadowed Home Office affairs, while his Defence duties were to be handled by Soames, so long 'Mr Agriculture' in and out of power. By those thought knowledgeable Soames at forty-four was regarded as the dark horse in the leadership stakes should Sir Alec retire.

Macleod was left high, dry, and frustrated. The cutting edge of his oratory was deflected from the steel nationalization Bill because the Committee stages were being taken 'upstairs', out of the public eye. He was to be heard plaintively asking his leader, 'What can I do next?'

In February Sir Alec announced the new method by which in future a Conservative leader was to be chosen. It was to be done, in the Socialist fashion, by ballots of M.P.s. The first ballot would be sufficient if No. 1 had an overall majority of not less than 15 per cent. If not there would be a second ballot with all candidates having to be re-nominated; and a third in case of a close result between two favourites.

Sir Alec himself had pressed for a change because he had been wounded by suggestions that he himself had got in 'by the back door'. He did not particularly like the new method, but 'I didn't think that any election held after my election by the same methods would ever carry any public confidence again.' Always it would be said that there was jobbery behind the scenes.

There *was* a real reason to change since the Party depended on how the Press presented such matters. This influenced public opinion, which as a result would not believe that under the old system the business was not done behind the scenes. It must be *seen* by the public to be above board. Otherwise the selected leader would always suffer.

Yet the old 1963 process was more obviously democratic since the whole Party, the Lords, the constituencies, Cabinet as well as M.P.s were consulted. Now it was the Parliamentary Party that decided. But Sir Alec thought this still gave time for the National Union of Conservative and Unionist Associations to make their representations to M.P.s, and plenty of time for the people who used to go into a huddle before to do so.

'But a Leader must feel that people *know* he's got the confidence of the Party. People outside thought that I had not got the confidence of the Party. They thought the matter had been—jobbed. I was perfectly happy with the old method but I wasn't happy from a future leader's point of view.'

When the new method was made public, some suggested that Sir Alec should submit himself to the ballot. This suggestion he ignored: the mechanism was intended to apply only to the choice of future leaders. Perhaps this was a mistake. He would certainly have been elected and probably with no other candidate offering himself, for it is a bold, or excessively foolish, colleague who stands up publicly to challenge his leader. So Sir Alec would have become virtually unchallengeable for a long time to come. Pride would not allow him even to consider such a course; nor, in any case, was he willing to remain leader by stifling opposition.

That there was opposition to him, however muffled and rudimentary, Sir Alec recognized. From early in January he was aware that a few M.P.s were muttering their dissatisfaction with his leadership. Maudling chose to condemn, but thereby to spotlight, the rumours on 19th January.

'I have grown sick and tired of the constant harping on personalities, the repeated speculation on the so-called "leadership issue", and what are supposed to be the manœuvrings and stratagems of rival candidates. I would like to make it clear that, from my point of view, I do not consider there is any such issue. And I have seen no evidence of such manœuvrings. Sir Alec Douglas-Home is, and will remain, at the head of our Party. He is a leader of outstanding qualities and strength of character.'[1]

When others took up the tale, Sir Alec simply asserted his intention of remaining leader. The Socialists seized the chance to distract public attention from their own woes by spreading dissension among their opponents. Sir Alec as leader was worth fifty seats to the Socialists, proclaimed Wigg, the M.P. who had led the Profumo campaign and was now Wilson's adviser, with the title of Paymaster-General. The Labour ruse was obvious: 'If the Prime Minister is prepared to go to such lengths to try to discredit Sir Alec, he must fear him as a dangerous opponent,' wrote Sir Alec's cousin, Lord Lambton, and, he added pointedly, 'Of this the Conservative Party should take note.'[2]

The majority *did* take note; only a tiny minority—an 'infinitesimal' number of M.P.s, Sir Alec wrote to a friend[3]—continued to murmur and perhaps to plot.

That did not, however, mean that the silent majority of the Party were entirely content with the leadership. Few of them knew quite why. They did not for a moment doubt that Sir Alec was a man of complete integ-

[1] *Daily Express*, 20th January 1965.
[2] *Evening Standard*, 8th March 1965. Viscount Lambton, heir to the Earl of Durham, was Tory M.P. for Berwick-upon-Tweed from 1951.
[3] Letter to J. C. Masterman, 15th April 1965.

rity, and that his reflexes and instincts were truly Conservative. He was for most of them the only possible leader. Yet he gave them little or no lead on the greater themes of the day: the sheep looked up to the shepherd and were not fed.

'The original middle-classes get small dividends for their Conservative investment,' wrote *The Times* political correspondent. It was up to Sir Alec to 'go deeper than pragmatism to show what Conservatism is today. British politics would be the better for it.'[1]

What the public wanted without consciously realizing it was a leader who would lift his eyes to the hills whence, they hoped, would come a salvation truly Conservative. Sir Alec did not. Yet in private, as we saw, he pondered the deeper issues of British politics. He understood the dangers of the Party not making its 'policies sufficiently distinctive for the ordinary worker to understand the difference between the Left-wing Conservative and the Right-wing Socialist.'[2] In his 'candid minute', he showed concern about the Tory yielding to expediency, and at the same time enunciated an inspiring faith in Britain's future: 'I believe that Britain has a fine part to play on the world stage. Not as a "trimmer" in international politics but as a country standing for true values . . . Neutralism . . . is not in the British character. We cannot lead from behind or from the middle ranks—we must be in front.'[3]

With such 'simple, clear' words, spoken out loud, Sir Alec might have had the Party and the country at his feet. Was he too shy to speak them, to reveal his innermost thoughts in public or was he too involved in the daily detail of Opposition? It is more likely that he simply did not hear the plaintive ba-ba-ba from the patient sheep so far from the purlieus of Westminster.

So that when the murmurings against him began inside Westminster he took them at face value, believing that he was being criticized for his supposed lack of parliamentary *brio*. Mystified, he wrote to Masterman that admittedly 'factious opposition does not come easily to me, but is that what the country wants?' It was not. He saw only the 'infinitesimal' number of restless Tory M.P.s, bemused by talk of technology, by muzzy ideas of progressiveness or driven by crude covetousness, and did not perceive that their captious criticisms were but the scum thrown up by a deeper tide.

[1] *The Times*, 15th March 1965.
[2] See p. 182 above.
[3] See p. 191 above.

On 17th March the 'infinitesimal number' held an ill-attended meeting at Westminster which came to no conclusion except that the situation required a latter-day Bishop of Bradford to sound the call that would precipitate Sir Alec's abdication.[1] However ill-attended, the meeting was given full coverage in most newspapers, including the *Spectator*, then edited by Macleod.

Better perspective was maintained by *The Times*: 'That Sir Alec Douglas-Home is under criticism or wry surveillance by his rank and file, just as Sir Winston Churchill, Sir Anthony Eden and Mr Macmillan were in their days, need not be doubted. That thought is being given to the qualities of the obvious candidates for the succession is certain.

'But that the mass of Conservative M.P.s is publicly breathing fire upon Sir Alec is nonsense. Publicly they are closing their ranks and swearing allegiance. We need not invest too much credence in that either, except that every intelligent Tory knows Mr Wilson will ruthlessly exploit any precipitate attempt to change the leadership.'

All the same, it helped neither Sir Alec nor his Party when the Tories were unseated and a Liberal elected in a by-election at Roxburgh, Selkirk and Peebles—Sir Alec's own corner of Scotland—on 25th March 1965. Some papers speculated on his 'personal' humiliation.

He was not humiliated and asserted at Leicester on 26th March that he was still 'impatient for the election in which I shall lead you to victory'. But the minority chuntering became more audible and the Tory M.P. Sir Gerald Nabarro implored his colleagues not to 'shoot the pianist, he is doing his best,' emphasizing that any leadership crisis would 'give hostages to Wilson, precipitate a snap election and lead to another Labour victory by a larger majority'.

There was no 'crisis', but Patrick Wall, a Right-wing Tory M.P., thought fit on 1st April 1965 to appeal to those who believed they had a chance of succeeding Sir Alec to follow Maudling in pledging their loyalty. He named one: 'Such action will be particularly appropriate for Mr Iain Macleod, whose friends never fail to seize the opportunity of putting forward his claims to the succession.'

Overt defence was as embarrassing as covert attack. Sir Alec was a

---

[1] On 1st December 1936 the then Bishop of Bradford, Dr A. W. F. Blunt, said that he wished King Edward VIII, not yet crowned, would give 'more positive signs' of his awareness that he needed 'God's grace' to rule the country. His words, almost accidentally, opened the way for newspapers to write of their knowledge of the King's determination to marry the twice-divorced Mrs Simpson. (See *Blunt*, by J. S. Peart-Binns, Mountain Press, Queensbury, Yorks, 1969.)

sensitive man. He was also a proud one. If the Party did not want him he would certainly not outstay his welcome. None near him suggested that he should go, but what, Sir Alec asked himself uneasily, were the real feelings of the mass of Conservatives, what was being said in the constituencies, in the privacy of M.P.s' 'surgeries', at the meetings, social or otherwise, of chairmen and the Party faithful in Hull North, Meriden, Maidstone, Westmorland?

The thick-skinned do not inquire: they survive. Sir Alec was not one of them. He sought reports from du Cann, the new chairman, on Party morale, and, as part of this, on Party attitudes to himself. This was neither self-conscious anxiety nor vanity. He really wanted to know whether as leader he was help or hindrance in making the Party palatable to the electorate.

Du Cann's inquiries were totally informal. This was no full-scale Central Office examination of Sir Alec's standing, as some papers hinted. In the normal course of a chairman's duties, du Cann toured the country, making himself known to area chairmen, agents and constituency workers. Over lunch or a beer in the Conservative club, they naturally spoke of the leadership.

But, du Cann emphasized later, few had emphatic opinions. Generally they asked questions: was it true, as the newspapers suggested, that some Tory M.P.s criticized Sir Alec's leadership, did he intend to carry on as leader, why were his television broadcasts so commonplace? [1]

All this du Cann faithfully reported to Sir Alec at a weekly private meeting. Sir Alec recalled that du Cann told him that he had 'found the constituencies wobbly. (How these inquiries went I don't know.) This did surprise me. I didn't allow this to influence me very much, but he did report this as a factor one had to consider.' Usually Sir Alec made no comment but once, du Cann remembered, he asked whether it was true that a change of leadership generally boosted a Party's fortunes.

A welcome fillip to morale came in May 1965, when the Conservatives gained 562 seats and Labour lost 419 in the borough elections. But by this time the small group of Tory M.P.s had the bit between their teeth. They confided to newspaper correspondents that these very successes indicated that Sir Alec was still a serious liability; local elections, they argued, were fought on material grievances—the Budget, higher prices, rates, immigration—but a General Election would be fought on the personalities of the two leaders.

[1] Du Cann to the author.

For Sir Alec the borough election results had another significance: the Labour *débâcle* meant that Wilson would not contemplate a snap election in June. At the earliest it would come in the autumn. Thus, if he were to resign the leadership, it should be before the House rose for the summer recess so as to give the new leader a breathing space to establish himself before the autumn session.

By July Sir Alec had another factor to consider. So far there had been three possible successors to the leadership, none with much advantage over the others. The position changed during the protracted debates on the Finance Bill. Heath, so recently made Treasury spokesman in place of Maudling, put on a brilliant and masterly display, fighting the Bill every inch of the way, and causing the defeat of the Government by Opposition majorities of fourteen and thirteen in the early hours of 7th July. It was Heath now, backed by the delighted Tories, who demanded that the Government should resign—'They have lost control of the House of Commons. They have lost their majority and can no longer continue their business.' The Opposition cheered him to the echo: this was really getting the Government on the hop.

Seeking to create a diversion Callaghan, the Chancellor of the Exchequer, turned to a curiously abstracted Sir Alec and said sarcastically: 'Why look so gloomy? You have won a great victory.'

Sir Alec was not gloomy. He was thinking that his moment of decision had been brought nearer. A credible successor had emerged. He could, if he chose, now depart with an easier conscience; but did he really so choose?

More openly now, Heath's supporters decided to try to make up Sir Alec's mind for him, though they were not of course aware of the way he was thinking. Led by Anthony Kershaw, Heath's former P.P.S., their aim was to generate a head of steam among Back Benchers for a change of leadership, believing that Heath would win the ballot. M.P.s were lobbied, the Press cultivated with some effect. One of the Heath group was reported as saying that there was a growing trend against Sir Alec in Party opinion throughout the country. There was even talk of a delegation to the Shadow Cabinet to demand a leadership election—if it could be shown that there was a Party consensus in favour.

'There was a band of young people in the House of Commons who showed that they wanted a younger leader in Opposition,' Sir Alec recalled, four years later. 'They thought that the Opposition as organized by me wasn't hitting the Socialists hard enough and that more "instant politics" was wanted.' This 'band' thought that Heath would supply it; they might have preferred Maudling but Heath's performance on the Finance Bill put him in the lead. Heath's supporters began to push their candidate and to agitate for Sir Alec's removal.

But there was no Party consensus, nor anything approaching it. A small meeting of Back Benchers, a week after Heath's parliamentary triumph, was still unmistakably in favour of Sir Alec. This was reported to him and during the weekend of 11–12th July he again declared his intention to continue as leader.

In his heart he was less certain. A National Opinion Poll credited the Socialists with an increased lead and showed Sir Alec himself falling yet farther behind. There were heavy leaders in heavy newspapers urging that it was time for a change.

He became tense and abstracted, hating the feeling that his colleagues were murmuring—'shrieking and squeaking, in fifty different sharps and flats'—perhaps even plotting against him and that he was no longer wanted. Even in the House he seemed singularly dejected, and during a heated debate on Vietnam had to be jogged into speech by William Whitelaw, the Chief Whip—and even then what he had to say was flat and inept.

Sir Alec was facing the biggest test of his career. Many friends—Lloyd, Anstruther-Gray, Mott-Radcliffe, and Whitelaw himself—sought to hearten him but, like his old master Chamberlain, he was a difficult man to talk to on subjects so intimate and personal. It was not in his nature, or upbringing; personal crises were to be met alone, not to be displayed to anyone.

Yet if his internal struggle was kept to himself it could not be kept from his demeanour. He was visibly jaded, his skin pallid and tauter than ever. He began to look more dead than alive and unable to conceal it. One M.P. privately observed to the Chief Whip: 'It's just cruelty—he can't go on.'

A decision one way or the other had to be taken. Sir Alec's advisers, although reluctantly, believed that he should make his mind up. Whitelaw in fact was seriously perturbed about Sir Alec's state of mind and thought fit to suggest that one way or another the issue should be resolved—preferably by Sir Alec staying—for otherwise he feared the parliamentary position might get out of hand.

Sir Alec, who had been accustomed to throw off his cares by plunging enthusiastically—and bloodily—into the pruning of roses, found no comfort now. A weekend at the Hirsel brought neither relief nor decision. He returned to London on Monday 19th July more sick at heart than ever.

This was the crucial week because Parliament was shortly to adjourn. If he were to resign, M.P.s would require time for balloting for a new leader before the recess: they could not easily be brought together once they had dispersed. If on the other hand he stayed he might well find himself leading the Party into another General Election and catastrophe.

On Monday 19th July he saw du Cann and Whitelaw, both of whom were convinced that any leadership change would smash the Party, and with them drafted a strong speech challenging his critics to stand up and be counted. It was intended that he should deliver it at the end-of-session meeting of the Back Benchers' 1922 Committee, due to take place three days later, on Thursday 22nd July. Next morning well-informed newspapers forecast 'Sir Alec will be tough', and headed their stories with 'Sir Alec angry with the rebels'.

But old friends, lunching with the Douglas-Homes on Tuesday, found Sir Alec quite unlike himself, gloomy and taciturn. He did not look like a man who has come to a decision and is therefore released from doubts. The mental wrestling continued.

Some time between Tuesday afternoon and Wednesday morning it ended. He was going—and at once. Otherwise he would find life intolerable.

Now he told his wife, who had throughout been determined that he should stay, just as she had been determined twenty months before that he should become Prime Minister. 'She was very annoyed,' Sir Alec remembered, and so were others let into the secret that day: 'There were a lot of people who came and begged me not to do it.'

Not however until Thursday morning, the day of the 1922 Committee meeting, did Sir Alec tell each colleague in turn of his decision. To his friend Selwyn Lloyd his opening words were: 'I'm sorry—I've let you down.' Lloyd was shocked and distressed and attempted to remonstrate.[1] To no avail; perhaps purposefully Sir Alec had kept it to the last from this old friend and admirer, so that it was too late for his persuasions to have effect.

[1] Selwyn Lloyd to the author.

Very few of the parliamentary party yet knew of his decision. They assembled in the Commons Grand Committee room at 6 p.m. expecting a strong speech with a few rockets for the critics. Sir Alec arrived promptly and as promptly gave them the shock of their lives. He was resigning then and there. No one, he said, 'suggested to me that I should go but there are those, who, perfectly properly, felt that a change of leadership might be for the best.' The stunned M.P.s were silent; but at the end cheered him to the echo.

Even for a man like Sir Alec lacking the last ounce of ambition, it is hard to give up the leadership of a great Party, a Party moreover which in July 1965 could still feel hopeful that it would turn a four-seat loss into victory at an election which could scarcely be long delayed. 'I don't deny it was a hard decision,' he wrote to Masterman ten days later, 'but I am convinced it was right.'

Why did he do it? 'I didn't see why after doing Commonwealth and Foreign Secretary and Prime Minister I should, so to speak, have to fight for position as Leader of the Opposition. It didn't attract me. I think I would have stuck it if I hadn't had that gruelling twelve years. If I'd been ten years younger I'd have seen it through.' But he was not going to be chivvied by his Party and its junior members.

That was the heart of the matter: why should *he* have to fight for place? To compete, manœuvre, kow-tow was beneath him. Though the least arrogant of men, Sir Alec had an inborn consciousness that while noblesse oblige, noblesse does not strive for position: it *has* position: 'A man who is born in Boston has no need to be born again.' Sir Alec would oblige, indeed, at no matter what cost to himself, even to the shedding of ancient peerages and sweating under television lights; he would fight the Opposition because that was like fighting in a cricket team to score more runs than the other team. But to remain top dog only by snarling and biting the dogs beneath him— no!

Yet those who knew him best were certain that he would have swallowed his pride, even though it meant distasteful stratagems, if he believed that he would serve his country and Party best by remaining. He did not. The hungry sheep must find another shepherd to lead them to greener pastures.

Edward Heath, then just forty-nine, was chosen leader by a ballot of Tory M.P.s a few days later. Not unnaturally he was suspected by a number of M.P.s of backstage wire-pulling, since those loudest against

Sir Alec were his supporters. Asked about this later, Sir Alec was scornful of those who suggested that Heath had engineered a plot. He was conscious that some of the younger M.P.s around Heath had schemed but refused to listen to any suggestions of Heath's personal involvement; he dismissed them with the curt words, 'I acquit him absolutely.' He was the first to congratulate Heath on his Finance Bill and had always had the highest opinion of him since they worked as 'partners' in the Foreign Office.

This exoneration of Heath is supported by Sir Alec's most fervent supporters. Heath's friends acted on their own. The worst that can be said is that Heath did not discourage them. But others in the Shadow Cabinet did not exert themselves greatly to squash criticism of their leader; nor, as we saw, did some of his colleagues impress themselves as active opponents in the Commons of a Government wide open to criticism. This could not be said of Heath.

For days, indeed weeks, after his resignation, Sir Alec was deluged with horrified and reproachful letters. Why had he done it? Who were the shady creatures who had conspired against him? Some, like Sir Alec's old friend James Stuart (Viscount Stuart of Findhorn) blamed the press: 'They got down our best man of his time—and a popular Leader —Sir Alec Douglas-Home, who had sacrificed himself in the national interest. Why, I ask again? Some ass or asses said he didn't photograph or televise well! And a lot of silly young Back-Bench M.P.s followed this absurd line. I wonder how Disraeli, Gladstone or Salisbury [the P.M.] would have fared and what difference their pretty or ugly pictures would have made to their ability to perform their onerous duties.'[1]

Sir Alec's brother William Douglas-Home took up the 'image' theme in the Liberal monthly, *New Outlook*. 'Suicide,' he wrote, was on Sir Alec Douglas-Home's death certificate as Conservative leader, but it was 'murder none the less'. He was dispatched by the Tories because his image was wrong.

'Is the image in the minds of the electors what the rebels think it ought to be? Or is it still deep-rooted in the true tradition of the Tory Party? If the former, then the rebels, though their methods may be questioned, have performed a signal service to the Party.

'If the latter, then all they have done is to set off the Party on the high road to Philippi and they only have themselves to blame for a

[1] James Stuart, pp. 158–9. See note p. 81 above.

233

disastrous miscalculation.'[1] The disaster came eight months later when the new-image leader led his Party to a crushing defeat, although in reality no leader could have done any better since, once the Labour Party were in, the electorate were unlikely to turn them out again after seventeen months in office working on a majority of four.

Though Sir Alec had not given them the lead they wanted, large numbers of Conservatives never ceased to believe that he was the only man who could. Sir Alec himself did not agree. Indeed he came to doubt the whole accepted mystique of leadership.

How much *does* a leader matter? By April 1969 the Conservative Opposition was, according to opinion polls, leading by twenty points, though Heath's personal popularity lagged behind. Yet even if it had not, even if he had been the most popular leader in the world, his Party could hardly have led by more than twenty points. Much of the success of a leader in Opposition resulted from a Government's failures, and the general impact of an Opposition in suggesting itself as a competent alternative.

All the same, Sir Alec would scarcely have disputed de Tocqueville's observation that 'Without ideas and leaders, a people cannot truly be said to exist.'

[1] *New Outlook*, 14th January 1966.

23. The People's Alec: 1965 – 7

*Hero at Tory Conference. Into the Rhodesia trap. General Election failure
and glory. Heath analysed. 'Boo to you'. Powell defended. George Brown.*

If the months of May, June and July 1965 found Sir Alec on the road
to Golgotha, the years that followed were roses, roses all the way. It
was very odd. Having resigned the leadership, he remained at Heath's
request in the Shadow Cabinet as foreign spokesman, ranking No. 3.
That was probably without precedent.[1] Yet more unprecedented was
the fact that the fallen leader became the idol of the Conservatives, the
people's Alec, his popularity far exceeding that of the man who had
taken his place.

The phenomenon burst upon Sir Alec, and the public at large, at the
Conservative Conference in the old Brighton ice rink in October 1965.
As he slid quietly into his chair on the platform, the whole audience,
like a sudden hurricane, rose to cheer, to shout, even to cry, and the
proceedings were held up for long minutes. His survey of foreign
affairs later in the week roused enormous enthusiasm, little connected,
it must be said, with the content of his speech. It was the man they
wanted more than his words.

When he stood up again to ask the Conference to pledge its loyalty
to Heath 'through thick and thin', the delegates were transported to
the seventh heaven of delight. He was the hero of the Conference.
There was even a hint of hysteria; many ladies present privately confessed their desire to embrace the former leader. To have accepted the
call to renounce his ancient titles to lead the country; then to have been
cast aside, and yet to have been humble and noble enough to serve
under another leader: such modesty of conduct appealed to every
instinct of chivalry in the Conservative psyche. Sir Alec had served the

[1] A. J. Balfour, having resigned the leadership in 1911, remained active in support
of the new leader, A. Bonar Law, but had no specific 'Shadow' post.

Conservatives better than they served him and a sense of guilt for the shabby way he had been treated augmented the delirium of his reception by the delegates.

The rapture was exaggerated. Sir Alec was a good and able man but no twice-as-large-as-life colossus towering above his generation like a Churchill. He was also a sensible man. He took the adulation with equilibrium: he had after all watched two much eulogized leaders, Baldwin and Chamberlain, pass swiftly into the outer darkness of contempt. His head was not turned:

'If applause is genuine it cheers you up because you know you've got across, and done your job,' he later remarked. 'I suppose it elates to some extent, but you mustn't allow yourself to be over-elated by it.'

The Brighton Conference of 1965 was not all triumph for Sir Alec. He led the Party into the trap laid by Wilson in connection with Rhodesia which, three weeks later, on 11th November 1965, would unilaterally declare her independence of Britain. Cautiously enough on 5th October the Shadow Cabinet, with Sir Alec present, issued a statement that a Rhodesia U.D.I. would have no legal validity and would have the gravest consequences. They did not, however, approve the Government's handling of the talks then taking place with Ian Smith, the Rhodesian Prime Minister.

But would they support sanctions against Rhodesia in case of U.D.I.? At the Conference Lord Salisbury declared: 'We will not have any lot or part in the Rhodesian hour of trial in turning on them and stabbing them to the heart', and he demanded that this amendment be made to the motion.

Sir Alec, however, insisted that a vote against the possibility of sanctions could, at that moment in time, be misrepresented as an encouragement to a Rhodesian declaration of independence. In the end, no vote was taken, but Sir Alec's refusal to vote against sanctions was to be exploited again and again by the Socialist Government and was to lead to fissure in the Tory party and humiliation in Parliament. It was curious too since Sir Alec always, as we saw, refused to countenance sanctions as an instrument of coercion.

When U.D.I. came on 11th November Sir Alec and the Party found themselves led by the nose into supporting the Government. Sir Alec tried to wriggle by drawing a distinction between penalties the Rhodesians had brought upon themselves, such as the end of Commonwealth preference and Bank of England credits, and sanctions which,

as Wilson at first conveniently agreed, would be 'vindictive and puni-
tive and designed to wreck Rhodesia's economy and bring chaos'.
But Wilson did not wish or intend to draw such a line; once the Opposition had agreed to consequential acts against Rhodesia they were
irretrievably tied to his cartwheel.

Wilson had it all his own way. When he forced along oil sanctions
in the wake of others, the Opposition split:

> . . . the little rift within the lute,
> That by and by will make the music mute . . .

By the time Wilson revealed that he had considered bombing the
electric cables providing power for Rhodesia from the Kariba Dam,
the Tory concerto was totally silenced. Triumphant, Wilson cuttingly
observed that Heath, when Chief Whip at the time of Suez, had done
far more to keep his Party together than he had over Rhodesia.

The humiliation was complete. Of course the Conservatives were in
a difficulty, partly as a result of their failure to seize the Rhodesian bull
by the horns at an earlier stage, and partly because they could not
condone a unilateral rupture of the bonds between Rhodesia and Britain.
There was too a difference between sanctions operated by Britain and,
as later, by the United Nations. All the same, the line was too thin; it
was incontrovertibly bad politics.

In his heart Sir Alec knew that the Government's designs were not
exactly as stated; he revealed, and condemned, the truth when he said
in New York to the Economic Club on 19th January 1966: 'Majority
rule in Rhodesia today or tomorrow would bring collapse and ruin.
Africans cannot live on slogans or disorder or political posturing, and
the harsh reality for the new countries of that continent is that nothing
matters to the people except food and education and the exploitation
of basic resources.'

For its own imperialist ends, Russia 'encouraged peoples who
throughout history had failed to gain mastery over their environment
to believe that all the benefits of civilization were theirs as of right, and
at their command by the turn of a switch or the push of a button. And
anyone who questioned these glib assumptions was labelled an enemy
of progress.'

Here indeed was the true voice of Conservative commonsense
speaking with limpid clarity. Yet had he vouchsafed such truths in the
House of Commons he would have been unable to make himself heard

above the din—while a majority of his own side would have sat in embarrassed silence.

A General Election was announced for 31st March 1966, and Sir Alec worked as hard as he had done in 1964, making not far short of sixty speeches. While in 1964 as Prime Minister he had gone campaigning in a motorcade with a police escort, lights flashing, and twenty press cars following, now he was followed by one press car and stood on farmcarts and beer crates to address as few as twenty people.

No, he did not like 'this opposition life', he frankly told reporters. 'Our Central Office is always telling you to attack in the House of Commons. "Have a go at Wilson", they say. Why should there be all this personal controversy?

'If the electorate is supposed to be better educated, why should we not give them our policies straight?'[1]

The Opposition decided that the right attitude for the House of Commons was to support the Socialist Government when it acted in the national interest but, where it did not, strongly to oppose. With these high-minded tactics, the Conservative voters became impatient, and the Tories lost not this time by four seats but by over a hundred, though whether any leader could have done better in the circumstances is very doubtful. The defeat heralded an almost continuous series of disasters for Britain—economic, foreign, social and a decline in the quality of life such as had rarely if ever been known in peace-time. Well might Sir Alec give warning to his fellow-countrymen that there was no control or direction at the helm, only vacillations and contradictions.

'If only Sir Alec had stayed leader' was the common cry, and the cynical observed that the first to bemoan his departure were those who had most vocally demanded a change. Conversely with the slump in the Party's fortunes, Sir Alec reached the heights of popularity. There were many in the Party who continued to hope that he would return to lead it, a fact that Sir Alec could scarcely help noticing. But he knew that unless the proverbial bus ran down his successor, the leadership of the Conservative Party was a once-for-all event.

To Heath his loyalty never wavered. He recognized that his style of leadership differed from his own and that of his other predecessors. His approach was that of a technocrat, producing programmes for

[1] *Sunday Times*, 27th March 1966.

problems rather than election speeches. Like Chamberlain, he would probably not get the emotional contact with the masses.

Sir Alec's opinion has been constant that Heath would make a very efficient P.M. and administrator, and that, Sir Alec ruminated, was more important than 'emotional contact'. Neville Chamberlain had not had what is called 'public appeal'—and yet would, if he hadn't got mixed up with foreign affairs, have been a highly successful P.M. Baldwin had the appeal—but it was not revealed to the public until he gained the confidence which comes to a Prime Minister.

Television had made people more conscious of a few individuals in the political firmament but politicians are not film stars: 'The P.M.'s job is to preside over the nation's "Board of Management",' Sir Alec believed; 'business comes before advertisement.'

As for the conduct of the Opposition, it was never easy to judge the right moment to launch policies; the good shells should not be fired away too early. It was a very delicate balance to find. Sir Alec had always doubted whether the country really wanted ding-dong parliamentary battles—'Boo to you, then boo back again.' But it was difficult to find the half-way house in Opposition.

There was the affair of Enoch Powell. He had always played a lone hand and his well-thought-out speeches caused a flutter which spread far beyond the Conservative dovecotes. This reached a climax in April 1968, with his speech on immigration and its references to the 'River Tiber foaming with much blood'. For this Heath promptly dismissed him from the Shadow Cabinet.

Sir Alec understood Heath's reaction: 'He thought the Party would be dubbed racialist ever afterwards if Enoch continued to be one of its Shadow Cabinet figures.' Sir Alec accepted Heath's verdict. Nevertheless he recognized Powell's intellectual contribution to Conservative thought and hastened to his defence. Speaking at York he denied that Powell was a racialist and said it was ridiculous to pretend that he was. But of course the damage had been done—once that "blood flowing in the streets" had been uttered, the emotions, the blood-pressure, rose too high all over the country.

Sir Alec himself had made several speeches in the same year insisting that the number of immigrants should be strictly controlled. On one occasion he advocated that no more immigrants should be allowed into the country over a five-year period than the number which went out. In a sense this was a more extreme view than Powell's but, he later observed, 'no one took the slightest notice.' Even so, he could not condone language which so stirred emotions that people were in danger of 'seeing blood'. That was not, he believed, a legitimate way to 'wake people up'.

Sir Alec was quick to defend his colleagues, though not all had fallen over themselves to back him when he was leader. Central Office too found a champion in him, despite his earlier irritations. In January 1967 some Conservative M.P.s thought the Central Office news-sheet, *Weekly News*, had gone too far in describing Wilson as 'the man you cannot trust'. Sir Alec publicly disagreed:

'If double-talk is consistently used in politics, then every example of it should be exposed because it debases the political currency.' Wilson had gone back without hesitation on his promises that grammar schools would be abolished over his dead body, that wage claims would never be frozen, that there would be no increase in general taxation, that interest rates would be kept down: 'People must not be allowed to forget these things or they will be duped again.' [1]

Sir Alec, as we saw, thought life too short to dislike his opponents, even Wilson, and for some had a qualified regard. For George Brown, for example, he felt affection. He was, however, highly sceptical of his flair: 'You can't charm a de Gaulle or a Nasser off his perch.'

On at least one critical occasion Sir Alec stepped in to divert mounting criticism of Brown. The respect of the two men was mutual: 'I reckon that of all my predecessors he did as well as anybody,' Brown said on 9th November 1967. 'I regard him very highly indeed. There are some fights I enjoy having but I don't enjoy having any with him.' Sir Alec, who was present at this meeting of the British Society for International Understanding, replied that their both appearing together was evidence of the miracles of co-existence.

Sir Alec believed that Opposition and Government should operate the amenities of civilized relationship. But if any of his political opponents seemed to be ignoring the national interest they 'could expect to get it in the neck'. His stance was that of patriot and gentleman. Both qualities were rare enough in the late 1960s to ensure him an attentive, often enthusiastic, hearing both inside and outside Parliament.

---

[1] At Peebles, 21st January 1967.

24. Intentions Abroad : 1966 – 9

'East of Suez' decision. China and Vietnam. Anzus and Britain. The Gulf. Inside and outside South Africa. Rhodesia policy. U.N. and U Thant.

As the Socialist years dragged on, Sir Alec Douglas-Home began to look at the field of foreign affairs from a slightly different angle. A snap General Election might precipitate him and his colleagues suddenly from criticizing into doing. Whether he entered a new Tory Cabinet as Foreign Secretary or as overlord of Foreign, Commonwealth and Colonial Offices he would be the guiding light in all the ticklish problems the Wilson Government would leave in its wake.

In most cases, Sir Alec knew exactly what he would do the first day back in office. There was, for example, the Far Eastern or, as it was sometimes called, the 'East of Suez' policy. The Socialists with their neutralist aims, were bent on scuttle; so too were such Tories as Enoch Powell.

Would Sir Alec reverse the Socialist scuttle? He recognized that the precipitate decision of the Socialist Government to evacuate the British 'presence' from South-East Asia by 1971 created a tricky situation which would need the maximum finesse and skill. His response was an unequivocal, though carefully defined, 'Yes'.

He had always insisted that a little power deployed in the right place at the right time could achieve political results far in excess of the numbers and effort expended. By withdrawing troops from South-East Asia before those living there could provide their own security, the Socialists he thought had done enormous damage. Eventually these countries must stand on their own feet. Meantime there was a gap in which a 'presence' could be of value.

Sir Alec did not believe that in the future great European or American armies would be deployed on the mainland of Asia: the Vietnam war had shown how unsatisfactory that could be, although a precipitate

American withdrawal could mean massacre of South Vietnamese on a scale comparable with Russian or Nazi atrocities—something that the American conscience would find intolerable.

Rather, he saw Britain's role and 'presence' as being confined, as he put it in his Ditchley Foundation lecture on 19th July 1968,[1] to taking 'an active hand' in the formation of a collective security system of Asians for Asians, based in the first instance on Malaysia, Singapore and Thailand. He hoped that Australia would influence Indonesia to join in.

Presumably, therefore, Britain would supply substantial training missions of Army and R.A.F. to be stationed in Singapore and elsewhere. But Sir Alec's conception of Britain's role went farther than that: 'I would like to see the United States, Japan, Britain, Australia and New Zealand accept the responsibility for keeping open and free the Indian Ocean, the Indonesian Seas and the Pacific, using their combined sea and air power to do so.' To do this, as he realized, 'implies a reorganization, indeed a replacement, of Seato, and Anzam and Anzus,[2] but such action would I believe pay an enormous dividend in peace and stability.'

This would evidently be a major British initiative involving both naval and air force units. Britain had originally been kept out of Anzus by the United States; by 1970 the United States, over-extended financially and militarily, would probably welcome British participation. It would mean too that Britain could more easily aid Australia and New Zealand, her Commonwealth partners, in case of war.

Could Britain afford even these participations in South-East Asian affairs? Even the Government had admitted that the net annual profit from the Gulf and Singapore area was £300 million a year. It was 'nonsense', Sir Alec believed, to say that Britain could not afford it though the Socialists might argue that a military presence would do no good. Moreover:

'It is a fair forecast that were we to leave these areas entirely, profit would diminish and a part of it would be taken by other people, who would come in and take the British place . . . Leave a gap and somebody else fills it', he wrote in 'Britain's Place in the World', a Conservative pamphlet published in August 1969.

For all such developments, Sir Alec thought there would be a 'time scale of up to fifteen years'.[3] Up to that time he did not believe China

[1] 'An International Weather Forecast', published by the Ditchley Foundation.

[2] The military defence pacts between Australia, New Zealand and the United States.

[3] Ditchley Lecture, p. 9.

could become a 'serious makeweight in the scales of power' because her material progress was slow; 'though she will retain an active nuisance value, she cannot challenge the dominance of the two great powers.'[1]

Not all the experts would agree with Sir Alec but it was certainly possible to make out a case for believing that China had no intention of moving armies towards Vietnam, Laos and Cambodia. She wanted reasonably friendly governments there. She might support a solution of the Vietnam situation by the creation of a belt of non-aligned states, followed by neutrality internationally supervised.

On this view, China's real drive was towards the rich central Asian provinces of Russia, which she claimed as part of her previous empire —parts of which she was already in the process of getting back, as in Tibet and from India. It was the mutual 2,000-mile frontier between China and Russia which would preclude the patching up of their relations.

While it would be Conservative policy to consult with the governments concerned in South-East Asia, a more difficult problem arose with the Gulf of Aden. There would be consultations with the Rulers but the Conservatives would have to face the question whether their East-of-Suez policy would be practicable in the Gulf. The Socialists' withdrawal of the British 'presence' there appeared to most observers in 1970 as almost irredeemable. It had been done partly on doctrinaire grounds, partly because insufficient pressure has been brought to bear on the United States to show them the importance of the Middle East to the grand, Western strategy.

The previous Conservative Government could rightly claim that they had not sacrificed Aden and would have continued to impress the American administration with the importance of Aden and the Gulf to both sides from the point of view of trade routes.

But if as seemed likely the loss of the Gulf bases was irretrievable and the closure of the Suez Canal almost permanent, how then were Indian and Pacific waters to be kept open to the West?

Here South Africa became of immense importance to Britain and Europe, faced by what Sir Alec called Russia's 'new forward, if not offensive, oceanic naval strategy based on the long-distance submarine'. He gave details of this vast development: 'They have 160 long-range submarines of which two-thirds are deployed in European waters.

[1] Ditchley Lecture, p. 9, see note, p. 242 above.

New completions including replacements number about ten each year and most of these are nuclear-powered. The relative strengths of the Russian and American submarine fleets are:

U.S.S.R. 35 nuclear   U.S. 80 nuclear
U.S.S.R. 320 conventional   U.S. 120 conventional
A total of Russian 355 to American 200.'[1]

Europe, Sir Alec believed, faced by such a submarine fleet, oceanic in range and embracing the oil routes, would have to think in terms of 'extended defence'. The Simonstown[2] agreement between South Africa and Britain, which gives Britain in the event of hostile action east of Suez the use of all South African ports including Durban, was likely to become a 'useful extension' to NATO's defence responsibilities:

'I forecast that this facility will be of great value in terms of the defence of Western Europe from interference with her oil supplies and that it will in effect become an informal extension of the NATO defences, though it will remain a bilateral agreement.'[3]

Sir Alec was very firm on what the next Tory Government would do about South Africa: 'We should immediately resume the practice of previous Conservative governments and sell arms to South Africa for use against external aggression and for the defence of the sea routes'. The sale had been banned by the Wilson Government immediately they came to power in 1964 in accordance with a Security Council resolution of the year before. At the end of 1967 the South African government had sought to buy naval vessels from Britain and, in the depressed state of the economy and growing unemployment, there had been pressures within the Cabinet to sign a contract. Wilson refused, and George Brown shortly afterwards resigned.

'Does the Prime Minister,' Sir Alec asked in the Commons, 'recognize that the Charter of the United Nations allows both for the export and reception of arms for external defence, and can he say what harm it does to any African for South Africa to order submarines?'

As a result of the Socialists' intransigence, the South Africans had bought three submarines not, as they would otherwise have done, from their ally, Britain, but from France. Even when the Conservatives

[1] Ditchley Lecture, p. 5.

[2] Simonstown, near Cape Town, is the main South African naval base.

[3] Ditchley Lecture, p. 5.

altered the policy, the South Africans would have to stick to the French pattern of submarine since the cost of chopping and changing and re-training would be prohibitive.

The South Africans also wanted frigates—and were willing to wait until, as they hoped, the British election brought a change of Government. The frigates were even more important for defence than the submarines.

Sir Alec became interested in South Africa itself. Strangely enough he had never visited the country; he had planned to go when he was Commonwealth Secretary but 'Suez' had intervened.

In the spring of 1968, he toured the Republic and saw some of its leaders, including the Prime Minister, B. J. Vorster.

Everyone who goes to the continent of Africa finds himself caught up in its emotions. Sir Alec was no exception. He found the South Africans reticent in public about the racial problems of their country but in private they would scarcely talk of anything else.

When he returned Sir Alec analysed the situation as he saw it. He was not one of those who forecast revolution and take-over by the Bantu hordes. The African was busy making money in circumstances of which he had never even dreamed in his tribal state. But if South Africa was to be a nation at harmony with itself, then the European population had to devise a way to give status to the African of quality and attainments. Education would produce many Africans and Coloured people as gifted as any white man and these people would have to be integrated into society.

Sir Alec was under no illusions as to the difficulty of the operation after the long history of separate development but he had no doubt that in the end it would have to be done. He found the administration totally unrealistic in their belief that Africans could all be transplanted from the cities into Bantu reserves such as the Transkei. There would certainly be millions who could not be so settled and who would continue to work in the towns.

It was here that he foresaw the eventual solution. Industry had increasingly been forced to use the African with ability and to place him in positions of increasing responsibility. Not for the first time the hard facts of economic and bread and butter would triumph over political theory.

On Rhodesia, Sir Alec was determined to take decisive, and controversial, action immediately he was back in the Foreign Office. He had watched with dismay the mishandling by the Socialists and strongly condemned Wilson for pledging that there would be no independence before majority rule (Nibmar): 'Wilson made a terrible mistake with Nibmar. He ought never to have allowed the control of Rhodesian affairs to pass out of Britain's hands.'

When in June 1969 the Rhodesian referendum showed an over-whelming majority in favour of Rhodesia's becoming an independent Republic, Sir Alec thought it 'very regrettable', but dismissed the closing down of the British mission in Salisbury as 'senseless', and observed: 'In other cases even where we strongly disapprove of a country's policies, we retain contact.'[1]

By September 1969 Sir Alec saw that it was all over, but he preferred not to oppose—nor, of course, to support—the renewal of the sanctions orders: 'I would rather say that we reserve complete right to re-assess policy when we return to power, and that we would never have got into this position, so let them get on with it.'

Sir Alec in the Commons and elsewhere has refused to define the line he would advise a Conservative Government to take on return to office. At the Foreign Office he was never prone to give away points of negotiation in advance. All he would say publicly was that the Conservatives reserved the right to deal with any situation they might inherit in the way that seemed best to them when the time came.

This refused to give hostages either to the Socialists or the future. The shape, however, of a Conservative Government's policy towards Rhodesia would obviously be based on the reality of the situation: the Rhodesian Government had won its independence, become a Republic and, as its budget was to show in 1970, was flourishing despite sanctions. Smith would discuss the renewal of relations with Britain—and nothing else. He did not expect, nor wish, to join the Common-wealth and 'preferences' were affairs of the past since other nations had taken the place of Britain as Rhodesia's trade and economic partner.

In the opinion of most commentators, including the present writer, Sir Alec and the Conservatives would have to reap where they had sown. There was no alternative to giving *de facto* recognition to the Republic of Rhodesia, without approval but without negotiation. There would be trouble. The new government would have to request the Security Council to lift mandatory sanctions, more damaging to Britain than to Rhodesia, and the request might be vetoed though to

[1] Speech at Cheltenham, 27th June 1969.

do so would be a serious step. There is little doubt that these moves would take place rapidly, following the return of a Conservative Government. So would end an unnecessary and miserable chapter in Britain's late colonial history.

Wilson's involvement of the United Nations in British-Rhodesian affairs was foolish and its legality under the Charter disputed. By 1965 Sir Alec's opinion of United Nations' methods had, in any case, worsened. The so-called Six Days' War between Israel and Egypt in May and June 1967 had reinforced his doubts. U Thant's personal and unauthorized withdrawal of the peace-keeping force facilitated Nasser's aggression. He did not believe that Hammarskjöld would have been 'old-soldiered' by Nasser as U Thant had been.

'There is no denying,' said Sir Alec in a new look at the United Nations six years after his famous Berwick-upon-Tweed *exposé*, 'and it is useless to conceal it, that the authority of the Secretary-General and the credibility of the United Nations itself was gravely damaged by the withdrawal of the protecting force from the Arab-Israel border at the first drop of a hat by one of the parties in dispute.'

To be fair, however, if member countries approached any international dispute with built-in prejudices how, he asked, could the Secretary-General command support for impartial action?

Sir Alec noted, in this address to the United Nations Association at Oxford on 1st November 1967 that while Russia's use of the veto had become less frequent it was now more subtle: 'She is willing to operate the peace-keeping system when it suits her political book. For example, the Indian-Pakistan war was a grave embarrassment and she connived at a Security Council intervention to stop it.

'Again if her support for a resolution moved by an Asian or African country is likely to confuse or confound the West, she is inclined to support it, while in the opposite case if the United States or United Kingdom want to act, she will refuse to co-operate or to pay for joint action. That, one might call Russian flexibility.

'But she did not, for example, oppose the despatch of observers to the Lebanon in 1958, nor veto the Congo operation in 1960, while Cyprus is policed. She will not pay for peace-keeping operations but nor will France.'

For the first time publicly, Sir Alec drew the clear conclusion: 'The United Nations cannot undertake and should not be asked to undertake ambitious peace-keeping adventures. Its activities are not, and need not be, negligible, but for peace-keeping, so long as Russia is a casual player, its role will be severely curtailed.'

He regretted also that as in 1961, most Asian and African countries, some newly independent, still carried the prejudices of the past to the point of a vendetta. The Committee of 24 [the General Assembly's 'colonialist' sub-committee] totally lacked impartiality. Again he drew a firm conclusion:

'If we are continuously to be made the target of double standards of behaviour, then we should do well no longer to provide a platform for prejudice and dissension and discord.'

25. Britain the Outsider: 1967-9

A revealing lecture. 'Cold war won by the West'. Healey criticized. Commonwealth doubts. His European dilemma, tact and hopes.

A few days after his sixty-fifth birthday on 2nd July 1968, Sir Alec gave a graceful and revealing lecture to the Ditchley Foundation,[1] from which quotation was made in the last chapter. It contains the maturity of his thought on international politics; with its blend of shrewd *realpolitik* and underlying optimism it faithfully pictures Sir Alec as statesman. He called his lecture 'An International Weather Forecast', explaining that an old Scottish countryman, when asked by a stranger what the Home family was like, replied 'They always know which way the wind blows'. The Homes, he added, were compelled to: 'If we did not, we lost our heads.'

Sir Alec began with the Pax Britannica. In its heyday the British Empire, backed by capital generated by the industrial revolution and commerce generated by the exploitation of physical assets far and wide, seemed to point forward to an unending vista of prosperity and peace. Doubtless there were examples of colonial exploitation of human beings —'which, incidentally, were only a pale image of what happens today' —but there were also high ideals and high achievement: 'In the British Empire at the end of the nineteenth and twentieth centuries, the Bible was certainly as influential as the sword. In many ways, socially, economically and politically the barometer was set fair at "evolution".'

Then in 1914 the world was 'knocked off course'. So-called civilized Europeans could not discard war—and even brought in Asians and Africans to 'watch them in mortal contest'. Communism challenged religion and applied its dogmas by force. By a coincidence 'surely designed by the devil', Communism's coming coincided with the beginnings of the emancipation of colonial territories from imperial

[1] 19th July 1968.

rule. Unfortunately too its doctrine of materialism superficially seemed to fit in with the new teachings of science and technology: 'If man can do so much, what is left for God to do?'

So the Communists posed as champions of the underdog, the friends—modern and progressive—promising to the newly independent nations 'in the twinkling of an eye' benefits for which others had toiled for generations. Evolution was turned into revolution, the world's desire to organize collective security thwarted.

Has Communism now done its worst, he asked? The balance, he thought, was nicely struck. Russia was still at it—increasing her budget for conventional arms, rearming Egypt after her defeat of the year before, using force in Czechoslovakia. She vetoed the reform of the United Nations, refused to use her influence to end the Vietnam war,[1] and pursued a 'forward' oceanic naval strategy based on the long-distance submarine. Navies would play the decisive role in the future as they had under the Pax Britannica, and 'Russia has always harboured imperialist ambitions'.

On the credit side was the fact that Russia continued her 'political dialogue' with the United States. She was apparently willing to co-operate in keeping down the ceiling of expenditure on nuclear weapons. Sir Alec believed that such expenditure would be fixed at a ceiling below that of the anti-missile missile. It might even be that Russia of the future would decide that '*comparative* political stability will pay the highest dividend. If so, the Western world will be given room to breathe'. It seemed that—because of the development of the Six and the rapprochement of France and Germany—'war with the West is no longer on the Soviet programme of options'. In fact the West had won the 'cold war' even though Germany remained divided.

So, he concluded, the international barometer was low. There was a trend to co-existence—was that optimism, or was it faith, or were they perhaps the same thing?

'On a very close reading of the weather graph, I conclude that one can just perceive a slight turn upwards towards fairer times in international affairs.'

Then Sir Alec made a forecast about himself: 'For fifty years I have tapped the barometer every morning and because I have to sustain

[1] Russia refused to join the British Foreign Secretary as Co-chairman of the Geneva Conference on South-East Asia, which had been kept in being from the early 1950s for just such a purpose.

something known as a grouse-moor image, I am going on tapping it for the rest of my active life.'

Even though Sir Alec believed that war with the West was no longer 'on the Soviet programme of options', he was far from suggesting that Western Europe, and Britain in particular, could lower their guard. Indeed, as we saw in the last chapter, Sir Alec thought that NATO defences should be extended, particularly East of Suez, and that a new strategy would have to be developed in which British sea and air forces would be required to play a greater part than they had done when defence was focused on Europe.

He was, therefore, deeply alarmed by the policy of the Socialist Government. Defence was not Sir Alec's Shadow Cabinet job. But, as in the debate on the Queen's Speech in October 1969, defence and foreign matters were often closely meshed. Sir Alec accused Stewart, the Foreign Secretary, of allowing 'the Secretary of State for Defence [Healey] so to reduce the forces of this country that his foreign policy may be totally nullified'.

How could Stewart uphold even a European policy, he asked, when disturbances on the scale of Northern Ireland led to a warning that Britain might have to withdraw her troops from NATO? How could he conduct an Atlantic policy if he allowed Healey to scrap the aircraft-carriers just when they had been refitted and before the Government had sanctioned the ships which would carry the aircraft in future for the defence of the sea routes in the Atlantic and elsewhere? How did Stewart propose to honour the defence obligations he had undertaken in Malaysia, Brunei, Mauritius, Caribbean, Hong Kong, Gibraltar and elsewhere?

Many Britons found it sinister that, though the Government might plead the imperative need to save millions of pounds on defence, they should ruthlessly disband practically costless, voluntary services ranging from the Royal Observer Corps to the Territorial Army. The Tories would re-embody the Terriers, and Sir Alec thought it 'really extraordinary' that the Socialists should have abolished the service since 'it is voluntary, the quality is good and cheap at the price'.

The larger issues of defence would require close consideration by a Conservative administration. While NATO with American membership was regarded as essential, the question would be to what extent would the Americans feel it necessary to withdraw land forces and arms from Europe? It would be the subject of consultation but it might be that Europe would have to assume a greater responsibility for its own defence.

If so, Anglo-French understanding would be of 'absolute importance for they are the two powers in Europe which command a nuclear capacity.' Neither Sir Alec nor any other knowledgeable observer thought that a transition from a NATO defence system with full American participation to a purely European defence system would be anything but a very slow and difficult process.

It was not certain whether the Americans would be willing to give France the latest nuclear knowledge; it had been given to Britain but Britain was not entitled to pass it on to a third party.

There would be a West German reaction. They would need much persuasion to believe that an Anglo-French nuclear defence system by itself would be adequate to defend West Germany. Fearing that in case of war they might be regarded as expendable, they would seek to acquire nuclear weapons of their own and this would reopen the old controversy about arming Germans and exacerbate Russian fears and suspicions.

With the possibility of America's withdrawing from European defence, Britain herself would be more isolated. She was outside Europe, outside the American orbit and, of course, outside the Iron Curtain. There remained the Commonwealth.

Sir Alec had once been its saviour. Since his rescue operation after Suez, however, it had become bigger and even more disunited. Two of its member countries had fought each other; some had broken off diplomatic relations with Britain; few of the more recently joined countries were in any sense democracies and some were dictatorships.

Could it and ought it to be kept in being? 'If the Commonwealth is going to exact the sort of penalty from one or other partner as they did over Rhodesia [i.e. Nibmar], then it could not be held together. One rule is absolute: non-interference in each other's internal affairs,' Sir Alec believed.

Nor did he believe that the Commonwealth could ever be an economic bloc, although it was valuable that, for instance, the Commonwealth Finance officials met twice a year, and were able to make, for example, the Sugar Agreement, through which the Commonwealth countries have been able to influence the world price. Commonwealth self-sufficiency was, however, a mirage. It had worked well when the Commonwealth was exporting goods and raw materials to Britain.

In more recent times the aim of the old Commonwealth countries was to become manufacturers and it was unlikely they would be able to export their manufactures into Britain. Through E.F.T.A., for example, Scandinavian timber was cheaper than Canadian. As for importing more food from them, the tendency was for Britain to increase her agricultural production here, and this could push her self-supporting position from about 50 per cent to something like 75 per cent of her needs. In general, however, if the Commonwealth was to exercise influence in the world in future it would, he believed, be as an organization where race and colour and different political systems could meet and take counsel—without a veto. He saw no incompatibility in Britain remaining a loyal member of such a Commonwealth and British membership of the Common Market, particularly when the pattern of trade was changing so fast, with all the Commonwealth countries, Canada inevitably, being so interested in the American market, Australia with Japan and S. E. Asia, the African countries—Nigeria and Ghana—making arrangements with the Common Market. A regional pattern was developing.

In short, though Sir Alec did not spell it out, it was unlikely that the Commonwealth could ever have the coherence the Empire and Dominions once had. Militarily, many of its members were neutralist and, except Australia and New Zealand, none would be likely to come to Britain's aid in war. Presumably a Conservative Government would help Australia and New Zealand were they to be threatened; but many doubted whether a Socialist Government would do so.

'The bonds are visibly slack, it is clear. The Queen is not Queen of some of the Commonwealth countries; English as a lingua franca within the Commonwealth is fading and so is the Christian religion. What remains in many of the newly independent countries, in Ghana and Nigeria for example, is a foundation of British Law upon which, it is possible, some sort of democratic machinery might be built.'

Britain's future, Sir Alec believed as he had believed since 1961, lay with Europe. Even though he added that a Britain richer by market membership would be more valuable to the Commonwealth as an economic partner and ally, it was only in Europe that she would once again spark on all six cylinders.

Nevertheless by 1969, when he spoke on the subject at the Conservative Conference in Brighton during October, he sounded a note of caution. For the Conservative leadership, thoroughly committed to the

European idea, was embarrassed by the facts that the public at large had lost interest in the subject, that many Tories—including Enoch Powell—had reneged on their former faith, and that the Socialist government had also espoused the European cause. In short, public and politicians were out of step with party leaderships, so that no matter for what party—except the Communists—an individual might vote at a General Election he would be underwriting a pledge for Britain to seek entry into the European Economic Community. In such a situation, one-man-one-vote democracy resembled Byron's archangel Michael who 'grew pale, As angels can'.

Sir Alec's speech to the Conservative delegates was a miracle of tact. He trod as warily as a Royal Engineer advancing to defuse an unexploded bomb. He had, he told the Conference, 'deliberately drained his speech of all emotion'. Peering coolly over his 'Homes', he claimed that the facts upon which to take a decision whether or not to enter the Common Market were not available and therefore the time for a decision was not 'ripe'. The 'facts' could be discovered only by discussion and negotiation. As far as a Conservative Government was concerned, nothing would happen until Parliament judged the results of negotiations with each of the 'Six' separately and with the Commission in Brussels.

The industrial gains from entry would be large but a Conservative administration would have to calculate whether the country could afford the immediate and short-term cost. But even a high premium might well be worth while and 'good business' in the long term. The size of the market made available to Britain by joining 'matters supremely'. Either way, it would be for Britain an 'historic decision'.

It was a 'holding' speech, just as had been Sir Alec's discussions with Ian Smith in September 1964. Sir Alec received his usual standing ovation but it was noticeably more perfunctory than his reception by Conference four years earlier, and the effect was spoiled by some delegates insisting on raising points of order and holding a ballot. 'Tact' is an admirable quality but some of those listening uneasily felt a temporizing about the speech which had been notably absent from Sir Alec's utterances in the past, a fact which had marked him out so clearly from some other politicians.

In truth, Sir Alec said nothing he did not believe though he did not say all he believed. To say all was not judged politic because the public was bored and antipathetic and an Election was in the offing, which, the Conservatives believed, it was essential they should win. Essential not for the sake of the ambitions of the leadership but, they genuinely believed, because another five years of Socialism would probably spell the end to the British form of democracy and, with 'permissiveness' rampant, to the British way of life.

Was Sir Alec right to temporize? The question would be irrelevant if asked about most other leading politicians: Sir Alec, however, had a reputation for telling the truth and shaming the devil. His dilemma was real: to say frankly that although he knew the public had turned against the idea of joining the E.E.C., the Conservative leadership intended to press on with the project was scarcely obeying the will of the people and might damage the Party's electoral chances. Was it not better to hedge if hedging would ensure that power returned to men of integrity? With justice did Professor G. Wilson Knight write that 'all worldly power is sin-struck at the core'.

Sir Alec would not have described his attitude as 'trimming'. The Common Market itself had run up against difficulties, particularly on the agricultural side, and their solution, as proposed by the Commission of the E.E.C. in Brussels, seemed to be a long process since it meant reducing the number of small farmers on the Continent and gradually amalgamating farms. Price levels would be fixed lower. Agriculture—and Britain's special arrangements with New Zealand—along with currency questions would be the main areas requiring settlement.

Neither Sir Alec nor any other responsible person denied that Britain, once in the Common Market, would pay more for food, though how much more could not be accurately estimated. On the other hand, Britain would be able to trade her industrial goods more easily and more advantageously once the tariff barriers were gone and—the point Sir Alec always emphasizes—Europe with Britain part of it could mobilize the sums of money required to compete on equal terms with the United States in the great projects, dependent on re-search, which would dominate the future of civilization. But, in Sir Alec's view, common prudence required that with so much unknown and so much of the cost unquantified a decision should be delayed.

Sir Alec was aware that many people in Britain, from left to right of the political spectrum, were chary of the loss of sovereignty they suspected was implied in the Treaty of Rome to which Britain would be obliged to subscribe. He pointed out, however, in the Europe House lecture of 13th November 1969 that the authors of the Treaty, mindful of 'the extraordinary political delicacy of this balance between the requirement of the individual nation and the Community', had stopped short of recommending the future political structure of Europe. The Council of Ministers was a check and, 'for as far ahead as we can see' would retain the ultimate say.

Under the rules of the Treaty, majority voting was possible over 'a limited range of economic decisions'; in practice the Council of Ministers had found it necessary to proceed by unanimity: 'That may not always be so, as confidence leads to the recognition of mutual benefits.' Nevertheless, 'none of the machinery established has been, or looks like being, Federal. The central bankers meet. The monetary committees meet; the Commission is in permanent session; and the Council from time to time. But this network of relationship is not Federal.'

Certainly it went beyond anything at present existing in a regional grouping of states. Yet as Burke said, every human benefit and virtue was founded on 'compromise and barter'. Such would be the subject of a running debate for many years ahead—and this 'process of evolution, adaptation and compromise is right up Britain's street'.

Sir Alec hoped Britain would take part in 'this great adventure', but he firmly asserted that when the Conservatives returned to power the matter would be reviewed afresh to decide whether the time was ripe for entry.

26. New Battle for Britain: 1967 – 70

Cricket and politics. Election 'rigging'. Bastards and drug-takers. Future of the Lords. 'Nasty Mess'. Trade Unions. Victory, June 1970.

One of the great loves of Sir Alec's life was cricket. Although he had not played since he was fifty, he was President of the M.C.C. for 1966–7 and he watched the game whenever he had chance.

But to his dismay first-class cricket began to bore him. Was it a sign of old age? Apparently not, for when he diagnosed the malady, and proposed a therapy in the 1967 winter annual of *The Cricketer*—in which he himself had figured as a useful player fifty years before—the experts agreed.

'Club cricket,' he wrote, 'commands widespread support and the Gillette Cup draws the crowds. So why is it that first-class cricket is relatively dull?

'On the evidence, the verdict must be that for too many captains and players the first objective is to avoid defeat rather than go all out to win. Batsmen too often seem to forget that they are there to make runs at a pace which will give the bowlers time to get the other side out. The better the wicket the faster the pace which must be set as the bowlers need longer to complete their task.

'To play to win it is necessary to start from the first ball. The captain must see to it that every member of the side carries out his tactical scheme and plays the kind of cricket he requires.

'This goes to the root of the matter, because if spectators are not going to see a competitive game they will . . . stay at home with the television and switch on to some other sport which gives them action, entertainment, and value for money.'

Alas, cricket and other sport too, under Socialist influence, became permeated by politics. South African and Rhodesian tours were officially frowned upon. As a committee member of the M.C.C. Sir

Alec found himself in an invidious position when the club was invited to play in Rhodesia, a country it had for many years past included in its South African tours.

He advised the M.C.C. against accepting the invitation and the team did not go. His reason for doing so is revealing if not immediately convincing: the Socialists were the British Government. He could not countenance going against the *diktat* of any British Government in international affairs, however much he disagreed with it, just as his father had for long refused to evade death duties, however unjust. To do so, according to his upright code, would be destructive of the institution of Government, a Government duly elected by a majority of the people.

But supposing that duly elected Government was prepared to 'rig' the next elections? 'Four years ago anyone would have scoffed at such an idea,' Sir Alec said at Huddersfield on 26th July 1969. Nevertheless it was happening. It had been agreed by all parties in 1954 that an impartial, judicial Commission should recommend alterations to constituency boundaries when they were made necessary by movements of population.

The Commission reported in spring 1969. Callaghan, the Home Secretary, neglected, however, to lay all the draft Orders in Council before Parliament, and thus frustrated the intentions of the Redistribution of Seats Act of 1949. He had, as Quintin Hogg commented, 'changed the rules in the middle of the game'. Moreover, he selected a few constituency changes for implementation, thereby, the Tories claimed, preventing possible Tory gains.

'One of the penalties which people are paying in many countries derives from the scant respect of governments for democracy,' Sir Alec said. 'We had always taken pride in this country, which did so much to fashion democracy, that governments of all parties would respect the Constitution. That they would rise, for example, above the temptation to fix elections in their favour. But recent events show that in Britain we are not immune.'

Nor, it appeared, was Britain immune from other antidemocratic assaults of a more violent nature. A new breed of anarchist was at large, said Sir Alec on 24th September 1969, at Berwick: 'He has no creed and no coherent philosophy. He sets out to overthrow and to hell with the future.' The riots in Northern Ireland showed, as the Cameron Report said, that 'the anarchist will take advantage of any opening to promote chaos'. He had seized 'the opportunity provided by the thoughtless' in the universities; so it was too with the hippie take-over of an empty house which was not their property.

'Always the exploiter is on the spot ready to stir the pot of trouble. Once violence takes charge it is the innocent, the onlooker, the passive, the majority, who only want a quiet life, who are the victims.

'It was the Communists who started the techniques of subversion and exploitation. With a Communist at least you know where you are. He will employ any means with the purpose of substituting his own order and way of life for yours.'

Sir Alec found repellent 'the idea of the sit-in on a diet of drugs', as had happened at some universities and elsewhere.[1] Those concerned were the weaklings, the victims of a 'national malaise'—due to the aftermath of war, loss of empire, change of standards brought by science and technology and 'ignorantly interpreted as a challenge to religion', and 'to boredom with undiluted technology or diluted art'.

The result was 'a loss of faith by the individual in his future and a loss of confidence by the public in the destiny of Britain. If that is allowed to persist the country could sink into a state of lethargy, into an acceptance of mediocrity and decline.'

Sir Alec pulled no punches. The attack on the individual, on his right of choice and responsibility, on his freedom and self-discipline, was led not by anarchists but by Socialists: 'The basic concept is challenged by Socialism for they look upon the individual as a nuisance and choice as an interference with the orders and will of the State. In our British democracy such a creed can be challenged on stated occasions at local and national elections.

'But in recent years Conservatives have learned that a political platform can be taken by stealth between times. In education, for example, uniformity was nearly imposed through the control and management of the local authorities by the Socialists, and that while Parliament slumbered.'

With Sir Alec the way in which the Socialists had distorted facts in order to gain office and then to keep it always rankled. Putting it in parliamentary language, he referred to the Prime Minister, on 30th October as 'regrettably open-minded about facts. His facts are so

[1] Address to Young Conservatives, Eastbourne, 9th March 1969.

selective to suit his own case that no one in the country takes what he says at its face value'.[1]

Sir Alec was bred in another school; he would not be compared with Abraham Lincoln, the man who never told a lie, but, to make political speeches deliberately to mislead the electors was to undermine democracy. Like Achitophel they were 'resolved to ruin or to rule the state.'

The veniality of their elders bore heavily on the young who, Sir Alec thought, had a greater share of kindliness and were more tolerant than their ancestors. Nor was it helpful to the young to hear such people as Jenkins, Chancellor of the Exchequer, describe the general decline in morals and conduct as 'civilized', and to read or listen to the would-be 'progressive' views of elderly men determined, even if it was with their last breath, to out-shock their juniors.

At one university discussion, the claim was made that the values of parents were useless to undergraduates and that they must find their own by experiment. Sir Alec asked how many illegitimate children would society have to keep before a decision was taken on a code of pre-marital conduct. It is about 2 per cent was the reply. 'That I suppose, is now entered as a university statistic,' he commented drily, 'but why not 4 per cent or 6 per cent—who decides?'

Then again, he said in an address at Great St Mary's Church, Cambridge, on 19th November 1967, 'How many drug-takers are tolerable before we decide where to draw the line against general corruption? Or how much licence is given to hooliganism before crime threatens to destroy the right of the individual to go his daily round in peace?'

These questions, said Sir Alec, were not asked. They ought to be asked and answered because: 'Unless the individual can reconcile his individual behaviour with the interests of society as a whole, then life is devalued and social anarchy prevails, and the majority are the victims.'

After all, 'if there is no external code of morals what is wrong with dictatorship? What's wrong with *apartheid*? Why should the developed countries help the developing?' Why, come to that, *shouldn't* the nuclear bomb be used for blackmail?

Logically the destruction of a moral code led to self-destruction, universally as well as individually, while social happiness, progress and security were conspicuously lacking.

'To what values do we turn to regain balance and poise?' he asked.

[1] This referred to Wilson's claim that overseas aid had not been cut. The figures showed that it had.

'I am told that this problem was got over the other day by setting a paper on the Ten Commandments with a note at the bottom saying "only four of these should be attempted". I am going to be more modest.

'We should begin by adding only one of the old Christian values to the new experiments and giving that one a fair trial.

'It is this: that in everything we do we should ask, how does my action affect my neighbour? For the ills of society today are not due to the failure of technical accomplishment, but to a failure of human understanding and a failure of the individual to reconcile his interests with those of others.'

Ask the question, how does my action affect my neighbour in the matter of sex, drugs, crime, industrial relations, international diplomacy, and 'in nine cases out of ten the answer will be clear and the individual will know what the right answer is.'

Of course, that 'our performance in society fell far short of the precept cannot be challenged. For example, the social conscience was slow to adapt itself to the casualties of the industrial revolution coming as they did, fast, quick and hard after years of an agricultural economy.' Yet the Indian Civil Service was 'the greatest example of disinterested service in the history of any nation', and the crusade for the emancipation of slaves began here.

The 'great deeds of Englishmen were inspired by faith in God,' and in British history 'the Bible is at least as influential as the sword.' Nor was it true that science had killed faith by demanding proofs: 'The existence of God the Creator, for whom all men have searched by instinct for protection and comfort, is not disproved, nor is Christ's teaching of a relationship between earthly performance and heavenly salvation.'

Above all, Sir Alec said, the Christian religion commands us to hope in spite of things looking wrong and gloomy and black; sometimes it was difficult 'and there's no denying that unless we handle things wisely, nuclear annihilation might come.' Nevertheless 'I am not a prophet of doom. I am one of those who has faith in the individual and my country.'

Throughout his life Sir Alec, as we have seen, bore public witness to his faith but always rather reluctantly. He received many letters asking him to make 'homilies, moral stands', and held back because he thought it 'rather an arrogant thing to do. For any political party to arrogate to itself the Christian principles is a pretty intolerable thing to do because the suggestion is these other fellows are not as I am or we are, but a lower form of animal life. And they are not.'

Apart from that, 'one feels very diffident individually about such things'. Sir Alec disclaimed any special illumination, any religious superiority. He told his Cambridge congregation the story of 'an earnest-looking woman who stopped a man in the street with the question "Are you saved?" Hoping as most of us would to get by without a fuss he answered, "Yes". But she persisted, "Why then are you not dancing in the road and praising God for joy?" He replied, "Because I thought it was so narrow a squeak that I'd better keep quiet about it."' The imaginary man bore a close resemblance to Sir Alec Douglas-Home.

Ever since he had ceased to be Leader Sir Alec had confined his speeches in the Commons to foreign and Commonwealth affairs—with the exception of one speech on the future of the House of Lords in early 1969.

The Government proposed to reduce the number of peers entitled to vote in the Lords from some 1,050, mostly Conservative, to about 250, who would be nominated. Sir Alec was rather in favour of the scheme. 'First of all the existing hereditary peers would go on till they die. So, since quite a lot of them are young or middle-aged, you would have some thirty years still with the hereditary peers in the Lords.

'Then during these thirty years, if we were in office, we should nominate quite a lot of hereditary peers—not *make* them hereditary peers but put them into the nominated Chamber. I don't see how *Wilson* could avoid doing it: they are people who take part in every kind of public service—there are experts on forestry, agriculture, science, the Commonwealth and every aspect of foreign affairs.

'They would all be life peers, in the sense that they would be there only for life. But some of the nominated peers would be drawn from the territorial hereditary peerage which under the scheme goes on.

'It's certain that under Wilson's scheme of a nominated House of some 250, no Prime Minister could escape appointing hereditary peers —it would be almost impossible.'

Under the Socialist scheme the Lords would have had a six-month delaying power, and non-Party peers would have had greater power. The preamble of the Bill stated clearly that the Government in the

Lords shall have a majority but *not* a majority over the Opposition plus the Crossbenchers. This would have avoided the danger of an overwhelming Conservative majority.

In short, Sir Alec thought that the Bill was the best that could be expected and 'would keep us going for about fifty years'. Unfortunately it met opposition from Back Benchers of both parties. The most skilful debaters on both sides conducted a filibuster and in April 1969 the Bill was lost. There were few mourners. But Sir Alec, though wasting no time in weeping, was one of the few.

The Socialists did not then threaten to deprive the Lords of all their powers, as he had feared they might. It was not that he was particularly in favour of the *status quo* in the Lords. It was not, he thought, possible to perpetuate the hereditary principle, at least in the sense that an eldest son should succeed by right to a seat in the Lords on the death of his father. What could be done was to create a House of Lords in which there were certain to be a number of hereditary peers. Before the war, leaders of the Lords simply read out official briefs. This led to absurdity. There was, for example, the classical story of the lord who read to the end of his brief—including his secretary's private note that 'This is a bad argument I know but good enough for their Lordships on a hot summer afternoon.'

Since then the House of Lords has been very efficient and Conservative leaders found their built-in majority an embarrassment. In Opposition they could always defeat the Government of the day on anything, and were therefore obliged to 'hold their horses' on many issues because a Government elected by the country had to be allowed to govern.

There were some Conservatives who thought that the leadership in the Lords had erred in this respect in 1968 by opposing the renewal of the statutory sanctions orders made against Rhodesia. It would, they argued, have been better to have let the technical order go, and had a two-day debate of censure on the Government's general Rhodesia policy with a vote at the end. There was always the dilemma of rejecting a Bill and then having to accept it a few months later.

Sir Alec himself, when in the Lords, had devised with Lord Salisbury a scheme according to which there would be a House of Lords numbering 400 with 200 hereditary peers elected by themselves, and 200 life peers, plus Crossbenchers. This scheme might form the basis of reform in agreement with the Labour Party.

During the Socialist Government no hereditary peers had been created though some Socialists were known to prefer hereditary titles for themselves. There seemed no reason to suppose that a new Conservative Government would continue the Socialist policy, even though what some Tories regarded as the over-lavish creations of the past were unlikely to be repeated.

Sir Alec Douglas-Home was too well accustomed to the see-saw of opinion polls to throw his cap over the moon when in 1968 they suggested that the Conservatives would win a General Election by a majority of 230 or more seats. Thus, he was not deflated when at the end of 1969 the pollsters thought the lead was no more than a few dozen, nor elated when once more a landslide was predicted in early 1970. Sir Alec was not by nature a see-saw man however much he hoped that 'Jacky shall have a new master.'

He knew, however, that the public, properly preoccupied with its own private affairs, had a short memory, and they were optimists. Fed by a few bonbons, such as the ending of the £50 travel allowance and wage increases, they might forget some of the disasters with which five years of the Socialist leadership had assailed them and brought the country low.

Sir Alec did not intend that they should be allowed to forget and, as a General Election became an ever larger light at the end of a long, dark tunnel, he played a full part in the rescue operation, aptly named the 'new battle for Britain'. He was in demand everywhere as a speaker; he visited abroad both, as in Yugoslavia, to 'show the flag', and as in his trip to Australia and New Zealand, to become acquainted with a new generation of politicians.

At home, he was indefatigable in spelling out the extent of the 'nasty financial mess' the Government had created. He welcomed signs of improvement in the balance of payments but this did not alter the fact that while prices had risen $2\frac{1}{2}$ per cent a year the last six years of Tory Government, they rose by $4\frac{1}{2}$ per cent a year under the Socialists:

'For every £175 taken by the Conservatives in taxes, the Socialists grab £240,'[1] he said in Richmond on 18th June 1969. 'The value of money has fallen by 4·2 per cent each year since 1964. Gross monthly

[1] By 1970 the position was worse: for every £1 taken by previous Conservative Governments in taxes the Socialists took £2. In terms of rates, the Socialists had increased taxes by £3 for every £2 the Conservatives had reduced them.

mortgage payments on the value of an average-priced house have risen from £18 7s. 0d. in October 1964 to £30 9s. 0d. today. Under Socialism the employee is already paying 40 per cent more on his weekly stamp than he paid in 1964.'

For all the vaunted improvement in the balance of payments, interest rates were so high that industrial expansion to create more wealth and give more employment was almost impossible. Taxes—including the iniquitous S.E.T.—showed the 'dreadful record': petrol tax up five times; car licence up £10; television licence up; National Insurance contribution up three times; Purchase Tax up three times; tax on beer and tobacco up three times; Income Tax up—a tax reduced five times in thirteen years by the Tories.

One of the worst scourges which the Socialists had brought to Britain was bureaucracy and paper, he said at Carlisle on 1st November 1969. The Civil Servants multiplied like locusts—there were 54,000 more of them than in 1964—and farmers and industrialists were snowed under with forms. They had to employ people whose sole activity was form-filling. Yet everyone knew that it was not possible for those who interpreted the forms to deal with more than a fringe of the mountains of paper. 'A Conservative Government will make war on forms and free labour for productive industry,' he promised. (He had once contemplated putting Duncan Sandys in charge of a Whitehall *épuration*.) 'The best Government is the least Government' might well be our motto, he said on 28th November 1969, quoting the chairman of the Monday Club, George Pole, whose annual dinner he addressed.

Sir Alec recognized that certain Socialist acts were irreversible, and that it was better to suffer nationalization rather than to disrupt large industries, such as steel, by chopping and changing from national to private ownership after each change of Government. He had not changed his opinion about the evils of nationalized industries he had so strongly condemned in 1950. Yet it was, he thought, obvious that private enterprise would hardly wish to buy back the railways or the coalmines, as some supporters of free enterprise proposed.

Nothing would be plain sailing for a new Tory administration. For instance, the leadership were pledged to legislate to make contracts entered into between employers and employees enforceable at law so as to avoid the wild-cat strikes that damaged the economy and annoyed the public. The Government in 1969 had proposed something similar —except that the appropriate Minister rather than the law courts was to decide the sanctions—but under pressure from the unions they had dropped the idea. A rash of unofficial strikes followed.

Some thought a Tory attempt would be even less likely to succeed and even cause a General Strike from which the country had been free since 1926. If a whole union went on strike after the due processes of law, including distraint of union funds, it was difficult to see what sanctions a government could invoke. On the other hand, if the electorate decisively supported a party which clearly stated that its policy was to make a signed contract enforceable by the processes of law, then to try to defeat the will of the people by strikes would be difficult. What frightened a lot of trade unionists, he thought, was the Socialist Government's proposal to give the power of enforcement to a Minister rather than to a judge.

It was peculiarly appropriate that Sir Alec, who had been dispatched as Minister of State for Scotland nearly twenty years before with Winston Churchill's blunt brief, 'Go up to Scotland and see if you can get rid of this embryo Scottish nationalist thing', should be chairman of the Heath-inspired Scottish Constitutional Committee which in March 1970 issued its report, *Scotland's Government*.[1] Skilfully guided by Sir Alec, a Scotsman born if not entirely bred who always felt happiest north of the border, the Committee took a wide look at Scottish affairs as a whole discovering, for example, that it would be almost impossible to unscramble the immensely intricate industrial and economic ties between Scotland and the rest of the United Kingdom. This alone would preclude an 'independent' Scotland. Nor would a federation of Scotland, England, Wales and Northern Ireland be any more practicable; and the Northern Ireland, Stormont system 'would be a poor exchange for the loss of Scotland's voice where it really matters—in the political and administrative machinery at the centre.'

A great deal of decentralization and administrative devolution already existed but, the majority of the Committee suggested, more was possible. The most striking proposal was for a Scottish assembly, to be called 'The Scottish Convention', whose members would be directly elected at the time of parliamentary elections. The 'Convention' would co-ordinate regional views, question the Scottish Ministers, discuss government proposals at an early stage and participate in the framing and passage of Scottish legislation.

Did the proposal go far enough to meet the often reiterated com-

[1] Edinburgh: the Scottish Constitutional Committee, 1970.

plaints of individuals who felt government from London to be remote and intangible; or too far so that the next step might be a demand for 'Convention' to become a parliament? It would be for the next Tory government to decide; the bases for such a decision were fully and fairly established in the report of Sir Alec's Committee.

When Wilson called a General Election for 18th June 1970, Sir Alec set to work with a will, speaking mainly in Scotland but also in England and Belfast. Despite almost universally depressing opinion polls, he buoyantly plugged the themes of Socialist failure in wage inflation, industrial relations, £3,000 million additional taxation, and a steep rise in unemployment—the biggest since the 1930s. He asserted his belief in the 'Responsible Society'—a Government which keeps its word, cares for the poorest and weakest, and allows the individual scope for his talents and initiative.

In his campaigning the turning point came when he realized that 'Emperor' Wilson had no clothes: he was proposing no policies at all, merely demanding *carte blanche*. At the last moment the electorate took the point, and the Conservatives were returned with an overall majority of thirty. Sir Alec, fighting Scottish Nationalist, Labour and Liberals, was returned with an increased majority of 9,764, compared with 9,582 in 1966.

He was at once appointed Foreign and Commonwealth Secretary, and early on Monday morning, 22nd June, he strolled across the Park, through the archway into the Foreign Office and up the broad stairs to the great room with its red leather furnishings that he had vacated almost seven years before on becoming Prime Minister. To this return he had looked forward with calm confidence. There would be many rapids to be shot and not a few bridges to be burned; but his policy as always would be 'conciliation based on strength'.

The country at large heaved a sigh of relief, and Foreign Office officials must have been tempted to signal embassies abroad rather as the Navy signalled the return of Churchill to the Admiralty in 1939: 'Alec's back.'

27. Sir Alec the Ageless: 1970

Agreeable prospect of office. 'Cutting the guff'. His detachment. The role. The true patriot.

Sir Alec found the prospect of a new term of office agreeable: 'participation at the centre' had lost none of its allure over the years. In foreign affairs he had no equal; no one in any country had either his experience or his wisdom. He would be sixty-eight on 2nd July 1971. Unlike Lord Vaux he could not complain that

> Age with stealing steps,
> Hath clawed me with his clutch.

Debonair and casual as ever, he sauntered hand-in-pocket down the corridors of the Commons or across the lawns of the Hirsel, tall shoulders bowed, large head questing forward as though still peering for the Chalk Blues of his nonage. His once sandy hair was a trifle greyer and sparser, the strong bone structure of his tanned face with its great forehead and deep eye-sockets more stark. About his lips and eyes a smile hovered ready to break into a boyish grin; and his sense of humour was as easily roused as when he burst out laughing at the practical jokers of Christ Church fifty years before.

He was, as R. A. Butler had said, ageless. To talk to him was, apart from his slight deafness, to talk to a young man who happened to have had years of experience in the world and among the world's top men. Though he was Britain's most eminent statesman, he gave no impression of being a man of weighty consequence. Conversation with him was a two-way affair, never a monologue. 'I' and 'me' were usually replaced by the modest 'one'. He did not assert. When he knew that he was *en rapport* with his companion, his sentences—delivered in that clear voice with its 'sh' for 's' and its occasionally plosive consonant—

simply faded out. He marked the end of a spoken paragraph with a faint two-note clearing of the larynx: 'hr-hum'.

As always he worked, one leg over the other and pad on knee, with family and friends around him, whether in his twelfth-floor flat in Victoria or in the long drawing-room at the Hirsel. Neither small grand-children, demanding interviewers nor the insistent telephone disturbed his phenomenal powers of concentration. He retained the incomparable gift, as a Shadow Cabinet colleague observed, of 'cutting out the guff and getting to the heart of the matter'. Dealing with political papers, as Morley said of Balfour, 'Every word showed a hard grip of the matter in hand. In business, he is absolutely without atmosphere.' He never gnawed at a subject: he dealt with it and passed on to the next, or to the House, to a cocktail party, to answering letters which continued to flood in upon him, to speak at a coffee-morning in Carlisle or a college in Cambridge. He never in his heart believed that anything could ever be quite so serious as some would make it; but, then, from birth he had been shielded from the more atrocious of life's slings and arrows—shortage of money, inferior housing, poor food. Serious illness alone he shared with common humanity—that and those emotions which have always been outside class or race.

He was not an inquisitive man, personally or intellectually. He seldom cross-examined, perhaps because he was himself reticent and shy about his deepest feelings, to expose which he would find as excruciatingly embarrassing as any Old Etonian of his generation. From many mundane matters he had always been detached. He did not reach out for things, ideas, or people. They came to him, floated into his awareness; he was polite to them, considered them, made a judg-ment, took a decision; and out they floated again. His life had a disciplined casualness which was almost the trade mark of the British aristocracy in the mid twentieth century. It was made possible not by butlers, footmen and valets, of which he had none, but by the organiz-ing genius of his wife Elizabeth, who was so skilled at the job that she herself appeared to be the most casual of all.

On his frequent trips abroad he had always been packaged and dispatched by his aides and secretaries like a top-secret letter, sealed and stamped with the highest insignia. He himself had neither schedule nor note of his engagements. He visited countries of whose exact position on the globe—or how to get there—he was unaware. But, strategically, he knew exactly where they lay in relation to the centres

of chief power, and exactly where they stood politically and economically. Though totally devoid of pomp or circumstance, he had sufficient
sense of his own importance, of *amour propre*, to refuse to visit a
country if its king, president or prime minister had not arranged to
receive him.

Yet, in another sense, his 'importance' meant nothing to him. He had
been Prime Minister, Foreign Secretary, Leader of the Opposition but,
unlike all his twentieth-century predecessors, carried away very few
documents, official papers, notes; his own half century of correspondence with the great and the less great was 'all over the place'. What
he knew he carried in his head, and despite his disclaimers his memory
was remarkable. Though he thought best on paper, he did not hoard
it; of *paperassie* he was totally free.

Sir Alec intended to retire when the leather boxes, the to-and-fro
of the Commons, the travel abroad by air began to pall. In 1970, far
from palling, they were the promised sweet after the medicine of
Opposition. When he did retire, an awkward problem would arise,
though he did not think about it much. As an ex-Prime Minister, who
had been an M.P. for almost forty years, he could expect to be translated to the Lords with an Earldom so that the fullness of his experience would not be quite lost to the nation.

But having popped out of an Earldom and the Lords in 1963, could
he decently pop back in again ten years later? To reappear under yet
another title, even Earl Douglas-Home, would have the flavour of
French bedroom farce where the hero under various guises is to be
found in every room but his own. A life peerage would be less osten-
tatious, almost endearingly middleclass. His own earldom was gone
beyond recall; for that there was no repining.

Under whatever guise, however, Sir Alec, who had most of the time
enjoyed politics, looked forward to enjoying them, in however dimin-
ished a capacity, to the end. His forbears had been generally long-lived
and his way of life—with its sport ('the secret of one's interests lies
out of doors'), its kaleidoscopic variety and warm family atmosphere—
was conducive to psycho-physical health. Country, the Borders,
Lanarkshire, drew him still, but he would never vegetate. At seventy
he would be no more the vegetative type than he had been at twenty-
six when he was 'discontented' with the country landlord role and
'felt it wasn't going to be enough'.

He did not worry about death for he was a Christian and would still say 'Yes, I am a religious man in the sense that I could not do without it.' But the grave illness of thirty years ago, which in a sense had annealed him, also left him sensitive towards health, his own and that of others: he knew what ill-health meant.

Sometimes he worried about poverty—or at least spoke of it. Barring complete Communism or rampant Socialism, such a condition for him was scarcely possible and might appear a mere, though not uncommon, vagary of the well-to-do.

It was not quite that. In terms of the Border, where dukes and earls throng the telephone directory, Sir Alec was not particularly rich. He had uncomfortably witnessed the reduction of the estates by two-thirds in his lifetime and the consequent fall in income. The new taxes of the last five years had not exactly buttressed his fortune; he had sold 1,000 or more acres of woodland in 1968. It was not ruin but of his possessions he had said: 'I would passionately keep things together. The history has gone back such a long way. One would feel guilty if one had to liquidate it.' Some liquidation had occurred.

But he had little with which to upbraid himself. Lucky in birth, lucky in love, he had made mistakes over specific acts in his political career—which he was the first to acknowledge—but he had always pursued an honourable course, serving God, Queen and country in that order, with self-interest well in the dusty rear. His conscience was clearer than a politician had any right to expect.

And what, as a politician, was his achievement? He had seldom bubbled with new ideas and fresh initiatives; he had no mania for legislation, believing with the great Lord Salisbury that government should interfere with men's lives only when urgently necessary. Sir Alec's role had been largely that of a saver of situations, an aristocratic trouble-shooter, humanizing relations between central government and disgruntled Scots, picking up the Commonwealth pieces after Suez, uniting the Tory Party when its leadership threatened to splinter after Macmillan's resignation. Then, like Kipling's 'Saviour of 'is country', when the guns had ceased to shoot it was 'Tommy this, an' Tommy that an' Tommy go away'.

As Foreign Secretary, he stood pat for Britain at a time when her prestige was being given away in handfuls. He boldly condemned that nest of Britain's enemies hiding behind the title of the peace-loving United Nations; he refused to countenance the disarming of his country. By personal diplomacy he set the American ally right on the true situa-

271

tion in Malaysia and Indonesia. But his writ was more confined than that of any of his predecessors because of the emergence of the 'super-powers'. His weapon was the tongue not the gunboat, and

> 'on the enlightened wind, with winning art,
> His gentle reason so persuasive stole
> That the charmed hearer thought it was his own.'

He believed that Britain's future lay in leading the Western European nations towards an Atlantic-Pacific community; he never doubted that she could and would remain in the 'First XI'.

His touch in foreign affairs was sometimes uncertain, for instance with regard to Africa. His view did not always prevail either with the Americans or with his Cabinet colleagues. He was not, however, a resigner or a 'last ditcher'; he would accept a majority view of the Cabinet since he never regarded himself as the fount of all wisdom, and loyalty to the leader was second nature.

Sir Alec was an excellent chairman rather than a go-getting man-aging director. His strength as a leader lay in his modest judiciousness, unaffected by dogma and totally free of self-seeking, his clear thinking devoid of passion or prejudice. Sir Alec was a stranger to the arts of publicity and the public—contrasting him with his political opponents —liked him the better for it. Given a second term of office, freedom from election pressures and a ministerial team of his own choice, there is every reason to believe that he would have steered the ship of state with safety and success.

A true patriot, in an age of increasing venality, of double-talk and double-think, of a new barbarism hailed as progress, he stands out as a slender pillar of probity, looked up to by his countrymen, his integ-rity unquestioned even by those who disagree with him, whether in Westminster or in the world at large. In politics, he is the last of the disinterested: the levelling-down of Socialism would see to that.

'Not a man of strong passion nor of bold measures; not a genius but a great talent; cool, calm, imperturbable': these words written about Prince Clement von Metternich could apply to some aspects of Sir Alec the statesman. As a description of the man himself they would satisfy no one who knew him well for, above all, he is kind, fair and humane. If beneath his portrait the painter allows himself one single sentence it must be: A Gentleman *sans peur et sans reproche*.

Select Bibliography

Unless otherwise stated all titles are published in London.

ALINGTON, C. A. (1933). *Eton Fables.*

ALINGTON, C. A. (1936). *Things Ancient and Modern.*

AMERY, L. S. (1955). *My Political Life*, vol. 3, *The Unforgiving Years.*

BARMAN, T. (1969). *Diplomatic Correspondent.*

BEVINS, R. (1965). *The Greasy Pole.*

BIRKENHEAD, 2nd Earl of (1969). *Walter Monckton: The Life of Viscount Monckton of Brenchley.*

BRITTAN, SAMUEL (1965). *The Treasury under the Tories, 1951–64.*

BUTLER, D. E., *and* KING, A. (1965). *The British General Election of 1964.*

CHANNON, Sir HENRY (1967). *Chips: The Diaries of Sir Henry Channon,* ed. R. R. James.

CHURCHILL, RANDOLPH (1959). *The Rise and Fall of Sir Anthony Eden.*

CHURCHILL, RANDOLPH (1964). *The Fight for the Tory Leadership,* 2nd edn.

CONNOLLY, CYRIL (1938). *Enemies of Promise.*

CONSERVATIVE RESEARCH DEPARTMENT (1964). *Campaign Guide: The Unique Political Reference Book.*

COOPER, A. DUFF (1953). *Old Men Forget.*

COOPER, LEONARD (1959). *Radical Jack: The First Earl of Durham.*

COOTE, COLIN R. (1965). *A Companion of Honour: The Story of Walter Elliot.*

COOTE, COLIN R. (1965). *Editorial: The Memoirs of Colin R. Coote.*

CROZIER, BRIAN (1969). *The Masters of Power.*

DAALDER, H. (1964). *Cabinet Reform in Britain, 1914–63.*

DE LA TORRE, LILLIAN (1952). *Heir of Douglas,* New York.

DICKIE, J. (1964). *The Uncommon Commoner: Sir Alec Douglas-Home.*

EDEN, Sir ANTHONY (1960). *Memoirs: Full Circle.*

ELIOT, T. S. (1939). *The Idea of a Christian Society.*

EPSTEIN, L. (1964). *British Politics since Suez.*

FEILING, KEITH (1946). *The Life of Neville Chamberlain.*

GARDNER, B. (1968). *Churchill in His Times: a study of a reputation, 1939–1945.*

GILBERT, M. *and* GOTT, R. (1963). *The Appeasers.*

HILL OF LUTON, Lord (1964). *Both Sides of the Hill.*

HOFFMAN, J. D. (1964). *The Conservative Party in Opposition, 1945–51.*

HOME, W. D. (1939). *Home Truths.*

HOME, W. D. (1954). *Half Term Report.*

HOWARD, A. *and* WEST, R. (1965). *The Making of the Prime Minister.*

JAMES, R. R., *see under* Channon.

KILMUIR, Earl of (1964). *The Memoirs of the Earl of Kilmuir: Political Adventure.*

MACMILLAN, HAROLD (1969). *Tides of Fortune, 1945–55.*

MEDLICOTT, W. N. (1968). *British Foreign Policy since Versailles, 1919–63,* 2nd edn.

MENZIES, Sir ROBERT (1967). *Afternoon Light: Some Memories of Men and Events.*

SAMPSON, A. (1967). *Macmillan.*

SKELTON, A. N. (1924). *Constructive Conservatism.* Edinburgh.

STUART, J. (Viscount Stuart of Findhorn) (1967). *Within the Fringe.*

TAYLOR, A. J. P. (1965). *Oxford English History, 1914–45.* Oxford.

THOMAS, HUGH (1967). *The Suez Affair.*

WELENSKY, Sir ROY (1964). *Welensky's 4,000 Days.*

WEST, R. ed. *see* Howard.

WOOLTON, the Earl of (1959). *Memoirs.*

WRIGHT, Sir MICHAEL (1964). *Disarm and Verify.*

Index